LIFE AND DEATH

ANDREA DWORKIN

THE FREE PRESS

New York   London   Toronto   Sydney   Singapore

THE FREE PRESS
A Division of Simon & Schuster Inc.
1230 Avenue of the Americas
New York, NY 10020

Manufactured in the United States of America

10   9   8   7   6   5   4   3   2   1

Library of Congress Cataloging-in-Publication Data

Dworkin, Andrea.
    Life and death : unapologetic writings on the continuing war
against women / Andrea Dworkin.
        p.   cm.
    Articles originally published 1987–1995.
    Includes index.
    ISBN 0-684-83512-6
    1. Women—Crimes against.   1. Sex discrimination against women.
3. Feminist theory.   I. Title.
    HV6250.4W6D86   1997
    362.88′082—dc20
                                                96-38335
                                                  CIP

PUBLICATION DATA

ORIGINS

My Life as a Writer

First published as "Andrea Dworkin (1946–   )" in *Contemporary Authors Autobiography Series,* Volume 21, March 1995 (Gale Research Inc.). Copyright © 1995 by Andrea Dworkin.

EMERGENCIES

In Memory of Nicole Brown Simpson

First published in the *Los Angeles Times* as three essays: "Trapped in a Pattern of Pain Where No One Can Help" (June 26, 1994), "In Nicole Brown Simpson's Words" (January 29, 1995), and "Domestic Violence: Trying to Flee" (October 8, 1995). Copyright © 1994, 1995, 1997 by Andrea Dworkin.

Living in Terror, Pain: Being a Battered Wife

First published in the *Los Angeles Times,* March 12, 1989. Copyright © 1989 by Andrea Dworkin.

The Third Rape

First published in the *Los Angeles Times,* April 28, 1991. Copyright © 1991 by Andrea Dworkin.

Gary Hart and Post-Pornography Politics

First published in an altered version as "The Right to Know How Women Are Humiliated" in New York *Newsday,* March 13, 1987. Copyright © 1987 by Andrea Dworkin.

A Government of Men, Not Laws, Not Women

First published as "Political Callousness on Violence Toward Women" in the *Los Angeles Times,* May 14, 1989. Copyright © 1989 by Andrea Dworkin.

Portrait of a New Puritan—and a New Slaver

First published in an abridged version as a letter in *The New York Times Book Review,* May 3, 1992. Copyright © 1992, 1997 by Andrea Dworkin.

Free Expression in Serbian Rape/Death Camps

First published as "The Real Pornography of a Brutal War Against Women" in the *Los Angeles Times,* September 5, 1993. Copyright © 1993 by Andrea Dworkin.

Beaver Talks

First published as a new introduction to *Pornography: Men Possessing Women* (New York: Plume, 1989). Copyright © 1989 by Andrea Dworkin.

RESISTANCE

Mass Murder in Montréal: The Sexual Politics of Killing Women

Speech at the Université de Montréal, December 7, 1990, organized by The Day After Committee to mourn the mass murder of fourteen women students on December 6, 1989, at the

— FOR NIKKI CRAFT —

— IN MEMORY OF MY BROTHER, MARK, 1949–1992 —

In analyzing women's thinking about what constitutes care and what connection means, I noted women's difficulty in including themselves among the people for whom they considered it moral to care. The inclusion of self is genuinely problematic not only for women but also for society in general. Self-inclusion on the part of women challenges the conventional understanding of feminine goodness by severing the link between care and self-sacrifice; in addition, the inclusion of women challenges the interpretive categories of the Western tradition, calling into question descriptions of human/nature and holding up to scrutiny the meaning of "relationship," "love," "morality," and "self."

—Carol Gilligan, *Mapping the Moral Domain*

Let there be no mention of the war. If it were not for those few who could not repress their experiences, the victims themselves would have denied the horror.

—Aharon Appelfeld, *Beyond Despair*

CONTENTS

PREFACE

I have spent the last twenty-five years as a writer, and during most of it I rejected first-person nonfiction writing by contemporary women. Even though I was riveted by, and learned much from, speak-outs, Take Back the Night rallies, and talks in which the point was first-person experience, in literature I regarded this as the back of the bus, for women of all colors. No woman had an "I" that swept up populations as Whitman's did, such that he could embrace them; nor did women have Baudelaire's cruel but beautiful "I"—so eloquent, so ruthless—which made God's world spoil in front of you, become ruined and rotting yet entirely new. The woman's "I" was trivial—"anecdotal," as the guardians of white-male writing put it. The "I" of a woman said, "My husband likes his shirts ironed this way; my teenage son is sulking but I remember him when he was three; I am the second daughter of my mother's fourth husband; and on Sunday, after making love, my husband and I had croissants." The "I" of a woman always had to be charming; the prose, feminine and without aggression; the manner of writing, gracious or sweet or unctuous. There had better be no hint of Whitman's grandiosity or Baudelaire's bitterness. Even if a girl could write "Spleen," it could only be experienced as an appalling breach of civility. Women's writings—like women—are judged by the pretty surface. There is no place for the roiling heart.

Yet as I organized this, my third collection of writings—after *Our Blood* (1976) and *Letters From a War Zone* (1988)—I saw with some shock that my "I" is everywhere in these essays and speeches, referring directly and explicitly to my own life. The experiences I have chosen to write about are not polite—they include being raped, battered, and prostituted—and I have not been polite about them; although I hope that in my telling I have honored intellect, veracity, and language. Like many male writers from a previous time, I have used portions of my life for evidence or emphasis or simply because that's what happened, which must matter. Some autobiographical facts and events are reiterated, like a leitmotif pointing to a pattern, a theme with variations. In each context the events are refracted from a slightly different angle, with more detail or deeper knowledge or another pitch of feeling.

I love life, I love writing, I love reading—and these writings are about injustice, which I hate. They are a rude exploration of it, especially its impact on women. This is the "I" forbidden to women, the "I" concerned less with ironing (and I have ironed *a lot*) than with battery. It is an "I" indifferent to the passions of popular culture but repelled by this culture's insistent romanticization of violence against women. This is the forbidden "I" that names the crimes committed against women by men and seeks redress: the "I" male culture has abhorred. There is nothing trivial about it.

In the first section, "Origins," I tell how I became a writer and why, and I say what I think my work is worth and why. I expect this autobiographical self-appraisal may be more accurate than that of critics, friend or foe. Mostly, of course, critics have been foes, too prejudiced against the reason I write to read with clarity or understanding, let alone to appreciate the writing itself. I'm the expert on me: not Freud, not *Playboy,* not *The Nation,* not *The National Review.*

In the next section, "Emergencies," I write about crises, many of which stirred public feeling to a fever pitch—the abuse of Nicole Brown

Simpson, for instance, or Hedda Nussbaum, or the genocidal rape of women and girls by Serbian fascists in Bosnia-Herzegovina. Here, too, I write about contemporary abuses of women that have been kept hidden—the attempted murder of Pamela Small by then House Speaker Jim Wright's top aide, John Mack, himself a formidable power and protected by both the political establishment and the media until Wright's fall on ethics charges. I suggest that the privacy of then presidential hopeful Gary Hart should not have been invaded by the press—but that John Mack's should have been. I suggest that the values and perceptions of a younger generation of male journalists have been significantly formed by their use of pornography such that they are now mostly voyeurs, not heroes of democracy. And I report the stories of truly anonymous, unimportant, uncared-for women—those used in pornography, those on whom pornography was used in sexual abuse or battery or to push them into prostitution. "Emergencies" is about the day-to-day lives of ordinary women, their lives degraded or destroyed by exploitation or violence.

"Resistance" is a selection of six speeches, each taking a public stand out loud in a public place, often in the face of some tragedy or atrocity—for instance, the mass murders in Montréal of fourteen female engineering students by a man whose motives were both political and woman hating. Here the terrorism of male violence against women is reported as being far from anomalous; and the dynamics of aggression and violence in pornography, prostitution, battery, and marital rape are made palpable. The last speech in this section—delivered in Toronto as part of an endowed, public policy lecture series at Massey College (founded by the writer Robertson Davies, who attended)—offers a summary of what we have achieved and makes clear where we have failed. The "we" in these speeches is feminists, which many people in their hearts consider themselves to be.

Three speeches were given in Canada—in Montréal, Québec; Banff, Alberta; and Toronto, Ontario—and three in the United States—Chicago, Illinois; Ann Arbor, Michigan; and Austin, Texas.

This geography should give the lie to the notion—reported in dozens if not hundreds of newspapers—that my colleague Catharine A. MacKinnon and I are not welcome by feminists in Canada because of the Canadian Supreme Court's *Butler* decision, which held that pornography violated women's equality rights. Canadian feminists invited me to speak; the speeches were received with enthusiasm and a deep commitment to making women's lives better. At least one was developed by Canadian feminists into a video project. By the same measure, the notion also fails that my feminist ideas are extreme or marginal: my work has been profoundly appreciated in the geographical heartland of the United States. Participants in the Texas event, for example, came from all over the state. "Resistance" represents the grassroots women's movement, made up of ordinary, hard-working, committed women and men everywhere who want an end to injustice. I have never been alone in this. I know that for a fact because of the audiences. They and their love, respect, and desire—to know and understand and act—are what can never come through to the reader of these pages. Especially they are women, and they want relief from male violence.

Still on the life-and-death terrain of violence against women but now going deeper, searching for its roots, is "Confrontations," a series of essays on why and how the perception of women as subhuman evolves such that violence and exploitation become habits rather than crimes. Here I examine women's exclusion from human status and women's political subordination in the United States, in the public domain in most Western countries, in the relatively young state of Israel, in the sparkling new Holocaust Memorial Museum in Washington, D.C. Here I also challenge women's exclusion from the right of speech as such—not simply from personal expression, from art or culture, but from creating the political premises we take for granted. In each essay, the silence or invisibility of women's experience and its meaning are shown as distorting, undermining, or destroying the political and moral integrity of a nation, an institution, a right, or an idea.

It is my hope that because of the political work of feminists over the last quarter of a century, these writings may at last be read and taken seriously. I am asking men who come to these pages to walk through the looking glass. And I am asking women to break the mirror. Once we all clean up the broken glass—no easy task—we will have a radical equality of rights and liberty.

—Brooklyn, New York
May 1996

ORIGINS

MY LIFE AS A WRITER

I come from Camden, New Jersey, a cold, hard, corrupt city, and—
now having been plundered by politicians, some of whom are in
jail—also destitute. I remember being happy there.

First my parents and I lived on Princess Avenue, which I don't remember; then, with my younger brother, Mark, at my true home, 1527
Greenwood Avenue. I made a child's vow that I would always remember
the exact address so I could go back, and I have kept that vow through
decades of dislocation, poverty, and hard struggle. I was ten when we
moved to the suburbs, which I experienced as being kidnapped by aliens
and taken to a penal colony. I never forgave my parents or God, and my
heart stayed with the brick row houses on Greenwood Avenue. I loved
the stoops, the games in the street, my friends, and I hated leaving.

I took the story of the three little pigs to heart and was glad that I
lived in a brick house. My big, bad wolf was the nuclear bomb that Russia was going to drop on us. I learned this at Parkside School from the
first grade on, along with reading and writing. A bell would ring or a
siren would sound and we had to hide under our desks. We were taught
to cower and wait quietly, without moving, for a gruesome death, while
the teacher, of course, stood at the head of the class or policed the aisles
for elbows or legs that extended past the protection of the tiny desks.

And what would happen to her when the bomb came? Never, I believe, has a generation of children been so relentlessly terrorized by adults who were so obviously and stupidly lying. Eventually, the dullest of us picked up on it; and I was far from the dullest.

I remember trying to understand what the bomb was and how it would come and why. I'd see blinding light and heat and fire; and when my brain got tired of seeing burning humans, empty cities, burning cement, I would console myself with the story of the three little pigs. I was safe because my house was brick.

It is that feeling of my brain meeting the world around me that I remember most about being a child. The feeling was almost physical, as if I could feel my brain being stretched inside my head. I could feel my brain reaching for the world. I knew my brain did more than think. It could see and imagine and maybe even create something new or beautiful, if I was lucky and brave. I always wanted engagement, not abstract knowledge.

I loved the world and living and I loved being immersed in sensation. I did not like boundaries or want distance from what was around me. I saw adults as gatekeepers who stood between me and the world. I hated their evasions, rules, lies, petty tyrannies. I wanted to be honest and feel everything and take everything on. I didn't want to be careful and narrow the way they were. I thought a person could survive anything, except maybe famine and war, or drought and war. When I learned about Auschwitz my idea of the unbearable became more specific, more informed, sober and personal.

I began to think about survival very early, because we were Jewish on the heels of the Holocaust; because of the ubiquitous presence of those Russian bombs; and also because my mother was ill with heart disease. She had scarlet fever when she was a child, and in her family, big and poor, both parents immigrants, one did not call the doctor for a girl. The scarlet fever turned into rheumatic fever, which injured her heart long before there was open-heart surgery. She had many heart failures, maybe heart attacks, and at least one stroke before I became officially adolescent. She would be short of breath, maybe fall down; then she'd be gone, to a hospital, but Mark and I never really had any way of knowing if she had died yet. We would be farmed out to relatives, separated most of the time. This could happen day or night, while doing homework or sleeping. We'd be told to get dressed fast because Mother was very sick and we couldn't stay here now; and Dad was at work or at the hospital and he would explain later: be quiet, don't ask questions, cooperate. We never knew anything we could count on. I usually didn't even know where Mark was. Or she might be sick, at home but in bed and off-limits, maybe dying. Sometimes I would be allowed to sit on her bed for a little while and hold her hand.

She was Sylvia, and I loved her madly when I was a child, which she never believed, not even by the time she did die, in 1991 at the age of seventy-six. I did stop loving her when I was older and exhausted by her repudiations of me; but it would not be wrong to say that as a child I was in love with her, infatuated. I remember loving her long, dark hair, and the smell of coffee, which she drank perpetually when she was able to walk around, and the smoke from her cigarettes. Maybe it was my child's fear of death, or her sudden, brutal absences, that made me adore her without ever flinching when she pushed me away. I wanted to be around her, and I would have been her slave had she been generous enough to accept me. She was my first great romance.

But I was the wrong child for my mother to have had. She preferred dull obedience to my blazing adoration. She valued conformity and never even recognized the brazen emotional ploys of a child to hold on to her. My emotions were too extravagant for her own more literal sensibility. One could follow her around like a lovesick puppy, but if the puppy peed on the floor, she thought its intention was to spite her. She saw malice in almost anything I said or did. When I would be stretching my brain in curiosity—and dancing my brain in front of her to dazzle her—she thought it was defiance. When I asked her questions, which was a way for me to be engaged with her, she considered the questions proof of rebellion, a wayward delinquency, maybe even treason to her authority. I could never excite her or make myself understood or even comfort her. I do remember her reading to me sometimes at night when I couldn't sleep, and I remember feeling very happy.

She often told me that she loved me but did not like me. I came to believe that whatever she meant by love was too remote, too cold, too abstract or formulaic to have anything to do with me as an individual, as I was. She said that a mother always loved her child; and since this was an important rule in her world, she probably followed it. I never understood what she meant even when I was fully grown up—which feelings this generic and involuntary love might include. But to the extent that she knew me, there was no doubt that she did not like me, and also that I could not be the child that she would find likable. I wasn't, I couldn't be, and I didn't want to be. She understood only that I didn't want to be.

I had to be independent, of course. I had to learn to live without her or without anyone special. I had to learn to live from minute to minute. I had to learn to be on my own, emotionally alone, physically alone. I had to learn to take care of myself and sometimes my brother and sometimes even her. I never knew what would happen next, or if she'd be sick or dying, or where I'd be sleeping at night. I had to get strong and grow up. I'd try to understand and I'd ask God how He could make her so sick. Somehow, in stretching my brain to beat back the terror, I'd assert my own desire to live, to be, to know, to become. I had many a Socratic dialogue in my head before I ever read one. I had a huge inner life, not so strange, I think, for a child, or for a child who would become a writer. But the inner lives of children were not an acknowledged reality in those days, in the fifties, before I was ten and we moved to the suburbs, a place of sterility and desolation where no one had an inner life ever.

I have idyllic memories of childhood in Camden: my brother, my father, and me having tickling fights, wrestling, on the living room floor; me in my cowgirl suit practicing my fast draw so I could be an Amerikan hero; a tiny sandbox on our front lawn where all the children played, boys and girls together, our Eden until a certain year when the girls had to wear tops—I may have been five but I remember screaming and crying in an inarticulate outrage. We girls played with dolls on the stoops, washed their hair, set it, combed it out, dressed the dolls, tried to make stories of glamour in which they stood for us. I remember being humiliated by some girl I didn't like for not washing my doll's hair right—I think the doll was probably drowning. Later, my grandfather married her mother across the street, and I had to be nice to her. I was happier when we moved from dolls to canasta, gin rummy, poker, and strip poker. The children on the street developed a collective secret life, a half dozen games of sex and dominance that we played, half in front of our mothers' eyes, half in a conspiracy of hiding. And we played Red Rover and Giant Steps, appropriating the whole block from traffic. And there was always ball, in formal games, or alone to pass the time, against brick walls, against the cement stoops. I liked the sex-and-dominance games, which could be overtly sadomasochistic, because I liked the risk and the intensity; and I liked ordinary games like hide-and-seek. I loved the cement, the alleys, the wires and telephone poles, the parked cars that provided sanctuary from the adults, a kind of metallic barrier against their eyes and ears; and I loved the communal life of us, the children, half *Lord of the Flies,* half a prelude to *Marjorie Morningstar.* To this day, my idea of a good time is to sit on a city stoop amid a profusion of people and noise as dark is coming on.

I would say that it was Sylvia who started fighting with me when I was an exuberant little pup and still in love with her. But eventually I started fighting back. She experienced my inner life as a reproach. She thought I was arrogant and especially hated that I valued my own thoughts. When I kept what I was thinking to myself, she thought I was plotting against her. When I told her what I thought, she said I was defiant and some species of bad: evil, nasty, rotten. She often accused me of thinking I was smarter than she. I probably was, though I didn't know it; but it wasn't my fault. I was the child, she the adult, but neither of us understood that.

Our fights were awful and I don't doubt that, then as now, I fought to win. I may have been around eight when I dug in; and we were antagonists. I may have been a little older. Of course, I still wanted her to take me back and love me, but each crisis made that harder. Because of the wrenching separations, the pressing necessity of taking care of myself or Mark or her, the loneliness of living with relatives who didn't particularly want me, I had to learn to need my mother less. When we fought she said I was killing her. At some point, I don't know exactly when, I decided not to care if she did die. I pulled myself away from her fate and tried to become indifferent to it. With a kind of emotional jujitsu, I pushed my mother away in my mind and in how I lived. I did this as a child. I knew that she might really die, and maybe I would be the cause, as they all kept saying. I also knew I was being manipulated. I had to make a choice: follow by rote her ten thousand rules of behavior for how a girl must act, think, look, sit, stand—in other words, cut out my own heart; or withstand the threat of her imminent death—give up the hope of her love or her friendship or her understanding. I disciplined myself to walk away from her in every sense and over time I learned how. She told me I had a hard heart.

I made good grades, though I had trouble conforming in class as I got older because of the intellectual vacuity of most of my teachers. I followed enough of the social rules to keep adults at bay. There weren't therapists in schools yet, so no adult got to force-fuck my mind. I was smart enough to be able to strategize. I wasn't supposed to take long, solitary walks, but I took them. I wasn't supposed to go to other parts of our neighborhood, but I went. I had friends who were not Jewish or white at a time when race and religion lines were not crossed. I knew boys who were too old for me. I read books children weren't allowed to read. I regarded all of this as my private life and my right. My mother simply continued to regard me as a liar and a cheat with incomprehensible but clearly sinister tendencies and ideas.

When I was ten we moved to Delaware Township in New Jersey, a place *New York Times* writer Russell Baker described in a column as "nowhere along the highway," after which the outraged citizens changed the name to Cherry Hill. It was an empty place with sporadic outbreaks of ranch-type and split-level housing projects. There were still wild cherry trees and some deer. With the deer came hunters who stalked them across flat fields of ragweed and poison ivy. It was virtually all-white, unlike Camden where the schools were racially and ethnically mixed even as residential blocks were segregated according to precise calibrations: Polish Catholics on one block, Irish Catholics on another. It was intellectually arid, except for a few teachers, one of whom liked to play sex-and-seduction games with smart little girls. It was wealthy while we were quite poor. We moved there because my mother could not climb steps and the good Lord had never made a flatter place than Delaware Township/Cherry Hill. I lived for the day that I would leave to go to New York City, where there were poets and writers and jazz and people like me.

Harry, my daddy, was not a rolling stone. He wasn't at home because he worked two jobs most of the time and three jobs some of the time. He was a schoolteacher during the day and at night he unloaded packages at the post office. Later he became a guidance counselor at a boys' academic high school in Philadelphia and also in a private school for dropouts trying to get their high school diplomas. I don't know what the third job was, or when he had it. My brother and I would go stretches of many days without seeing him at home; and when we were in other people's houses, it could be weeks. There were times when he would go to college classes on Saturdays in an effort to get his Ph.D. degree, but he never had the time to write a dissertation, so he never got the degree. My dream was that when I grew up I would be able to give him the money to write his dissertation; but I never did make enough money and he says he is too old now anyway (though he still goes to the library every week). He was different from other men in how he acted and how he thought. He was gentle and soft-spoken. He listened with careful attention to children and women. He wanted teachers to unionize and the races to integrate. He was devoted to my mother and determined that she would get the very best medical care, a goal entirely out of reach for a low-paid schoolteacher, except that he did it. He borrowed money to pay medical bills. He borrowed money to take my mother to heart specialists. He borrowed money for professional nurses and to get housecleaning help and some child care and sometimes to hire a cook. He kept us warm and fed and sheltered, even though not always at home or together. He was outspoken and demonstrative in expressing affection, not self-conscious or withdrawn as most men were. He was nurturant and emotionally empathetic. He crossed a gender line and was stigmatized for it; called a sissy and a fairy by my buddies on the street who no doubt heard it from their parents. He loved my mother and he loved Mark and me; but especially me. I will never know why. He said I was the apple of his eye from the time I was born and I believe him. I did nothing to earn it and it was the one great gift of my life. On Sundays he slept late but he and I would watch the Sunday news shows together and analyze foreign crises or political personalities or social conflicts. We would debate and argue, not the vicious arguments I had with my mother but heightened dialogue always touching on policy, ideas, rights, the powerful and the oppressed, discrimination and prejudice. I don't know how he had the patience; but patience was a defining characteristic. He enjoyed my intelligence and treated me with respect. I think that to be loved so unconditionally by a father and treated with respect by him was not common for a girl then. I think he kept my mother alive and I think he kept Mark and me from being raised in foster care or as orphans.

He was appalled by the conflict between me and my mother, and certainly by the time I was a teen-ager he held me responsible for it. He knew I was adult inside. He let me know that my mother's well-being would always come first with him. And I remember that he hated it when I would cry. He must have thought it cowardly and pitiful and self-indulgent. I made many eloquent but to him unpersuasive declarations about my right to cry.

I trusted and honored him. I guess that I trusted him to love me even more than to take care of us. In an honors history seminar in high school, the class was asked to name great men in history. I named my father and was roundly ridiculed by advocates for Thomas Jefferson and Napoleon. But I meant it—that he had the qualities of true greatness, which I defined as strength, generosity, fairness, and a willingness to sacrifice self for principle. His principle was us: my mother, Mark, and me. When I was an adult we had serious ruptures and the relationship broke apart several times—all occasions of dire emergency for me. I think that he did abandon me when I was in circumstances of great suffering and danger. He was, I learned the hard way, only human. But what he gave me as a child, neither he nor anyone else could take away from me later. I learned perseverance from his example, and that endurance was a virtue. Even some of his patience rubbed off on me for some few years. I saw courage in action in ordinary life, without romance; and I learned the meaning of commitment. I could never have become a writer without him.

I wrote my first novel during science class in seventh grade in the suburbs. My best friend, a wild, beautiful girl who wanted to be a painter, sat next to me and also wrote a novel. In the eighth grade, my friend gone from school to be with a male painter in his late twenties or thirties, I wrote a short story for English class so disturbing to my teacher that she put her feelings of apprehension into my permanent record. The ethos was to conform, not to stand out. She knew the writing was good, and that troubled her. There was too much vibrancy in the language, too much imagination in the physical evocations of place and mood. Highly influenced by the television series *The Twilight Zone* and grief-stricken at the loss of my soulmate girlfriend, I wrote a story about a wild woman, strong and beautiful, with long hair and torn clothes, on another planet, sitting on a rock. My story had no plot really, only longing and language. I remember getting lost in descriptions of the woman, the sky, the rock, maybe wind and dirt. In formal terms, I believe I kept circling back to the woman on the rock through repeating images and phrases that worked almost like music to my ear—a way of creating movement yet insisting on the permanence of some elements of the scenario. I had a picture in my mind, which was involuntary. I don't know why it was there or how it got there. The picture was stubborn: it didn't move or change. I could see it as if it were real with my eyes open, though it was conceptual and in my head. It wasn't in front of my eyes; it was behind them. I had huge emotions of pain and loss. I had the need to keep moving through life, not be held back or stopped by anything I felt. I remember finding words that resonated with the emotions I felt: not words that expressed those emotions or described them, but words that embodied them without ever showing them. It was the unrevealed emotion—attached to the words but invisible in them, then used to paint the picture in my head in language that was concrete and physical—that gave the prose an intensity so troubling to my teacher. Was she troubled by the homoeroticism of the story? I don't believe she recognized it.

In the eighth grade, of course, I did not have any consistent internal standards for how prose must be or what prose must do. But I did know much more about what I wanted from language when, thirty years later, I brought that same picture, the same wild woman on the same rock, into my novel *Mercy,* first published in 1990 in England.

The rock was Masada: a steep, barren mountain surrounded by desert, a refuge in ancient Palestine for a community of Jews known as zealots who committed, as the traditional story goes, mass suicide rather than surrender to the occupying Roman army. Ten men used their swords to slit the throats of everyone else; then one man killed the nine men and himself.

Mercy's narrator is a contemporary figure who in one of the novel's endings (it has two) sees herself as the wild woman on Masada at the time of the so-called suicides: "A child can't commit suicide. You have to murder a child. I couldn't watch the children killed; I couldn't watch the women taken one last time; throats bared; heads thrown back, or pushed back, or pulled back; a man gets on top, who knows what happens next, any time can be the last time, slow murder or fast, slow rape or fast, eventual death, a surprise or you are waiting with a welcome, an open invitation; rape leading, inexorably, to death; on a bare rock, invasion, blood, and death. Masada; hear my heart beat; hear me; the women and children were murdered."

I wasn't missing my old girlfriend. I didn't have the same picture in my head because I was feeling what I had felt in the eighth grade. In my experience nothing in writing is that simple. Both memory and consciousness are deeper and wider than the thinking mind, which might find meaning in such a facile association.

I felt, certainly, a much larger abandonment, a more terrifying desolation, essentially impersonal: how the lives of women and children were worthless to men and God. In the despair of that recognition, the barren landscape of the rock became a place to stare men and God in the face, and my wild woman the one to do it. When the picture first came into my head, I dismissed it but it would not go. When I started to work with it in words, I saw Masada, I saw her, and I saw the murders. I, the writer, became a witness. Real history out in the world and a picture etched in my brain but forgotten for three decades converged in words I felt compelled to keep bringing together. Each word brought with it more detail, more clarity. My narrator, who is a character in my book, knows less than I do. She is inside the story. Deciding what she will see, what she can know, I am detached from her and cold in how I use her. I do not ever think she is me. She is not my mouthpiece. She does not directly speak my views or enumerate my ideas or serve as a mannequin in words displaying my wounds of body or soul. I am more than the sum of all her parts; and she can live in the reader's mind but the reader's mind cannot know me through knowing her. I have never been to Masada. However dull it may seem, I am the person who sits at the typewriter writing words, rewriting them, over and over, night in and night out (since I work at night), over months or years. *Mercy* took three years to write.

In using the picture in my head from my eighth-grade story, I broke the picture open into a universe of complex and concrete detail dreadful with meaning, in particular about incest and the power of the father—the patriarchal right of invasion into the bodies of women and children. At the end of writing *Mercy*'s Masada chapter, I felt as if I had finally seen that earlier picture whole. When I was younger I could only see a fragment, or a line drawing, but now I had seen everything that had been implicit in the picture from the beginning, from its first appearance in my mind, as if I had uncovered something pre-existing. It was always real and whole; what I had done as a writer was to find it and describe it, not invent it. In the eighth grade, I had not known how to use my mind or language to explicate the picture in my head, which was a gift or a visitation; I couldn't see the human destiny that had been acted out on that barren rock. But the time between my childhood and now had collapsed. The time between Masada and now had collapsed.

This strange but not unusual aftermath of creating helps to explain why so many writers disclaim responsibility for their characters and ideas. The character made me do it, most writers say. But the truth is that one starts out with a blank page, and each and every page is blank until the writer fills it. In the process, the mind uses itself up, each cognitive capacity—intellect, imagination, memory, intuition, emotion, even cunning—used to the absolute utmost, a kind of strip-mining of one's mental faculties. At the same time, with the mind as scavenger and plunderer, one cannibalizes one's own life. But one's own life for the writer includes everything she can know, not just what happened to her in the ordinary sense. If I know about you—a gesture, an emotion, an event—I will use you if I need your gesture, your emotion, your event. What I take will seem to me to be mine, as if I know it from the inside, because my imagination will turn it over and tear it apart. Writers use themselves and they use other people. Empathy can be invasive. Friendship is sometimes a robbery-in-progress. This omniscient indifference takes a certain coldness, and a certain distance, which writers have and use.

Facts and details are the surface. The writer needs the facts and everything underneath them. One wanders, bodiless, or goes on search-and-destroy missions using one's mind. One needs a big earth, rich soil, deep roots: one digs and pulls and takes.

But after, when the writing is finished, one looks at the finished thing and has a feeling or conviction of inevitability: I found it, not I made it. It—the story, the novel—had its own laws; I simply followed them—found them and followed them; was smart enough and shrewd enough to find them and follow them; wasn't sidetracked or diverted, which would mean failure, a lesser book. Even with nonfiction, which in the universe of my writing has the same cognitive complexity as fiction, in the aftermath one feels that one has chiseled a pre-existing form (which necessarily has substance attached to it) out of a big, shapeless stone: it was there, I found it. This is an affirmation of skill but not of invention. At best, one feels like a sculptor who knows how to liberate the shape hidden in the marble or clay—or knew the last time but may not know the next, may be careless, may ruin the stone through distraction or stupidity. Once finished, the process of writing becomes opaque, even to the writer. I did it but how did I do it? Can I ever do it again? The brain becomes normal. One can still think, of course, but not with the luminosity that makes intelligence so powerful a tool while writing, nor can one think outside of literal and linear time anymore.

Writing is alchemy. Dross becomes gold. Experience is transformed. Pain is changed. Suffering may become song. The ordinary or horrible is pushed by the will of the writer into grace or redemption, a prophetic wail, a screed for justice, an elegy of sadness or sorrow. It is the lone and lonesome human voice, naked, raw, crying out, but hidden too, muted, twisted and turned, knotted or fractured, by the writer's love of form, or formal beauty: the aesthetic dimension, which is not necessarily familiar or friendly. Nor does form necessarily tame or simplify experience. There is always a tension between experience and the thing that finally carries it forward, bears its weight, holds it in. Without that tension, one might as well write a shopping list.

My fiction is not autobiography. I am not an exhibitionist. I don't show myself. I am not asking forgiveness. I don't want to confess. But I have used everything I know—my life—to show what I believe must be shown so that it can be faced. The imperative at the heart of my writing—what must be done—comes directly from my life. But I do not show my life directly, in full view; nor even look at it while others watch.

Autobiography is the unseen foundation of my nonfiction work, especially *Intercourse* and *Pornography: Men Possessing Women*. These two nonfiction books are not "about" me. There is no first-person writing in them. Conceptually, each involved the assimilation of research in many intellectually distinct areas using analytical skills culled from different disciplines. The research materials had nothing to do with me personally. They were freestanding, objectively independent (for instance, not interviews conducted by me). Yet when I wrote *Intercourse* and *Pornography: Men Possessing Women,* I used my life in every decision I made. It was my compass. Only by using it could I find north and stay on course. If a reader could lift up the words on the page, she would see—far, far under the surface—my life. If the print on the page turned into blood, it would be my blood from many different places and times. But I did not want the reader to see my life or my blood. I wanted her to see intercourse or pornography. I wanted her to know them the way I know them: which is deeply.

I'd like to take what I know and just hand it over. But there is always a problem for a woman: being believed. How can I think I know something? How can I think that what I know might matter? Why would I think that anything I think might make a difference, to anyone, any-where? My only chance to be believed is to find a way of writing bolder and stronger than woman hating itself—smarter, deeper, colder. This might mean that I would have to write a prose more terrifying than rape, more abject than torture, more insistent and destabilizing than battery, more desolate than prostitution, more invasive than incest, more filled with threat and aggression than pornography. How would the innocent bystander be able to distinguish it, tell it apart from the tales of the rapists themselves if it were so nightmarish and impolite? There are no innocent bystanders. It would have to stand up for women—stand against the rapist and the pimp—by changing women's silence to speech. It would have to say all the unsaid words during rape and after; while prostituting and after; all the words not said. It would have to change women's apparent submission—the consent read into the silence by the wicked and the complacent—into articulate resis-tance. I myself would have to give up my own cloying sentimentality to-ward men. I'd have to be militant; sober and austere. I would have to commit treason: against the men who rule. I would have to betray the noble, apparently humanistic premises of civilization and civilized writ-ing by conceptualizing each book as if it were a formidable weapon in a war. I would have to think strategically, with a militarist's heart: as if my books were complex explosives, mine fields set down in the culture to blow open the status quo. I'd have to give up Baudelaire for Clausewitz.

Yes, okay, I will. Yes, okay: I did. In retrospect, that is just what I did:

in *Mercy* and *Intercourse* and *Pornography: Men Possessing Women* and *Ice and Fire.*

I t was in Amsterdam in 1972 that I made the vow, which I have kept, that I would use everything I know in behalf of women's liberation. I owed the women's movement a big debt: it was a feminist who helped me escape the brutality of my marriage. Escape is not a one-time run for your life: you keep running and hiding; he shows up out of nowhere and beats you, menaces you, threatens, intimidates, screams a foul invective at you in broad daylight on crowded streets, breaks into wherever you find to live, hits you with his dirty fists, dirtied by your pain, your blood.

I left the marital home toward the end of 1971, some two months after I turned twenty-five. I fled the country in which I had been living for five years in November 1972. I have no continuous memory of the events of that year. Even with the events I can remember, I have no sense of their sequence. I was attacked, persecuted, followed, harassed, by the husband I had left; I often lived the life of a fugitive, except that it was the more desperate life of a battered woman who had run away for the last time, whatever the outcome.

I have written about the experience of being a battered wife in three nonfiction essays: "A Battered Wife Survives" (1978) and "What Battery Really Is" (1989), both of which are included in the U.S. edition of *Letters From a War Zone;* and "Trapped in a Pattern of Pain," published in the *Los Angeles Times,* June 26, 1994. I wrote "A Battered Wife Survives" to celebrate my thirty-first birthday. I still shook and trembled uncontrollably, but not all the time; had nightmares and flashbacks, but less. I had published two books: *Woman Hating* (1974) and *Our Blood* (1976). I had survived and was not alone in a universe of pain and fear. The other two essays were written in behalf of other battered women: Hedda Nussbaum and Nicole Brown Simpson. I felt the need to try to make people understand how destructive and cruel battery is—and how accepted, how normal, how supported by society. With enormous reluctance, I revisited the site of this devastation in my own life. I had to say what battery was from the point of view of the woman being hurt, since I knew.

Everything I have written in these nonfiction essays about myself is true. It would be wrong, however, to read my fiction as if it were a factual narrative, a documentary in words. Literature is always simpler and easier than life, especially in conveying atrocity. As the infrequency of my nonfiction essays about battery suggests, I am extremely reluctant to write about it: partly because I can't bear to think about it; partly because I feel physically ill when I literally trip over absent memory, great and awful blank areas of my life that I cannot recover—I am shaky with dread and vertigo; and partly because I still hide.

But the year of running, hiding, to stay alive is essential to the story of how I became a writer, or the writer I am, for better or worse. He kept our home; I was pushed out. This was fine, since I just wanted not to be hit. I had no money. I was isolated as battered women usually are but also I was a foreigner with no real rights except through my husband. My parents refused to have me back. His family was his—I was too afraid of him ever to tell them anything, though I believe they knew. I slept first on the floor of a friend's room—his friend, too—with her two dogs. Later, I slept where I could. I lived this way before I was married but not with an assassin after me, nor having sustained such brutality that my mind didn't quite work—it failed me in everyday situations, which it no longer recognized; it failed me with ordinary people who couldn't grasp my fear.

A feminist named Ricki Abrams helped me: gave me asylum, a dangerous kindness in the face of a battering man; helped me find shelter repeatedly; and together she and I started to plan the book that became *Woman Hating*.

I lived on houseboats on the canals—a majestic one near the Magere Brug, a stunningly beautiful bridge, a plainer one infested with mice. I slept in someone's kitchen. I lived for a while in the same house as Ricki, a narrow, teetering building on a cobblestone street that ringed a canal in Amsterdam's historically preserved old city. I hid on a farm far outside Amsterdam with a commune of hippies who made their own cloth with a spinning wheel and a loom. I slept in a cold and deserted mansion near the German border. In one emergency, when my husband had broken into where I was living, had beaten me and threatened to kill me, I spent three weeks sleeping in a movie theater that was empty most of the time. Experimental movies were shown in a big room where I hid. The whole building was empty otherwise. On some nights small audiences of artistes would sit and watch formless flashes of light. When the avant-garde cleared out, I was allowed to open a cot. I lived in a state of terror. Every trip outside might mean death if he found me.

No one knew about battery then, including me. It had no public name. There were no shelters or refuges. Police were indifferent. There was no feminist advocacy or literature or social science. No one knew about the continuing consequences, now called post-traumatic stress syndrome, which has a nice dignity to it. How many times, after all, can one say terror, fear, anguish, dread, flashbacks, shaking, uncontrollable trembling, nightmares, he's going to kill me?

At the time, so far as I knew, I was the only person this had ever happened to; and the degradation had numbed me, disoriented me, changed me, lowered me, shamed me, broken me.

It was Ricki who first gave me feminist books to read. I remember especially *Sexual Politics* by Kate Millett (whose class at Barnard Ricki had taken), *The Dialectic of Sex* by Shulamith Firestone, and the anthology *Sisterhood Is Powerful* edited by Robin Morgan. I had left the United States in 1968 a second time (the first being in 1965, after a rapelike trauma in Manhattan's Women's House of Detention, where I was taken after an arrest for protesting the Vietnam War). I had not read or heard about these books. I argued with them in Amsterdam. I argued with Ricki. Oppression meant the U.S. in Vietnam, or apartheid in South Africa, or legal segregation in the U.S. Even though I had been tortured and was fighting for my life, I could not see women, or myself as a woman, as having political significance. I did know that the battery was not my fault. I had been told by everyone I asked for help the many times I tried to escape—strangers and friends—that he would not be hitting me if I didn't like it or want it. I rejected this outright. Even back then, the experience of being battered was recognizably impersonal to me. Maybe I was the only person in the world this had ever happened to, but I knew it had nothing to do with me as an individual. It just never occurred to me that I was being hit because I was a woman.

Woman Hating was not a book written out of an ideology. It came out of an emergency, written half underground and in hiding. I wanted to find out what had happened to me and why. I knew *only* that it was impersonal. I made a list of what I thought might bear on what had happened to me, and that list became the table of contents in the published book. I looked at fairy tales—what did they teach about being female; at pornography—I was part of a generation that used it—what did it say about being female; at Chinese footbinding and the persecution of the witches—why was there culturally normalized violence against females; at androgyny—the myths and contemporary ideas of a community not organized on the principle of gender, the falseness of gender itself. I wanted to examine the culture: sex roles; sex; history; mythology; community.

Somehow, I had been given a key and access to a space in the basement of Paradiso, one of the clubs the Dutch government sponsored for counterculture, hashish-smoking, rock-and-roll–addicted hippies. The basement under the huge church building was dark and dank with a colony of misfits and homeless, mentally disoriented strangers, most of whom were hiding from someone, often the police. I was allowed to work there on the book—I had a desk and chair—but I was not supposed to sleep there, and I tried not to. My cohabitants did not inspire confidence, and my husband, who worked upstairs at night when Paradiso was open, was dangerous for sure. Like other escaping battered women (I have since learned), I lived in a shared or overlapping social and economic world with the batterer; I tried to believe it would be all right.

The book Ricki and I were going to write together became, of course, very important to me. I don't know if the attempt was interrupted by the violence or the violence was interrupted by the attempt. I know that I devoted myself to the book, even though it was hard for me to concentrate because I lived in constant fear. I held on to the book as if it were a life raft, even though I was drowning in poverty and fear. There were times of hope, near normalcy. At one point my husband got a new apartment and offered me our old one. I took it, for all the obvious reasons. He left a mattress; someone gave me a small radio; and I lived on potatoes. Then he started breaking in; and it was there that he bloodied me and said he would kill me, run me down when he saw me, and I knew it was true finally, and I had to hide in the movie theater after that for three weeks, the time it took to get a restraining order. My lawyer, assigned by the court, at first didn't believe me or didn't care when I told him about the beatings or how dangerous my husband was; but later my husband apparently roughed up the lawyer's secretary. This time, when driven from the apartment by my husband's threats to a phone in a store around the block, the lawyer told me to go somewhere else for a while, though he didn't know where or how and didn't care. I had had to go to the store to use the phone because the apartment phone was in my husband's name, and he had it disconnected and it was a two-year wait for a new line. As I came out of the back room of the store where the phone was, the woman who owned the store opened her cash register, grabbed a handful of bills, pushed them at me, and said: "Run for your life. Now." I did.

Through all this, I held on to this idea of a book; and I kept working on it. Ricki and I did research together and some writing together. But then she pulled away from it. The book itself, in taking on counterculture pornography, brought us into conflict with friends and acquaintances in the exilic, counterculture community in Amsterdam. Some of these folks produced a pornography tabloid called *Suck*. Ricki and I drafted a chapter on *Suck* and gave it to them to read. I, at least, believed that they would see the insult to women in what they were publishing, and that there was danger in some of their photographs—I remember in particular a photo of an Asian woman inserting a huge, glass, bowl-shaped jar into her rectum. I had begun to identify with other women. Our friends, the makers of the pornography, reacted with outrage to our effrontery in challenging them. They said they had always been for civil rights (against segregation based on race) and this was sex—what kind of chicks were we anyway? We thought we were perfectly fine chicks at the time, even though the word "chick" itself was beginning to have an ugly sound to it. Ricki decided that she couldn't take the social ostracism these folks threatened. We agreed that I would finish the book and get it published. I had to get out of there anyway or I'd be killed. I knew I had to disappear and that there could be no mistakes. I planned a secret escape and in November 1972 I disappeared suddenly.

The vow that I made—out loud, to myself but with Ricki as witness—was that I would become a real writer and I would use everything I knew to help women. I didn't know how much I knew, how valuable it would be; nor did she. But we both did understand that in 1972 what I knew was not part of feminism: what I knew about male dominance in sex or rape in marriage, for instance. The knowledge about male dominance in sex came not only from this one marriage but from several years of prostituting before I got married. I called it "being on the streets," and it consisted of equal parts whoring, poverty and homelessness, and just being a tough girl. I had never kept it a secret, not from my husband, not from any friend. Ricki and I both understood that I had experience that could be knowledge. I made a vow to use it for women.

Writers need to be damned hard to kill. So do women, of course. I have never believed in suicide, the female poet's alternative to standing her ground and facing down the power of men. I don't like it that Plath and Sexton wrote strong and beautiful poems capturing the horror and meanness of male dominance but would not risk losing socially conventional femininity by sticking around to fight it out in the realm of politics, including the politics of culture. I always wanted to live. I fought hard to live. This means I did something new. I have been bearing the unbearable, and facing men down, for a long time now.

I began messing with men when I was in high school, though, sadly, they began messing with me earlier than that—I was raped at nine, though not legally, since fingers and a hand were used for penetration, not the officially requisite penis. That ended up in my hand as he twisted and contorted with a physical omnipresence that pinned me and manipulated me at the same time. This breach of a child's body does count. It does register. The boundary of the body itself is broken by force and intimidation, a chaotic but choreographed violence. The child is used intentionally and reduced to less than human by the predator's intelligence as well as his behavior. The commitment of the child molester is absolute, and both his insistence and his victory communicate to the child his experience of her—a breachable, breakable thing any stranger can wipe his dick on. When it is family, of course, the invasion is more terrible, more intimate, escape more unlikely. I was lucky—it was a stranger. I was lucky by the standards of today: neither kidnapped nor killed. The man became part of the dark—not "the dark" in its usual symbolic sense, bad, with a racist tinge, but part of the literal dark: his body, almost distinct, got folded into every dark room like the one in which he hurt me and he got folded into the dark of every night I had to get through, with eyes open, waiting. I didn't like to sleep, because then I couldn't guard my mother against death. So I kept my eyes open. I could feel that the night was occupied with tangible creatures, and the man, hiding, was one of them.

As a child with an immense ambition to live, to know, to feel, I moved toward everything that frightened me: men, night, the giving up of my own body. I wanted to be an artist, by which I meant a writer. I despised commercial writing. My heroes were Rimbaud and Baudelaire. I had a paperback of Baudelaire's poems with me, in French with an English prose translation, when the man molested me. A few years later I had a high school teacher who said that most girls of my social class who worked (the ideal was not to work) became hairdressers, but I was so smart that I could become a prostitute, which at least was interesting. He was my tutor in sex; a guide; a charlatan and an exploiter. But he made the sameness of art and opening my legs palpable, urgent: there wasn't one without the other. I thought he was a philosopher and someday we would found a school of philosophy; I would be his acolyte. He introduced me to Camus and Sartre. I was a motherless child with spirit and intelligence in a world that abhorred both in girls. I wanted knowledge but distrusted formal education because the adults were enforcers and transparently wanted to break my spirit; except for the seducer. He wanted to appropriate it for his own purposes but I didn't begin to imagine that. I would find ways to go to New York City to find poems and on the bus I would find a way to get money from old guys who liked teen-age girls to touch them. I'd use the money to go to Greenwich Village and buy mimeographed collections of poems. I loved Allen Ginsberg especially. More than anyone he expressed the sense of pain I felt, the anger and rebellion, but also the undifferentiated infatuation I felt for the world of possibility around me. I had no sense of evil and I didn't believe that harm could defeat me—I'd make poems out of it. High school was hell, to be endured, the teachers behavior-police who took books away and tried to shut the mind down. For instance, a tenth-grade teacher in a study hall confiscated my copy of *Hamlet,* which I had been reading. She said we weren't allowed to read it until the twelfth grade. I told her that I had already read it several times so why take it from me? She did take it and countered with her certainty that one day she would read about me in the newspapers. In those days only politicians and criminals made news. Girls didn't become politicians. I was bad for reading *Hamlet.* Each day the enforcers pushed me into a sustained rage laced with contempt; and each day the seducer manipulated my anger and loneliness, pushed me further into experiencing intelligence as a sexualized mark of Cain and artistic ambition as a sexualized delinquency.

Meanwhile, my father worked hard so that I could have a formal education that would be excellent, not mediocre, on the college level. The high school guidance counselors wanted me to go to a state college for girls to get a teaching degree "to fall back on when your husband dies." My intelligence had no significance to them; my desire to write, which I confessed, was beneath consideration. My father knew I would not stay in any college that was high school redux. In September 1964 I went to Bennington College on scholarships and loans, loans he took out, not me. I did have jobs there for money but not enough to carry any of the real economic burden. I stayed there one year, left, returned for two years, left, mailed in my thesis from Amsterdam. In 1969 my father, fittingly, attended my graduation and picked up my diploma. I am considered a graduate of the class of 1968, however, because that is how Bennington keeps track of students. In those years, so many students left—some of the richer ones to Austin Riggs, a mental institution not too far away, some taking other detours—that the college always reckoned you a member of the class in which you entered and optimistically added four years to signify graduation; it would be hard for an already overtaxed administration to know who returned when, for how long, and to what end.

Bennington had a reputation for academic excellence and a bohemian environment. In fact, Bennington trained mistresses, not wives, for artists, not businessmen. To illustrate the ambience: the year before my first year, seniors in literature had, as a group project, recreated the brothel scene in Joyce's *Ulysses,* themselves the whores. A lot of the faculty preyed on the nearly all-female student body; and the deep conviction of most of the faculty that these girls would never become artists themselves was openly articulated when, in my third year of attendance, coeducation was discussed and eventually adopted. Students, including me, got to hear how useless the mostly male faculty felt teaching girls. We never became anything, they said, each a dozen times in a dozen ways. We seemed to be fine for fucking and serial marriage, some faculty actually going through as many as four marriages with successive students and countless adulteries. But we could never become what in our hearts we thought we were: creative, ambitious, risk-taking doers and thinkers and makers. I had three brilliant teachers at Bennington, each of whom was ethically scrupulous with respect to me; and I owe them a lot. They taught me with an astonishing intellectual generosity; they supported my aspirations; they even protected me, from other faculty and sometimes from myself. They extended friendship without the sexualization. The rest of it was intellectually boring. After my first few weeks there, my philosophy professor telephoned me at the student house where I lived and asked me please not to leave: she knew I was bored. I distracted myself with drugs, sex, and politics.

Bennington had a nine-week work period in the winter—a long two months—and long Thanksgiving, Christmas, and spring breaks, a big problem for a girl with no real home and no money. For my first work period in December 1964 I took marginal political jobs in New York City and fucked for food and shelter and whatever cash I needed. I worked with the Student Peace Union and the War Resisters League opposing the war in Vietnam. I had other jobs, too, for instance as a receptionist at a New York University institute for remedial reading. In February 1965 I was arrested outside the United States Mission to the United Nations for protesting Amerika's involvement in Vietnam. I had a book of poems by Charles Olson with me when I was arrested. I spent four days in the Women's House of Detention before I was released on my own recognizance. While in jail, in addition to the many strip-searches by hand that police and nurses made into my vagina and anus, I was brutalized by two male doctors who gave me an internal examination, the first one I ever had. They pretty much tore me up inside with a steel speculum and had themselves a fine old time verbally tormenting me as well. I saw them enjoy it. I witnessed their pleasure in doing it. I couldn't understand why they would like to hurt me. I began to bleed right after. When I came out of jail I was mute from the trauma. I wandered around the city, homeless and resourceless, silent and confused, for several days, until I showed up at the apartment of a stranger who had taken a bag I had packed for jail from me when, toward the end of the day, it seemed as if we would not be arrested. I sort of vaguely remembered her name and looked it up in the phone book when I needed underwear badly enough. She was the writer Grace Paley and this was before she herself had gone to jail to protest Vietnam. She made me come in and sit; I stared silently. Grace got me to talk but instead of normal talk I said what had happened to me. I didn't even know the words for speculum or internal examination, so I was exceptionally blunt and used my hands. She thought that what had been done to me was horrible and she immediately called a woman reporter to say that this monstrous thing had been done to this girl. The reporter said: so what? But that night I went to the Student Peace Union office and typed letters to newspapers to tell what had happened to me in the jail:

blunt letters. The antiwar boys, whose letters I typed during the day, whose leaflets I mimeographed, laughed at me; but I mounted a protest against the prison. *The New York Times,* the *Daily News,* and the *New York Post* carried the story. The city was forced to conduct a grand jury investigation. An assistant to the governor also investigated. A liberal Republican, John V. Lindsay, challenged entrenched Democratic incumbent Robert Wagner for mayor partly by holding Wagner responsible for the corruption in the jail and promising to shut it down. Lindsay won. Television news shows did documentaries on the prison, which had a long history of brutalizing women, some of whom had died. Eventually, the grand jury vindicated the prison, and the governor's assistant was defunded by the legislature. My parents were ashamed of my arrest and of the way in which I had been hurt. They were enraged with me and pretty much abandoned me. I left school, my parents, the country. I went to Greece with less than $100 in my pocket. I gave most of it to an old woman, Mildred, whom I met on a train. She said she had lost hers but had money waiting in Athens. I showed up at the appointed place, at the appointed time, but she never came. That night, my nineteenth birthday, I picked up a Greek army officer: I needed food and money. Since the hill overlooking Athens was beautiful and the night sublime, it was easy to pretend this was romance. I remember saying to him after, "You really hate women, don't you?" I hadn't anticipated woman hating but I recognized it in his abrupt post-coital tristesse. I learned not to voice the observation however many times I made it, whatever the post-coital mood. Men don't like to be seen or remarked on by what my friend Judith Malina, director of the Living Theatre, calls "talking women." I wrote poems and a novel called *Notes on Burning Boyfriend,* a surrealistic screed against the Vietnam War built on the self-immolation of protester Norman Morrison. I published a small collection of poems and Genet-like prose called *Child* (Heraklion, Crete, 1966). It wasn't until I published *Woman Hating* in 1974 that I became a talking woman who could say with some authority: you really hate women, don't you?

The authority was never my own plain experience. I always thought other people's lives were worth more than mine. As a matter of temperament I had an interest in the collective or communal, not the personal. I thought psychology was a phony science, and I still do. I didn't think something was important simply because it happened to me, and certainly the world concurred. I had learned that I would not be believed. I knew that from the world's point of view, though never my own, I was trash, the bottom. The prison authorities said I lied and the grand jury claimed to believe them, not me. No one really believed me about my husband. I had a deep experience of the double standard but no systematic understanding of it. The writers I had loved and wanted to emulate—Baudelaire or Artaud or Dostoevsky or Henry Miller or Jean Genet—were apparently ennobled by degradation. The lower they sunk the more credibility they had. I was lowered and disgraced, first by what was being called sexual liberation, then by the violence of domestic sexual servitude, without any concomitant increase in expertness: I paid my dues, baby, I know the price of the ticket but so what? When I emerged as a writer with *Woman Hating,* it was not to wallow in pain, or in depravity, or in the male romance with prostitution; it was to demand change. I wanted to change the power structure in the social world that had made degradation a destiny for many of us, or lots of us, or maybe even all of us—for women. I didn't want to write the female suicide's poem; nor did I want to write another male-inspired lyric celebrating the sewer. I wanted to resist male dominance for myself and to change the outcome for other women. I did not want to open my legs again, this time in prose. I did not believe that to do so would persuade or bring change. I found, then and over the next twenty years, a stubborn refusal to credit a woman with any deep knowledge of the world itself, the world outside the domain of her own introspection about romantic love, housekeeping, a man. This refusal was so basic and so widespread that it could stay an unspoken assumption. Women who wanted to write about social issues did it through anecdote. Books that could only have been written out of an extensive and significant knowledge of what it meant to be pornographized or sexually colonized—my books—were dismissed by patriarchy's intellectual ruling class as Victorian or puritanical—empirical synonyms for ignorant.

Instead of using my own experience as the immediate subject of discourse, I used a more complex method of exposing bone and blood: I found the social phenomena that could be pulled apart to show what I knew to be the essential heart of the experience—rape, prostitution, battery, for instance; woman hating, sexualized insult, bias, discrimination—and I found the language to carry it: to carry it far, way past where critics could reach or, frankly, most men could imagine. I had the luck of having my books last over enough time to reach women—not elite women but grassroots women and marginalized women. Slowly women began to come to me to say, yes, that's right; and I learned more from them, went deeper. I used writing to take language where women's pain was—and women's fear—and I kept excavating for the words that could bear the burden of speaking the unspeakable: all that hadn't been said during the rape or after, while prostituting or after; truths that had not been said ever or truths that had not been said looking the rapist, the batterer, the pimp, the citizen-john in the eye. This has been my contribution to literature and to the women's movement.

I saw my mother's strength. Illness seems a visitation, a particular affliction to test the courage of the stricken person, a personal challenge from God. It is hard to know what one can learn from the example even of someone as heroic as my mother surely was. In my mother, I saw Herculean strength in the face of pain, sickness, incapacitation, and the unknown. I have never thought that much of it rubbed off, because I am a coward in that realm: any minor illness makes me feel as if life has stopped. The heroic person, as I saw from my mother, never accepts even the suggestion that life might stop. She keeps pulling the burden, illness as a stone weight; she never stops pulling. Nothing in my mother's life suggested that women were wimps.

In school—grade school and college—my female friends were rebels with deep souls: bad children in adulthood; smart adults in childhood;

precocious; willful; stubborn; not one age or one sex or with one goal easily advanced by a conforming marriage and inevitable motherhood. Despite the best efforts of parents, teachers, to bind our feet Chinese-style, we kept kicking. Ain't none of us got out with unbroken feet; we all got some bones bent in half; we got clipped and pushed and stepped on hard to make us conform; and in our different ways we kept walking, even on the broken bones. It was a time when girls were supposed to be virgins when we married. The middle-class ideal was that women were not supposed to work; such labor would reflect badly on our husbands. Anyone pregnant outside of marriage was an outcast: a delinquent or an exile; had a criminal abortion or birthed a child that would most likely be taken away from her for adoption, which meant forever then. In disgrace, she would be sent away to some home for pregnant girls, entirely stigmatized; her parents ashamed, shocked; she herself a kind of poison that had ruined the family's notion of its own goodness and respectability. She would be socially reprehensible and repulsive— and the social ostracism would be absolute. I had close friends who resisted, who never quite gave in, despite appearances to the contrary. The cost was high sometimes; but it is my impression that my friends, like most women, paid the highest price when they did give in, not when they resisted. The cost needs to be spread out over time: the many marriages and the midlife depression. On the streets there were women who were both strong and fragile at the same time: immensely strong to bear the continuing sexual invasion, consistent brutality, and just plain bad weather (no joke); immensely strong to accept responsibility as the prostituting persona—I want this, I do this, I am this, ain't nothin' hurts me; and much too fragile to face either the cost of prostituting or its etiology. The cost was physical disintegration and mental splitting apart. The cost was getting dirtier and lonelier and anesthetizing pain with more and meaner drugs. The cost was accepting the physical violence of the johns, moving through it as if it didn't matter or hadn't happened, never facing that one had been hurt, then hurt again, nor asking why. Some girls were straight-out battered and forced. But even without a violent man in sight, the etiology always had to do with sexual abuse, in the present or in the past; also with homelessness and poverty; with the willingness of men to use any girl for small change; with abandonment—the personal abandonment of family, the social abandonment choreographed by the users. It may be harder to face abandonment than to endure exploitation; and there were no models for articulating the realities and consequences of sexual abuse. The point of dealing with political oppression has never been that the oppressed are by nature weak, therefore pitiful: the more injustice on one's back, the stronger one must be. Strong girls become strong women and use that strength to endure; but fighting injustice requires a dynamic strength disciplined to resistance, focused on subverting illegitimate power, eventually to level it. In a system valuing men over women, girls with piss and vinegar carried a heavier burden than girls brimming over with sugar and spice; the stronger were punished more, and still are. In this world, female friendships, deep and sustained loves, romances and infatuations, also love affairs, helped keep one's heart alive, one's sense of self, however unratified by the larger universe, animated and sensate. The political use of female strength to change society for the benefit of women is a different choice: a harder, better choice than endurance, however noble (or stylish) the endurance.

In my early adult life as a writer, there were three women especially who helped me and taught me and believed in me: Grace Paley, Barbara Deming, and Muriel Rukeyser. Each one sort of took me in and took me to her heart for some significant period of my life. Each one was mother and sister and friend. Each one was a distinguished and powerful writer, a social rebel, an original moral thinker. Each lived a life that combined writing and political action. Each put herself on the line for the oppressed, the powerless; was repelled by exploitation and injustice; and was devoted to women—had deep and intimate friendships with women and fought for women's rights. I met Grace in 1965, shortly after I got out of the Women's House of Detention. She fed me and gave me a bed to sleep in; I went to her when I was distressed, exhausted, in trouble—or more trouble than usual. She helped me when I came back from Greece; then again later when I came back from Amsterdam. I met

Barbara in 1965 a few months after I met Grace, on a television program about the Women's House of Detention, where she too had spent some time as a political protester (see "Letter to M.," *Lavender Culture,* edited by Jay and Young); and then we met again and became close after *Woman Hating* was published. In 1976, my friend John Stoltenberg (about whom more later) and I went down to Sugarloaf Key in Florida to live on shared land with Barbara and her lover, Jane Verlaine. I couldn't tolerate the subtropical climate so after five months John and I moved north to the Berkshires. I met Muriel in 1972 after I had returned to New York City from Amsterdam at an antiwar meeting. She tried very hard to help me survive as a writer, including by hiring me as her assistant (see "Introduction," *Letters From a War Zone*). My apprenticeship to her had a slightly formal quality, because she paid me for the duration. She opened her home to me and her heart; she advised me and counseled me; and she made sure I had a bare minimum of money. She was attuned to the concrete necessities. A woman who has been poor and entirely on her own, as Muriel had been, knows that one's life can slip through a crack; good intentions can't match the value of a dime.

These friendships were of enormous importance to me; I doubt I would have survived without them. But the friendships went far beyond any utility for survival. Each of these women had faith in me—and I never quite knew why; and each of these women loved me—and I never knew why. It was a lucky orphan who found each of these women and it was a lucky striving writer who found each of these writers. They are all taken more seriously now than they were then; but I had the good sense to know that each was an Amerikan original, wise with common sense and plan talk, gritty with life; they were great craftswomen, each a citizen and a visionary. I know what I took; I hope I gave enough back.

It is hard to say what keeps a writer writing in the face of discouragement. It helps to have had a difficult childhood; to have a love of writing itself, without regard to the outcome; and eventually to have an audience, however small, that wants you, wants those troublesome books, is like a lover to you, very intimate with enormous expectations—embraces you through the language you find and the truth you are willing to tell. I have had that audience, which I meet when I travel to lecture or to give readings, a U.S. underground unrecognized by the media in small towns, on college campuses, at political rallies, tender, luminous, brave women of all ages, and mostly but not exclusively young men who want fairness for women. They have shown me respect and love.

One can be derailed by savage reviews, certainly poverty, a ubiquitous cultural contempt, violent words or violent gestures or violent acts, invisibility as a writer or, in the Amerikan tradition, too much fame or notoriety. My own view is that survival is a matter of random luck: the right blow, the one that will finish you, does not hit you at the right time in the right place. I have not made money or had an easy time publishing my work, which has been anathematized. I had a hard childhood, which is good; and I have the audience that wants my work, which is essential; and I love to write regardless of the outcome in publishing, which is damned lucky or I'd have died of a broken heart. But especially I have had the love of John Stoltenberg, with whom I have lived now for twenty years, and the love and friendship of Elaine Markson, who has been my agent for the past twenty-two years. They are fierce and brilliant friends. Neither has been intimidated by the anger against my work or against me. Each has stayed with me when I thought they would leave or should leave. I love John with my heart and soul; but what is more extraordinary is the way in which he has loved me (see his "Living With Andrea Dworkin," *Lambda Book Review,* May/June 1994). I never promised him anything; but he promised me right from the beginning that he would stay with me for the rest of his life. I am just entertaining the idea that he might. He undertook to live the life I needed. He has taken on my hardships as his own; indeed, they have become his own. We share the circumstances created by the antagonism to my work on Grub Street. We share the politics of radical feminism and a commitment to destroying male dominance and gender itself. We share a love of writing and of equality; and we share each and every day. He is a deeply kind person, and it is through the actual dailiness of living with him that I understand the spiritual poverty and the sensual stupidity of eroticizing brutality over kindness. Elaine has been a loyal friend and colleague in circumstances both complex and difficult. She has stayed loyal to me and to my work through years when she didn't make enough in commissions to cover the postage she spent sending out my manuscripts. Pornographers and their flunkies have tried to bully and intimidate her; so have publishers, as if silencing me would further freedom of speech. She has kept sending out manuscripts of mine for years as publishers stubbornly refused them. It was she who finally made it possible for me to publish my work in England when U.S. publishers were a dead end. *Ice and Fire,* published by Secker & Warburg in the United Kingdom in 1986, was the first of several books to have widespread British distribution while remaining unsold in the U.S. I had written a good first draft in 1983, which Elaine tried to sell in the U.S., then a final version in 1984. *Ice and Fire* was finally published here in 1987—by an English company—but was never brought out in a paperback edition. The paperback is still in print in England. These are trying difficulties that no slick, money-driven agent would tolerate. Elaine will tell you that she doesn't always agree with me; but why should she—and why should anyone assume that she does? The assumption comes from the lazy but popular stigmatizing ploy of guilt by association, a form of hysteria that pervades any discussion of me or my work in publishing circles. She refuses to give in to this discrediting ruse. Her faith in me has sometimes had to stand in for my faith in myself: I have become shaky but she stands firm. Many times, in the quiet of the room where I work, I have had to face the fact that I would not still be writing—given how hard the hard times have been—were it not for Elaine's passionate commitment and integrity. We've walked many miles together.

So the right blow may still strike in the right place at exactly the right time: to break my writer's heart and stop me in my tracks. I do believe that survival is random, not a result of virtue or talent. But so far, especially in knowing John and Elaine, I have been blessed with monumental grace and staggering good luck.

On April 30, 1992, at the age of forty-two, my brother Mark died of cancer. This was exactly eighteen years after the publication date of *Woman Hating,* an anniversary that will never make me happy again.

He was living in Vienna when he died, a molecular biologist, married to his wife of ten years, Eva Rastl, also a molecular biologist, forty at the time of his death.

He was chair of the department of molecular biology at the Ernst Boehringer Institute of Vienna. He and Eva worked together there and also earlier at Columbia University in New York City. He had done postdoctoral work in biochemistry at the Carnegie Institution in Baltimore, the National Cancer Institute in Bethesda, and the University of California at Davis. At the time Mark got ill, he and Eva were doing research on the metabolism of cancer cells. They were wonderful together, sharing love, friendship, and work. She, a Catholic from Austria, he, Jewish, born in Camden in 1949, reconciled cultural differences and historical sorrow through personal love, the recognition of each other as individuals, and the exercise of reason, which they both, as scientists, valued. A belief in reason was key to a world view that they had in common.

When my brother died, part of me died. This is not hyperbole or cliché. I could feel some of the light that is life going dead inside me and when he died, it went out. He was a gentle boy, the one life I knew from infancy. I had a utopian memory of loving him, a kind of ecstatic love for him that was nonverbal, inexplicable, untouched by growing older. Although we were separated from the time I left home to go to college—there was a period of eleven years when I didn't see him at all, although we wrote each other—the closeness of early childhood never changed, his emotional importance to me, mine to him. But he didn't remember his early childhood or his later childhood; he didn't remember anything from childhood. This terrified me. Because we had usually been sent to stay at separate places when my mother was ill, I had no idea what might have happened to him. As an adult, he had recurrent nightmares that he couldn't understand. I was able to explain or identify the elements of one of them for him. He saw a big man dressed in black carrying a black bag and coming into the house at night—then he woke up in fear. This was my mother's doctor, a cold, frightening figure. I always thought of him as death but I did know who he was. My brother didn't. The childhood years were still blank when he died.

He was the kind child, the nurturer of my parents. As they grew older, he took care of them, with his company, his true concern. My mother died a year before Mark, and I don't believe he recovered from her death before his own. Like my father, like John, he was a good and giving man.

I saw him about three weeks before he died. He had asked me to come to Vienna in October 1990 to visit. I didn't want to go to Austria ever, but put these feelings aside to see him. Told in November 1991 he had cancer, he submitted to a major operation in which a large part of his esophagus near his stomach was removed. He recovered from the surgery but lost the use of his larynx. There were signs that the malignant cells had spread. I found myself the bearer of this knowledge, a confidant for Eva, the one who had to keep my father hoping and eventually the one who had to tell him that Mark would die soon, probably within a few days. In our childhood, Mark and I had learned to be alone with our troubles whatever they were. Mark undertook to die the same way. Eva was with him and they were close, tender, inseparable; but he didn't want family or friends to make the journey to see him. I told him that I was coming to Vienna and he didn't have to see me but I would be there; I had made the arrangements. I believe he was glad, but he got sicker much faster than he or Eva or I anticipated. When I went he was unbearably ill. He had asked me to bring him Skippy peanut butter, which was our staple as children. He was starving to death, a not unusual effect of cancer, and so Eva and I hoped he would eat it. But he couldn't. I also took him marbles, especially cats' eyes, which we had played with when we were children. Marbles and bottlecaps were currency among the kids in our neighborhood. Once he had stolen all

mine and my mother had let him keep them because he was a boy—
they were boys' wealth, not girls'. He smiled when I told him but I don't
think he remembered. He kept the marbles near him.

I sat with him during the day for as long as he would let me. Sometimes he could whisper—it was air, not sound, shaped by his mouth.
But sometimes he was too weak for that, and I sat at a table in the same
room—a modern living room with a large picture window that looked
out on trees and bushes, a room filled with daylight—and read, or tried
to read. I think it was only after he died and Eva sent me some photographs of him from those days of my visit that I realized how frail he
had been, how much I hadn't seen—how hard it had been for him to
appear clean and groomed and calm and smiling. The cancer had spread
to his liver. Tumors were growing on his neck, which he kept covered,
and on other parts of his body.

Then I'd go back to my hotel and I would wail; I'd scream and cry
and wail. I would call John—it would still be late afternoon in Vienna,
too expensive to call—and I'd howl and keen and cry wildly, again and
again, until I was worn out. Then I'd take a walk in the park across from
my hotel. The cold air would be bracing, and my head would stop hurting. Then I would return to my room and sit down to write. I had
brought a legal pad with me and also an article that John Irving had recently published in *The New York Times Book Review* castigating feminists for opposing pornography, charging that we were purveyors of a
new puritanism (see John Irving, "Pornography and the New Puritans,"
March 29, 1992). I knew that to survive the pain I felt on seeing my
brother dying I would have to find a way to use the pain. I truly thought
that otherwise it would kill me. I decided, coldly and purposefully, to
confront the most painful theme in my own life—repeated sexual
abuse. The logic of my answer to Mr. Irving was that no one with the
kind of experience I had could be called a puritan; and maybe I and
other women actually knew more about sexual violence than he did;
and it was the pornographers, not feminists, who punished women in
the public square, as puritans had, for being sexual. The narrative was a
first-person detailed telling of rapes and assaults (see *The New York*

Times Book Review, May 3, 1992). The day my piece was published as a nearly full-page letter edited from the article I had intended, my father and I were on a plane to Vienna to bury Mark at the Central Cemetery. The chief rabbi of Vienna conducted the service. My father simply refused to sit with the men, as is Orthodox practice, and sat with Eva and me. My brother wasn't religious but he loved walking in that great European graveyard. He was someone who walked miles for pleasure; and the Central Cemetery, miles from where he lived, had been one of his favorite places to walk to, then wander in. What does a man with no memory of childhood think of on long, solitary walks to the civilized, well-tended graves of the Austrians, the abandoned, overgrown graves of the Jews? My brother had taken me there on my first trip to Vienna—he had wanted me to see this place that was special to him. I had reacted with horror to the sight of the neglected Jewish graves, the latest stone I saw dated 1938. On my 1992 trip back to Vienna when Mark was sick, I saw on television that the mayor of Vienna had just made a speech acknowledging the importance of Jews, always, to life in Vienna, to its greatness as a city, and that a committee of non-Jewish Austrians was trying to make some restitution by cleaning up the abandoned graves and trying to find out what had happened to the families. Because of this change, we felt able to bury Mark in the Central Cemetery, in the contemporary Jewish burial ground, where he could rest near Eva, though she cannot be buried with him. I have gone back to visit his grave. Eva says it has helped her to have Mark buried there.

I am less alive because I lost my brother. Yet I used what I felt while I watched him dying to write something I considered necessary. I think this is a deep and perhaps terrible truth about writing. Surely, it is a deep and terrible truth about me. As long as I can, I will take what I feel, use it to face what I am able to know, find language, and write what I think must be written for the freedom and dignity of women.

EMERGENCIES

IN MEMORY OF
NICOLE BROWN SIMPSON

I. BEFORE THE TRIAL

It's the Perpetrator, Stupid

You won't ever know the worst that happened to Nicole Brown Simpson in her marriage, because she is dead and cannot tell you. And if she were alive, remember, you wouldn't believe her.

You heard Lorena Bobbitt, after John Wayne Bobbitt had been acquitted of marital rape. At her own trial for malicious wounding, she described beatings, anal rape, humiliation. She had been persistently injured, hit, choked by a husband who liked hurting her. John Wayne Bobbitt, after a brief tour as a misogynist–media star, beat up a new woman friend.

It is always the same. It happens to women as different as Nicole Simpson, Lorena Bobbitt—and me. The perpetrators are men as different as O.J. Simpson, John Wayne Bobbitt, and the former flower-child I am still too afraid to name.

There is terror, yes, and physical pain. There is desperation and despair. One blames oneself, forgives him. One judges oneself harshly for not loving him enough. "It's your fault," he shouts as he is battering in the door, or slamming your head against the floor. And before you pass out, you say yes. You run, but no one will hide you or stand up for you—which means standing up to him. You will hide behind bushes if there are bushes; or behind trash cans; or in alleys; away from the decent people who aren't helping you. It is, after all, your fault.

He hurts you more: more than last time and more than you ever thought possible; certainly more than any reasonable person would ever believe—should you be foolish enough to tell. And, eventually, you surrender to him, apologize, beg him to forgive you for hurting him or provoking him or insulting him or being careless with something of his—his laundry, his car, his meal. You ask him not to hurt you as he does what he wants to you.

The shame of this physical capitulation, often sexual, and the betrayal of your self-respect will never leave you. You will blame yourself and hate yourself forever. In your mind, you will remember yourself—begging, abject. At some point, you will stand up to him verbally, or by not complying, and he will hit you and kick you; he may rape you; he may lock you up or tie you up. The violence becomes contextual, the element in which you try to survive.

You will try to run away, plan an escape. If he finds out, or if he finds you, he will hurt you more. You will be so frightened you think dying might be okay.

If you have no money, can't find shelter, have no work, you will go back and ask him to let you in. If you work, he will find you. He may ask you back and make promises filled with repentance. He may beat you and force you back. But if you do stay away and make a break, he will strike out of nowhere, still beat you, vandalize your home, stalk you.

Still, no one stops him. You aren't his wife anymore, and he still gets to do it.

Nicole Simpson, like every battered woman, knew she would not be believed. She may have been shrewd enough to anticipate the crowds along the Orange County freeways cheering on O.J. Every battered woman has to be careful, even with strangers. His friends won't stop him. Neither will yours.

Nicole Simpson went to many experts on domestic violence for help but none of them stopped *him.* That's what it takes: the batterer has to be stopped. He will not stop himself. He has to be imprisoned, or killed, or she has to escape and hide, sometimes for the rest of her life, sometimes until he finds another woman to "love." There is no proof that counseling the batterer stops him.

It was Nicole who asked the police to arrest Simpson in 1989, the ninth time the police had been called. Arrest needs to be mandatory. The 1989 assault on Nicole Simpson should have resulted in O.J. Simpson's ninth arrest. We don't know by what factor to multiply the number nine: how many episodes of being beaten women endure, on average, per phone call to the police. In 1993 alone, there were 300,000 domestic violence calls to the police in New York City.

Wife-beating is not Amerika's dirty little secret, as the press and Health and Human Services Secretary Donna Shalala say. Feminists have spent two decades exposing wife abuse with insistence and accuracy, organizing refuges and escape routes and changing law enforcement practices so that, increasingly, wife-beating is recognized as a violent crime.

Wife-beating is commonplace and ordinary because men believe they have rights over women that women dispute. The control men want of women, the domination men require over women, is expressed in this terrible brutality. For me, it was for a four-year period, twenty-five years ago in another country. For 4 million women in the United States, one every fifteen seconds, it was yesterday and today.

What no one will face is this: the problem is not with the woman; it is with the perpetrator. She can change every weakness, transform every dependency. She can escape with the bravado of a Jesse James or the subtle skill of a Houdini. But if the husband is committed to violence and she is not, she cannot win her safety or her freedom. The current legal system, victim advocates, counseling cannot keep her safe in the face of his aggression.

Accounts of wife-beating have typically been met with incredulity and disdain, best expressed in the persistent question, "*Why doesn't she leave?*" But after two decades of learning about battery, we now know that more battered women are killed after they leave than before.

Nicole Simpson was living in her own home when she was murdered. Her divorce had been finalized in 1992. Whether or not her ex-husband committed the murder, he did continue to assault her, threaten her, stalk her, intimidate her. His so-called desire for reconciliation masks the awfulness of her situation, the same for every woman who escapes but does not disappear. Having ended the marriage, Nicole Simpson still had to negotiate her safety with the man who was hurting her.

She had to avoid angering him. Any hint that her amiability was essentially coerced, any threat of public exposure, any insult to his dignity from his point of view, might trigger aggression. This cause-and-effect scenario is more imagined than real, since the perpetrator chooses when he will hurt or threaten or stalk. Still, the woman tries. All the smiling photographs of them together after the divorce should evoke alarm, not romantic descriptions of his desire to reconcile. Nicole Simpson followed a strategy of appeasement, because no one stood between her and him to stop him.

Escape, in fact, is hell, a period of indeterminate length reckoned in years, not months, when the ex-husband commits assaults intermittently and acts of terrorism with some consistency. Part of the torment is that freedom is near but he will not let the woman have it. Many escaped women live half in hiding. I am still afraid of my ex-husband each and every day of my life—and I am not afraid of much.

Maybe you don't know how brave women are—the ones who have stayed until now and the ones who have escaped, both the living and the dead. Nicole Simpson is the hero. The perpetrator is the problem, stupid.

II. DURING THE TRIAL

In Nicole Brown Simpson's Words

Words matter. O.J. Simpson's defense team asked Judge Lance A. Ito to order the prosecution to say *domestic discord* rather than *domestic violence* or even *spousal abuse*—already euphemisms for wife-beating—and to disallow the words *battered wife* and *stalker*. Ito refused to alter reality by altering language but some media complied—for example, *Rivera*

Live, where *domestic discord* became a new term of art. The lawyer who successfully defended William Kennedy Smith on a rape charge also used that term systematically.

Where is the victim's voice? Where are her words? "I'm scared," Nicole Brown told her mother a few months before she was killed. "I go to the gas station, he's there. I go to the Payless Shoe Store, and he's there. I'm driving, and he's behind me."

Nicole's ordinary words of fear, despair, and terror told to friends, and concrete descriptions of physical attacks recorded in her diary, are being kept from the jury. Insignificant when she was alive—because they didn't save her—the victim's words remain insignificant in death: excluded from the trial of her accused murderer, called "hearsay" and not admissible in a legal system that has consistently protected or ignored the beating and sexual abuse of women by men, especially by husbands.

Nicole called a battered-women's shelter five days before her death. The jury will not have to listen—but we must. Evidence of the attacks on her by Simpson that were witnessed in public will be allowed at trial. But most of what a batterer does is in private. The worst beatings, the sustained acts of sadism, have no witnesses. Only she knows. To refuse to listen to Nicole Brown Simpson is to refuse to know.

There was a time when the law, including the FBI, and social scientists maintained that wife-beating did not exist in the United States. Eventually the FBI did estimate that a woman is beaten every fifteen seconds in the U.S., and the Justice Department concluded the same in 1984.

Such a change happens this way. First, there is a terrible and intimidating silence—it can last centuries. Inside that silence, men have a legal or a tacit right to beat their wives. Then, with the support of a strong political movement, victims of the abuse speak out about what has been done to them and by whom. They break the silence. One day, enough victims have spoken—sometimes in words, sometimes by running away or seeking refuge or striking back or killing in self-defense— that they can be counted and studied: social scientists find a pattern of injury and experts describe it.

The words of experts matter. They are listened to respectfully, are often paid to give evidence in legal cases. Meanwhile, the voice of the victim still has no social standing or legal significance. She still has no credibility such that each of us—and the law—is compelled to help her.

We blame her, as the batterer did. We ask why she stayed, though we, of course, were not prepared to stand between her and the batterer so that she could leave. And if, after she is dead, we tell the police that we heard the accused murderer beat her in 1977, and saw her with black eyes—as Nicole's neighbors did—we will not be allowed to testify, which may be the only justice in this, since it has taken us seventeen years to bother to speak at all. I had such neighbors.

Every battered woman learns early on not to expect help. A battered woman confides in someone, when she does, to leave a trail. She overcomes her fear of triggering violence in the batterer if he finds out that she has spoken in order to leave a verbal marker somewhere, with someone. She thinks the other person's word will be believed later.

Every battered woman faces death more than once, and each time the chance is real: the batterer decides. Eventually, she's fractured inside by the continuing degradation and her emotional world is a landscape of desperation. Of course, she smiles in public and is a good wife. He insists—and so do we.

The desperation is part fear—fear of pain, fear of dying—and part isolation, a brutal aloneness, because everything has failed—every call for help to anyone, every assumption about love, every hope for self-respect and even a shred of dignity. What dignity is there, after all, in confessing, as Nicole did in her diary, that O.J. started beating her on a street in New York and, in their hotel room, "continued to beat me for hours as I kept crawling for the door." He kept hitting her while sexually using her, which is rape—because no meaningful consent is possible or plausible in the context of this violence.

Every battered woman's life has in it many rapes like this one. Sometimes, one complies without the overt violence but in fear of it. Or sometimes, one initiates sex to try to stop or head off a beating. Of course, there are also the so-called good times—when romance overcomes the memory of violence. Both the violation and the complicity make one deeply ashamed. The shame is corrosive. Whatever the batterer left, it attacks. Why would one tell? How can one face it?

Those of us who are not jurors have a moral obligation to listen to Nicole Simpson's words: to how O.J. Simpson locked her in a wine closet after beating her and watched TV while she begged him to let her out; to how, in a different hotel room, "O.J. threw me against the walls . . . and on the floor. Put bruises on my arm and back. The window scared me. Thought he'd throw me out." We need to hear how he "threw a fit, chased me, grabbed me, threw me into walls. Threw all my clothes out of the window into the street three floors below. Bruised me." We need to hear how he stalked her after their divorce. "Everywhere I go," she told a friend, "he shows up. I really think he is going to kill me."

We need, especially, to hear her call to a battered-women's shelter five days before her murder. In ruling that call inadmissible, Ito said: "To the man or woman on the street, the relevance and probative value of such evidence is both obvious and compelling. . . . However, the laws and appellate-court decisions that must be applied . . . held otherwise." The man and woman on the street need to hear what was obvious to her: the foreknowledge that death was stalking her.

We need to believe Nicole's words to know the meaning of terror—it isn't a movie of the week—and to face the treason we committed against her life by abandoning her.

When I was being beaten by a shrewd and dangerous man twenty-five years ago, I was buried alive in a silence that was unbreachable and unbearable. Imagine Nicole being buried alive, then dead, in noise—our pro-woman, pro-equality noise; or our pro-family, pro–law-and-order noise. For what it's worth—to Nicole nothing—the shame of battery is all ours.

III. AFTER THE ACQUITTAL

Domestic Violence: Trying to Flee

Five days before Nicole Brown Simpson was murdered on June 12, 1994, she called a battered women's shelter in terror that her ex-husband was going to kill her. The jury was not told this, because she couldn't be cross-examined. Guess not. Most of the rest of the evidence of beating and stalking, from 1977 to May 1994, was also excluded.

O.J. Simpson had stalked her not once, as represented to the jury, but over at least a two-year period. Prosecutors had been permitted to introduce seven incidents of stalking, but they chose to admit only one into evidence. The jury, predominantly women, was not responding to the wife abuse evidence, said observers. In fact, during an interview late last week, one woman juror called the domestic abuse issue "a waste of time." Polls during the trial confirmed women were indifferent to the beatings Nicole Simpson endured.

As a woman who escaped an assassin husband and is still haunted by fear and flashbacks, I agreed with Deputy District Attorney Christopher A. Darden that, in 1989, Nicole Simpson knew someday her husband would kill her. She'd told many people, including her sister, Denise, that he'd kill her and get away with it. In fact, you can take a battered woman's knowledge of her abuser's capacity to inflict harm and evade consequences to the bank.

But five days before Nicole Simpson was murdered, she knew, for sure, she would die. How? Why? Something had happened: a confrontation, a threatening phone call, an unwanted visit, an aggressive act from Simpson directed at her. She told no one, because, after seventeen years of torment, she knew there was no one to tell. The police virtually everywhere ignore assault against women by their male intimates, so that any husband can be a brutal cop with tacit state protection; in Los Angeles, the police visited Nicole Simpson's abuser at home as fans.

Remember the video showing Simpson, after the ballet recital, with the Brown family—introduced by the defense to show Simpson's pleasant demeanor. Hours later, Nicole Simpson was dead. In the video, she is as far from Simpson, physically, as she can manage. He does not nod or gesture to her. He kisses her mother, embraces and kisses her sister, and bear-hugs her father. They all reciprocate. She must have been the loneliest woman in the world.

What would Nicole Simpson have had to do to be safe? Go underground, change her appearance and identity, get cash without leaving a trail, take her children and run—all within days of her call to the shelter. She would have had to end all communication with family and friends, without explanation, for years, as well as leave her home and everything familiar.

With this abuser's wealth and power, he would have had her hunted down; a dream team of lawyers would have taken her children from her. She would have been the villain—reckless, a slut, reviled for stealing the children of a hero. If his abuse of her is of no consequence now that she's been murdered, how irrelevant would it have been as she, resourceless, tried to make a court and the public understand that she needed to run for her life?

Nicole Simpson knew she couldn't prevail, and she didn't try. Instead of running, she did what the therapists said: be firm, draw a line. So she drew the sort of line they meant: he could come to the recital but not sit with her or go to dinner with her family—a line that was no defense against death. Believing he would kill her, she did what most battered women do: kept up the appearance of normality. There was no equal justice for her, no self-defense she felt entitled to. Society had already left her to die.

On the same day the police who beat Rodney G. King were acquitted in Simi Valley, a white husband who had raped, beaten, and tortured his wife, also white, was acquitted of marital rape in South Carolina. He had kept her tied to a bed for hours, her mouth gagged with adhesive tape. He videotaped a half hour of her ordeal, during which he cut her breasts with a knife. The jury, which saw the videotape, had eight women on it. Asked why they acquitted, they said he needed help. They looked right through the victim—afraid to recognize any part of themselves, shamed by her violation. There were no riots afterward.

The governing reality for women of all races is that there is no escape from male violence, because it is inside and outside, intimate and predatory. While race-hate has been expressed through forced segregation, woman-hate is expressed through forced closeness, which makes punishment swift, easy, and sure. In private, women often empathize with one another, across race and class, because their experiences with men are so much the same. But in public, including on juries, women rarely dare. For this reason, no matter how many women are battered—no matter how many football stadiums battered women could fill on any given day—each one is alone.

Surrounded by family, friends, and a community of affluent acquaintances, Nicole Simpson was alone. Having turned to police, prosecutors, victim's aid, therapists, and a women's shelter, she was still alone. Ronald L. Goldman may have been the only person in seventeen years with the courage to try to intervene physically in an attack on her; and he's dead, killed by the same hand that killed her, an expensively gloved, extra-large hand.

Though the legal system has mostly consoled and protected batterers, when a woman is being beaten, it's the batterer who has to be stopped; as Malcolm X used to say, "by any means necessary"—a principle women, all women, had better learn. A woman has a right to her own bed, a home she can't be thrown out of, and for her body not to be ransacked and broken into. She has a right to safe refuge, to expect her family and friends to stop the batterer—by law or force—before she's dead. She has a constitutional right to a gun and a legal right to kill if she believes she's going to be killed. And a batterer's repeated assaults should lawfully be taken as intent to kill.

Everybody's against wife abuse, but who's prepared to stop it?

LIVING IN TERROR, PAIN

Being a Battered Wife

On November 1, 1987, Joel Steinberg, a criminal defense lawyer, beat his illegally adopted daughter, Lisa, into a coma. She died November 5. Hedda Nussbaum, who had lived with Steinberg since 1976, was also in the apartment. Her face and body were deformed from his assaults, she had a gangrenous leg from his beatings. With six-year-old Lisa lying on the bathroom floor, Steinberg went out for dinner and drinks. Nussbaum stayed behind. When Steinberg came home, he and Nussbaum freebased cocaine. Early the next day, Lisa stopped breathing and Nussbaum called 911. She was arrested with Steinberg, then given immunity for testifying against him.

Steinberg had started beating Nussbaum in 1978. In that year alone, she reportedly suffered at least ten black eyes. In 1981, he ruptured her spleen. During this time, she worked as a children's book editor at Random House. She was fired in 1982 for missing too much work. Socially speaking, she was "disappeared."

Many say Lisa's death is Nussbaum's fault. They mourn Lisa; they blame Nussbaum. A perception is growing that Nussbaum is responsible legally and morally for the death of Lisa Steinberg.

I don't think Nussbaum is "innocent." I don't know any innocent adult women; life is harder than that for everyone. But adult women who have been battered are especially not innocent. Battery is a forced descent into hell and you don't get by in hell by moral goodness. You disintegrate. You don't survive as a discrete personality with a sense of right and wrong. You live in a world of pain, in isolation, on the verge of death, in terror; and when you get numb enough not to care whether you live or die you are experiencing the only grace God is going to send your way. Drugs help.

I was battered when I was married and there are some things I wish people would understand. I thought things had changed but it is clear from the story of Hedda Nussbaum that nothing has.

Your neighbors hear you screaming. They do nothing. The next day they look through you. If you scream for years they will look through you for years. Your neighbors, friends, and family see the bruises and injuries—and do nothing. They will not intercede. They send you back. They say it's your fault or you like it or they deny it is happening. Your family believes you belong with your husband.

If you scream and no one helps and no one acknowledges it and people look right through you, you begin to feel you don't exist. If you existed and you screamed, someone would help you. If you existed and were visibly injured, someone would help you. If you existed and asked for help in escaping, someone would help you.

When you go to the doctor or to the hospital because you are injured and they don't listen or help you or they give you tranquilizers or threaten to commit you because they say you are disoriented, paranoid, you begin to believe that he can hurt you as much as he wants and no one will help you. When the police refuse to help you, you begin to believe that he can hurt you or kill you and it will not matter because you do not exist.

You become unable to use language because it stops meaning anything. If you try to say you have been hurt and by whom and you point to visible injuries and are treated as if you made it up or as if it doesn't matter or as if it is your fault or as if you are worthless, you become afraid to say anything. You cannot talk to anyone because they will not help you and if you do talk, the man who is battering you will hurt you more. Once you lose language, your isolation is absolute.

Eventually I waited to die. I wanted to die. I hoped the next beating would kill me. When I would come to after being beaten unconscious, the first feeling I had was a sorrow that I was alive.

I would ask God to let me die now. My breasts were burned with lit cigarettes. My husband beat my legs with a wood beam so that I couldn't walk. I was present when he did immoral things to other people. When he hurt other people, I didn't help them. Nussbaum's guilt is not foreign to me.

A junkie said he would give me a ticket to far away and $1,000 if I would carry a briefcase through customs. I said I would. I knew it had heroin in it. I kept hoping I would be caught and sent to jail because in jail he couldn't beat me.

I had been sexually abused in the Women's House of Detention in New York City (arrested for an anti–Vietnam War demonstration), so I didn't have the idea that jail was a friendly place. I just hoped I would get five years and for five years I could sit in a jail cell and not be hit by him. In the end the junkie didn't give me the briefcase to carry, so I didn't get the $1,000. He did kindly give me the ticket. I stole the money I needed. Escape is heroic, isn't it?

I've been living with a kind and gentle man I love for the last fifteen years. For eight of those years, I would wake up screaming in blind terror, not knowing who I was, where I was, who he was, cowering and shaking. I'm more at peace now, but I've refused until recently to have my books published in the country where my former husband lives, and I've refused important professional invitations to go there. Once I went there in secret for four days to try to face it down. I couldn't stop trembling and sweating. I could barely breathe. There still isn't a day when I don't feel fear that I will see him and he will hurt me.

Death looks different to a woman who has been battered. It seems not nearly so cruel as life. I'm upset by the phony mourning for Lisa Steinberg—the hypocritical sentimentality of a society that would not really mind her being beaten to death once she was an adult.

If Lisa hadn't died, she would be on West Tenth Street being tortured—now. Why was it that we wanted her to live? So that when the child became a woman and then was raped or beaten or prostituted we could look right through her? It's bad to hit a girl before she's of age. It's bad to torture a girl before she's of age. Then she's of age and, well, it isn't so bad, because she wants it, she likes it, she chose it.

Why is it all right to hurt adult women? Those who love children but don't think adult women deserve much precisely because we are not innocent—we are used and compromised and culpable—should try to remember this: the only way to have helped Lisa Steinberg was to have helped Nussbaum. But to do it, you would have had to care that an adult woman was being hurt—care enough to rescue her.

There was a little boy there too, Mitchell, seventeen months old, tied up and covered in feces. And the only way to have spared him was to rescue Hedda. Now he has been tortured and he did not die. What kind of man will he grow up to be? I wish there was a way to take the hurt from him. There isn't. Is there a way to stop him from becoming a batterer? Is there?

THE THIRD RAPE

Rape victims find courtrooms are dangerous places—so most avoid them. Nine of ten rapes go unreported. For those that go to trial, annihilating the victim—through insult, innuendo, intimidation, forced repetition of every detail, the pressure of continuing public humiliation before family, friends, coworkers—is still the rapist's best chance for acquittal; and acquittal is the usual outcome. Feminists call the trial "the second rape."

Now, thanks to *The New York Times* and NBC News, both of which identified by name the victim in the William Kennedy Smith rape trial, there will be a third rape—by the media. If a woman's reporting a rape to the police means she will be exposed by the media to the scrutiny of voyeurs and worse, a sexual spectacle with her legs splayed open in the public mind, reporting itself will be tantamount to suicide. Because of my own experience with sexual abuse and media exposure, I know the consequences are unbearable.

In February 1965, I was arrested at an anti–Vietnam War demonstration in New York City. I was imprisoned in the Women's House of Detention for four days before a judge released me on my own recognizance.

In the jail, all the orifices of my body, including mouth, vagina, and rectum, were searched many times, by hand, by many persons. I was told the jailers were looking for heroin. My clothes were taken away because I was wearing pants and a men's sweatshirt. Only dresses were allowed in that house of rectitude.

I was given a flimsy robe that had no buttons or hooks—there was no way to close it. My bra, underpants, and the sash to the robe were taken away so I wouldn't kill myself. For four days, I had nothing else to wear.

To see whether I had syphilis, I was examined by two male doctors. They never did the blood test for syphilis; instead, they drew blood from my vagina. The brutal internal examination they forced on me, my first, caused me to bleed for fifteen days—when I finally decided it wasn't my period. My family doctor, a taciturn man whom I had never seen express emotion, even as he treated my mother's heart attacks, strokes, and experimental heart surgery, said he had never seen a uterus so bruised or a vagina so ripped. He cried. I was eighteen.

I came out of jail unable to speak. This is a frequent response to sexual abuse—but in 1965 no one knew that. Sexual abuse wasn't on anyone's map of the everyday world until feminists redrew the map.

I couldn't talk, I couldn't stop bleeding, I didn't know what they had done to me. The men I worked with against the war laughed at me—a girl struck dumb. But they knew someone had stuck something up me and they figured I deserved it. I lived with two men. They said I was sick and unclean—they thought the bleeding was some sexual disease—and they threw me out. My mother said I was an "animal," and my parents threw me out.

The writer Grace Paley took me in, in a sense taught me how to speak again by forcing me to tell her what had happened, convinced me that speaking was right by believing me. So I spoke out. I wrote *The New York Times* and the *New York Post*. I went through the Yellow Pages and wrote every newspaper listed. I wanted the prison torn down. I wrote a graphic letter—after all, I didn't know the word "speculum," and it was a speculum that had done most of the ripping.

I had a scholarship to Bennington College—this happened during the work term of my first year. The papers liked that: Bennington Girl

Brutalized in Internal Examination in Women's Prison. The doctors had liked it, too. During the assault, they joked about how they liked to go up to Bennington to find girls. Newspapers and rapists tend to find the same facts compelling.

I went to the newspapers because I was an idealist who wanted to stop prison abuses. I believed in sexual liberation, birth control, and abortion as a right. I believed in ending poverty, racism, and war. I loved reading and I wanted to be a writer. I'm not cynical now and I wasn't then; but I had had a tough childhood. I had learned to take a lot of pain and to do what was necessary to stay alive, including stealing food when I was hungry.

I had been raped twice before. No one used the word "rape." The first time I was nine; my parents didn't report it. The second time, a month before the jail incident, was what is now called "acquaintance rape." Yes, I fought; yes, he beat me; yes, he hurt me, and no, I never told anyone. Yes, there was blood; yes, there were bruises; but the unspeakable physical pain was between the legs—the *rape* part. Women are human down there, too.

After I went to the newspapers, I learned a new kind of hell. I didn't know that the facts about my imprisonment were sexually arousing—to me they were an anguish. I didn't know that in the public eye I became living pornography for men who liked to watch a frightened girl tell the story. I got hundreds of obscene letters from men, taunting, obsessive letters. The man would say what he wanted to do to me or what he was going to do to me when he came and got me and how he masturbated to what the prison doctors had done. The man would describe my genitals or threaten me with detailed sexual assault.

Each day there was another stack of letters. Every day I'd get person-to-person obscene phone calls from men all over the country. I was a student now, back at school. There were cameras everywhere I went. My name was everywhere.

This was when there were still standards, limits, protections—the media followed some rules. A constitutional lawyer wrote a letter for me that stopped someone from making a sensationalist film based on "my" story. But when I asked newspapers to leave me alone—when I explained that I was a student and had a paper due, for example—I was threatened: we will use a telescopic lens, we can see every move you make.

For months, I was followed nearly all the time. I would expect the frenzy to die down but it would only intensify. The women who lived in my dorm started screening my mail and phone calls. Nothing helped me stop shaking.

Investigations into conditions at the jail continued and I had to go to New York repeatedly to testify. People would run after me on the streets. I didn't have money for taxis. I'd run into the subway to escape and find myself trapped by a crowd, unable to get aboveground. Men approached me to offer safe passage. Within a few seconds, it was clear they were sexually excited by the public narrative of my abuse—they'd start talking about vaginal bruises and how they would like to rub their penises up against them.

I left school and I left the country. Photographs of me had been published as far away as Taiwan. I found a place where no one would ever know me. The rapes, of course, you take with you.

I chose to go to the media—in an age without satellite transmission. I am strong but there is no "strong enough." *Choice,* were *The New York Times* to grant it—an act of noblesse oblige, since they have the power to do what they want—is not the magic bullet. A rape victim needs *control*: privacy, dignity, lack of fear. The media use you until they use you up. You don't get to tell them to stop now, please.

Had *The New York Times*'s new woman-hating standard of going after the victim—the only way to characterize using a rape victim's name—been in force, I would have kept quiet about what happened in the jail.

Had *The New York Times*'s new tabloid standard of journalism been in operation, I would have been absolutely destroyed. I was no innocent. I was living with two men and had a third male lover at the time of my arrest; I smoked marijuana; I had already, by eighteen, spent many months on the streets, destitute. Despite my Bennington affiliation, I was desperate and poor.

I believed then, and I believe now, that still no one had a right to rip up my insides—nor the insides of the many hundreds of mostly black women, mostly prostitutes, in that jail. The City of New York, through its policies, tormented and injured women, based on the conviction that once a woman had had sexual experience, she was dirt. Woman as dirt sells; pornography proves that. *The New York Times* has just changed sides—from exposing abuse to exploiting it.

The Women's House of Detention was torn down in 1972. A community-run garden flourishes in its place.

GARY HART AND
POST-PORNOGRAPHY POLITICS

I'm a member of the public that the press pretends to represent, and I don't have a right to know what Gary Hart did Friday night or Saturday night, or if or how he masturbates, or how or with whom he makes love, or whether his personal friendships with men or women are sexual or not. His wife, Lee Hart, has a right to know. I do not. My rights meet up with hers only when or if Mr. Hart brutalizes or exploits women, because then he is not fit to govern. Using this novel standard, *The Miami Herald* should have many stories to tell about politicians in power now. Of course, that would be harder and more dangerous than doing bad imitations of *Miami Vice* and knocking off at midnight. News flash: lots of adults stay up, and dressed, past midnight. Actual conversations between men and women take place then too. And on boats.

Watching the in-depth television coverage of this spectacular non-event—two people, Mr. Hart and Donna Rice, walk through a door into a house—one thing was clear: the reporters and managing editor of *The Miami Herald* are young, members of the pornography generation, that segment of our population that came into adulthood with pornography saturating public places, legitimized, the courts defending it as speech and linking it in every breath they take to journalism, extending

60

to pornography the constitutional protections journalism has and thereby giving pornography a similar social value, a high value.

These men chanted two mantras: *the public's right to know* and *the character question*. They were exceptionally inarticulate except for this peculiar version of *Om*.

The public's right to know is the propagandistic slogan the pornographers have been using to justify publishing violating pictures of naked women, especially famous or near-famous women, who, in fact, do not consent; who are, in fact, humiliated and hurt by the publishing of them; and whose bodies become public property because the pornographers argue that a male public's prurient interest has more constitutional value than a woman's sexual privacy or integrity. The courts have agreed. The press has sided with the pornographers. Now there is a generation of male reporters nurtured on this cynical ethic of invasion: the violating exposure of anything sexually arousing. Gary Hart in his house with a woman not his wife—or, as one of the reporters kept saying on *Nightline* (May 5, 1987), "a *single* woman"—appears to be sexually arousing to these arrogant voyeurs who have taken the most banal circumstantial evidence and turned it into hard news. What's hard isn't hard to find. To them, Mr. Hart and Ms. Rice are pornography.

The character question, so-called, is also rooted in the way pornographers do business. Every sexual act that they sell in their magazines they also use as a form of insult and attack: for instance, they sell photographs of lesbian sex but attack those who oppose them as dirty lesbians. Any sex act, present or past, stigmatizes a person "exposed" by them; they make anything you are and anything you do dirty. So it is with these boys from *The Miami Herald*: Mr. Hart did something dirty, no matter what he did. We are to infer that that's the way he is.

The next step, of course, is to get photographs of Mr. Hart or other politicians engaged in sex acts. Without those photographs, the documentation, there is still only innuendo. Surely in this pornographer's paradise *the public's right to know* and *the character question* justify photographing Mr. Hart, by any means necessary. The use of photography to violate the sexual privacy of women—the publication of the photographs—has laid the groundwork socially and legally. Women used to be blackmailed. Now women are published. Politicians used to be blackmailed. Now they will be published. Blackmail is very cruel, but the politicians will find what women found—that being published is crueler.

This has been a circus of sadism, reprehensible in what it has done to Mr. Hart, especially in invading a domain of privacy that every human being must have, the privacy of chosen association, whether sexual or not; but it has been murderous toward Ms. Rice and Lee Hart. Ms. Rice is turned into meat; Lee Hart is humiliated beyond human endurance. Since it was done in the name of my right to know, I beg their forgiveness.

A GOVERNMENT OF MEN,
NOT LAWS, NOT WOMEN

There's no way to live with what John Mack did to Pamela Small in 1973. Mack—who resigned Thursday as House Speaker Jim Wright's main aide and executive director of the congressional Democratic Steering and Policy Committee—said his crime had been part of the public record for sixteen years. Mack had been protected by Wright, powerful Democrats in Congress, and a quiescent press willing to live with his crime against Small—protecting him, fraternizing with him, rewarding him. How could they?

John Paul Mack, then nineteen, managed a discount import store. Pamela Small, then twenty, bought some Venetian blinds there. There was something wrong with them, so Mack asked Small to come into the storeroom to pick new blinds. Then, he blocked the door and told her to lie down. She refused. He took a hammer and repeatedly smashed her skull. Then, he stabbed her five times with a steak knife in her left breast and shoulder and slashed her throat many times. Then, he put her body in a car and drove around. Then, he parked the car and went to a movie.

Small survived, escaped, pressed charges. Mack pleaded guilty to malicious wounding: specifically "that he did . . . stab, cut and wound one Pamela Small with the intent to maim, disfigure, disable and kill." He was sentenced to fifteen years, seven suspended, in the Virginia State Penitentiary.

He never did hard time or much time. He served less than twenty-seven months in a county jail where he worked as a cook. Then, he was paroled—to a job on Wright's congressional staff. Wright's daughter was then married to Mack's brother. Presumably not a consumer of discount venetian blinds, she was not in any immediate danger; or if she was, the speaker didn't seem to care. The *Washington Post* said that since Wright became speaker, Mack was "arguably the most powerful staff member on Capitol Hill."

Wright offered Mack a job before he was sentenced and wrote letters in Mack's behalf to the probation officer and sentencing judge. Only Wright's influence can account for the extreme leniency shown Mack for a crime of heinous brutality. Only complete indifference to the worth of a woman's life—a stunning callousness—can account for Wright's manipulation of the legal system such that, in fact, the perpetrator has been rewarded with political power for his carnage.

Mack said he "just blew my cool for a second." Examined by a psychiatrist nearly a year later, Mack said he had "reacted in a way in which any man would perhaps react under similar circumstances." The "circumstances" he was referring to were long work days and a failing marriage. Happily, he wasn't saying he had had an appropriate response to a woman choosing venetian blinds. Unhappily, he was saying that bludgeoning the skull of a woman with a hammer, slashing her throat repeatedly with a steak knife, stabbing her in the breast and shoulder repeatedly, then going to a movie with the body left in the car, was something "any man" would do if he were under pressure.

It's an interesting and eloquent assertion of gender, implying as it does that it is natural for a man to use massive, grotesque violence against a woman, any woman, when he is upset. Court psychiatrists said that Mack was sane when he committed the crime, that he knew right from wrong. In fact, he knew Wright from wrong. The speaker sprung him and he was protected by a network of male power. House Majority Whip Tony Coelho (D-Calif.) told the *Washington Post* two weeks ago that if Wright were to fire Mack, "members would be lined up to hire him." Because of the public outrage, that might no longer be the case.

Mack's sane, Wright's sane, Coelho's sane: what is a sane man? When men know right from wrong, what is it that they know? And why are these men running the country? How many sane men are there in government? How many use hammers; how many use fists?

In the city where I live, a major politician has a history of beating women. In each election for the past decade in which he has been a candidate, women's groups have taken documentation to the press—affidavits and testimony from women he has hurt. The press never thought it was worth a line of newsprint. The press, too, is composed of sane men. Between the male journalists who know right from wrong and the male politicians who know right from wrong, women are in a vise: information and public policy controlled by Mack's "any man"—men protecting men who hurt women because "any man" will or might or can.

If Wright's time had not come, if he were not under indictment by the House Ethics Committee, the public would not have been told about Mack. The sane men in the press who know right from wrong wouldn't have thought it was important. Congressional insiders knew Mack had committed a felony, some even knew about Mack's crime; they just didn't tell the rest of us.

The issue for the press was Wright's weakened political position. It wasn't that Mack committed an unspeakable crime of violence; or the meaning of the speaker's complicity in protecting him; or the meaning of the congressional support for him—legislators protecting a slasher when, not coincidentally, rape is epidemic, abortion rights threatened, and pornography legally protected.

Male dominance means that men who are sane the way Mack was sane run the country and control information; they are the government and the press; they shape reality through laws and perception. They protect "any man's" violence against any woman. Not by accident is the United States a nightmare of violence against women. Men in power make choices for violence. They protect violence in men because any man, under similar circumstances, would perhaps react the same way:

the way Mack did; the way Wright did; the way Coelho and other powerful Democrats did. It's the boys-will-be-boys theory of good government, a government of men, not laws, not women.

Coehlo says he is "very close" to Mack. "Rightly or wrongly," he said,
"under our system of law John Mack owed his debt to society, not to
this young woman." The woman is chopped liver to him. The question
is: what is any woman going to do about it?

PORTRAIT OF A NEW PURITAN—
AND A NEW SLAVER

As a woman determined to destroy the pornography industry, a writer of ten published books, and someone who reads, perhaps I should be the one to tell John Irving ("Pornography and the New Puritans," *The New York Times Book Review*, March 29, 1992) who the new Puritan is. The old Puritans wouldn't like her very much; but then, neither does Mr. Irving.

I am forty-five now. When I was a teen-ager I baby-sat. In any middle-class home one could always find the dirty books—on the highest shelf, climbing toward God, usually behind a parched, potted plant. The books themselves were usually *Ulysses, Tropic of Cancer*, or *Lady Chatterley's Lover*. They always had as preface or afterword the text of an obscenity decision in which the book was vindicated and art extolled. Or a lawyer would stand in for the court to tell us that through his mighty efforts law had finally vindicated a persecuted genius.

Even at fifteen and sixteen, I noticed something strange about the special intersection of art, law, and sex under the obscenity rubric: some men punished some other men for producing or publishing writing that caused erection in—presumably—still other men. Although Mrs. Grundy got the blame, women didn't make these laws or enforce them or sit on juries to deliberate guilt or innocence. This was a fight among men—but about what?

Meanwhile, my life as a woman in prefeminist times went on. This means that I thought I was a human being with rights. I even thought I had responsibilities—for instance, to stop the Vietnam War. Before I was much over eighteen, I had been sexually assaulted three times. Did I report these assaults?—patriarchy's first question, because surely the girl must be lying. When I was nine I told my parents. To protect me, for better or worse, they did not call the police. The second time, beaten as well as raped, I told no one. I was working for a peace group and I heard jokes about rape day in and day out. "What do you tell the draft board when they ask you whether you would kill a Nazi who was going to rape your sister?" "I'd tell my sister to have a good time" was the answer of choice. The third time, the sexual assault was reported in *The New York Times*, newspapers all around the world, and on television: girl in prison—New York's notorious Women's House of Detention—brutalized by two prison doctors. Neither prison doctor was charged with sexual assault or sexual battery; none dared call it rape.

I had always wanted to be a writer in the *Ulysses*/Lawrence/Miller mode but I learned without knowing it the first rule of speech for a woman, who is, after all, not quite a human being when a man is forcibly sticking something up her: keep your mouth shut, don't write it down, don't sign it, don't say it even if you can.

And at first I couldn't. I came out of the Women's House of Detention mute. Speech depends on believing you can make yourself understood: that a community of people will recognize the experience in the words you use and they will care. You also have to be able to understand what happened to you enough to convey it to other people. I lost speech. I was hurt past what I had words for. I lived out on the streets for several days, not having a bed of my own, still bleeding; and finally spoke because Grace Paley used kindness to make me tell her what had happened to me. She convinced me that she would both understand and care. Then I spoke a lot. A grand jury investigated. Columnists indicted the prison. But no one ever mentioned sexual assault. The grand jury concluded that the prison was just fine. I left the country—to be a writer, my human dream.

Now, to make this short if not sweet. A year later I came back having learned that the kindness of strangers is most meaningful when you get it in cash up front. I spent a lot of years out on the street, living hand to mouth, these New York streets and other streets in other hard cities. I can hide my prostituting because I went to college and no one ever looks for a woman's real life anyway. I thought I was a real tough-ass and I was: tough-calloused; tough-numb; tough-desperate; tough-scared; tough-hungry; tough—beaten-by-men-often; tough—done-it-every-which-way-including-up.

All of my colleagues who fight against pornography with me know that I prostituted. I know about the lives of women in pornography because I lived pornography. So have many feminists who fight pornography. Freedom looks very different when you are the one it is being done on. It's his, not yours. Speech is different, too. Those sexy expletives are the hate words he uses on you while he is using you; and your speech is an inchoate protest never voiced.

In my work, fiction and nonfiction, I've tried to voice the protest against a power that is dead weight on you, fist and penis organized to keep you quiet. I would do virtually anything to get women out of prostitution and pornography, which is technologized prostitution. With pornography, a woman can still be sold after the beatings, the rapes, the pain, the humiliation have killed her. I write for her, in behalf of her, to try to intervene before she dies. I know her. I have come close to being her. I read a lot of books. None of them ever told me the truth about what happens to women until feminists started writing and publishing in this wave, over these last twenty-two years. Over and over, male writers call prostituted women "speech"—their speech, their right. Without this exploitation published for profit, the male writer feels censored. The woman lynched naked on a tree, or restrained with ropes and a ball gag in her mouth, has what? Freedom of what?

I lost my ability to speak—became mute—a second time in my life. I've written about being a battered wife: I was beaten and tortured over a period of a few years. Amnesty International never showed up. Toward the end, when I would either die or escape, I lost all speech. Words were useless to the likes of me. I had run away and asked for help and had been sent back many times. My words didn't seem to mean anything, or it was okay to torture me. Taken once by my husband to a doctor when hurt I risked asking for help. He said he could write me a prescription for Valium or have me committed. The neighbors heard the screaming but no one did anything. So what good are words? I have always been good with them, but never good enough to be believed or helped. No, there were no shelters then. But I am talking about speech: it isn't easy for me; I come from under him, tortured and tormented; what he does to me takes away everything—he is the owner of everything—he hurts all the words out of me and no one will listen anyway. I come to speech from under the brutalities of thousands of men. For me, the violence of marriage was worse than the violence of prostitution; but this is no paradigm for choice. Men act out pornography. They have acted it out on me. Women's lives become pornography. Mine did. And so for twenty years now I have been looking for the words to say what I know. But maybe liberal men—so open-minded and intellectually curious—can't find the books to read. Maybe, while John Irving and PEN are defending *Hustler*, snuff films, and the coercion of Linda Marchiano into *Deep Throat*, a political dissident like myself is pushed out of publishing (in magazines for well over ten years now; books sold and published in England because here they are anathema, especially to the free speech fetishists): not because the publishing industry punishes prudes but because dissenters who mean it, who stand against male power over women, are pariahs. Either the words that I use in books to help people understand how pornography destroys women's chances in life are worthless—and I am pushed back into being mute, this time a function of despair caused by the refusal of liberals to see women's real lives even when we dare to show them—hard lives; or my work has been suppressed and stigmatized so successfully that John Irving and others do not know that in the world of women pornography is real—not ideas, not fiction, it is done to us; it is the real geography of how men use us and torment us and hate us.

With Catharine A. MacKinnon, I drafted the first civil law against pornography. It holds pornographers accountable for what they do: they traffic in women (contravening the United Nations Universal Declaration of Human Rights and the Convention on the Elimination of All Forms of Discrimination Against Women); they sexualize inequality in a way that materially promotes rape, battery, maiming, and bondage; they make a product that they know dehumanizes, degrades, and exploits women; they hurt women to make the pornography and then consumers use the pornography in assaults both verbal and physical.

Mr. Irving refers to a scene in *The World According to Garp* in which a woman bites off a man's penis in a car when the car is rammed accidentally from behind. (How pleasant that it is the car, not the woman.) This, he says, did not cause women to bite off men's penises in cars. Neither did my favorite women's movement button: "Don't Suck. Bite." I have written—in *Ice and Fire*, in *Mercy*, and in the story "the new womans broken heart"—about a woman raped by two men sequentially, the first aggressor routed by the second one to whom the woman, near dead, submits—and he bites viciously and repeatedly into her clitoris and the lips of her labia. When I wrote it, someone had already done it—to me. Recently I read a report of a report on rape that for the first time (to my knowledge) described this sadism as part of many rapes. The rapists didn't get it from me. But those working against rape finally understood that they had to say that this is often part of rape because it is. We know that serial killers frequently mutilate the genitals of women, including with their teeth. The violence, as Mr. Irving must know, goes from men to women. Women barely say what we know. Then even that is ridiculed or suppressed. A letter to me dated March 11, 1992, says in part: "The abuse was quite sadistic—it involved bestiality, torture, the making of pornography. Sometimes, when I think about my life, I'm not sure why I'm alive, but I'm always sure about why I do what I do, the feminist theory and the antipornography activism."

A letter dated March 13, 1992, says: "It was only when I was almost fucked to pieces, that I broke down and learned to hate. . . . I have never stopped resenting the loss of innocence that occurred the day I learned to hate." Male liberals seem to think we fight pornography to protect a sexual innocence, but we have none to protect. The innocence we want is the innocence that lets us love. People need dignity to love.

Mr. Irving quoted Hawthorne's condemnation of Puritan orthodoxy—the graphic description in the short story "Endicott and the Red Cross" of public punishments of women: bondage, branding, maiming, lynching. Today pornographers do these things to women and the public square is a big place—every newsstand and video store. A photograph immunizes rape and torture for profit. In defending pornography as if it were speech, liberals defend the new slavers. The only fiction in pornography is the smile on the woman's face.

FREE EXPRESSION IN SERBIAN RAPE/DEATH CAMPS

In Bosnia, women and children are 75 percent of the more than 2.5 million people driven from their homes—not by the random violence of war but by forced expulsion and mass killings—in the Serbian military effort called "*ciscenje prostora*," or what Amerikans have learned to call "ethnic cleansing." Ethnic cleansing, enunciated as policy by Serbian political and military leaders at the highest levels of authority, is genocide. It requires the removal or killing of all non-Serbs from the new republics of Bosnia-Herzegovina and Croatia, both formerly part of Yugoslavia.

The Serbian military has killed an estimated 200,000 people in Bosnia alone, perhaps 80 percent Muslim, in massacres, mass murders, and bombings aimed at civilians. Serbian military policy has mandated the systematic gang rape of Muslim and Croatian women and girls, their imprisonment in schools, factories, motels, arenas, and concentration camps for ongoing serial rape, rape followed by murder, sexual torture, and sexual slavery.

In addition to the estimated ninety concentration camps set up throughout Bosnia, there are more than twenty rape/death camps. Some hold fifteen to twenty-five women and look like brothels; others hold more than 1,000. More than 7,000 women were held as prisoners in a

Serbian-run prison-brothel near Brcko in northern Bosnia, and Muslim women are reportedly held in sexual slavery in the Sarajevo suburb of Grbavica. Young girls just reaching puberty appear to be specially designated targets for gang rape.

And then the Serbian soldiers started making pornography: well, why not? Are we Amerikans going to understand that the war against women—including the genocidal Serbian war of aggression against women in Bosnia and Croatia—is rape, prostitution, and pornography? Or do we think that Serbian-nationalist thugs are "expressing themselves" in the pornographic landscape of sex and murder with which our still-male government—not to mention the United Nations—is loath to interfere? Are the films of rapes being made now in the Serbian-run rape/death camps in occupied areas of Bosnia and Croatia—even of rapes staged in order to be filmed—trivial compared with the rape itself, which later will be blamed on the victims and called prostitution?

Most prostitution everywhere in the world begins with rape: a child raped by her father; a teen-ager gang-raped by half the number of men involved in a typical Serbian military gang rape (six instead of twelve at a time); a female child sold into sexual slavery; any girl or woman driven out of her home by male aggression, then pushed up against a wall or down on a slab of earth and used.

The aggressor spits "whore" and moves on to the next victim while the raped woman, her ties to a place and people destroyed, meets the next aggressor. She will be an exile, a stigmatized, shunned refugee, polluted—in ordinary language, a whore. His invective becomes her life.

Before this war, the pornography market in Yugoslavia was, according to critic Bogdan Tirnanic, "the freest in the world." Whatever the communists suppressed, it wasn't pornography—yet another example of folks who can tell the difference between pornography and literature.

The pornography was war propaganda that trained an army of rapists who waited for permission to advance. An atavistic nationalism provided the trigger and defined the targets—those women, not these women. The sexuality of the men was organized into antagonism, superiority, and hatred. The lessons had been learned—not an ideology but a way of being: dehumanization of women; bigotry and aggression harnessed to destroying the body of the enemy; invasion as a male right; women as a lower life form.

In this war, pornography is everywhere: plastered on tanks; incorporated into the gang rapes in the prostitution-prison brothels. Soldiers have camcorders to do the military version of "Beaver Hunt"—women tortured for the camera, raped for the camera, knifed and beaten for the camera; and of course, for the man behind it, the rapist-soldier turned—in Amerikan parlance—into an expresser. Of what? Oh, ideas.

In fact, acts of hatred often do express ideas; it is the Amerikan pathology to euphemize aggression by calling it speech. This may be why the U.S. press—with the exception of *Ms.*—has largely ignored the pervasiveness of the pornography used by the Serbian rapists and now being made by them. There is rape; that's bad. There is pornography; that's fun—adolescent, innocuous, endearing, as one writer in *Harper's* represented it.

Serbian soldiers using pornography reminded that writer of "a wretched teen-age camping trip"; the pornography they had he described as "ours." He and the soldiers played poker with "nudie cards."

Even during genocide, there is affectionate tolerance for a boys-will-be-boys behavior so close to the Amerikan heart.

The world of women is different. Azra, fifteen, a Muslim, was raped by eight men while conscious, "and I don't know what happened after that." Her breasts were cut by a man who "seemed to be playing," while another was still on top of her. Enisa, sixteen, also gang-raped, said, "In my world, men represent terrible violence and pain. That feeling is stronger than me. I cannot control that feeling."

And what will the land of the free and the home of the brave do when the pornography of genocidal rape reaches our own home-grown men—no strangers to aggression against women by all statistical representations?

The men will invoke their constitutional rights and consume it.

The courts will protect it. Rape will travel with that pornography, as it does with all pornography: the rape of the women used to make it, now flattened and two-dimensional to be enjoyed in perpetuity, whether the women are alive or dead; and the rape of new targets, three-dimensional and present in the flesh—nominally citizens but not so that anyone has to notice.

If the Constitution is ever to be women's too, it cannot protect—de jure or de facto—war on our bodies, the devastation of our dignity, the slow murder of so many of us through rape, prostitution, and pornography, the true trinity of woman-hating atrocity.

It is perhaps too horrific to wonder, but: were the 200,000 "comfort" women, raped by Japanese soldiers during World War II, lucky because the Japanese didn't have camcorders? They were turned into living pornography through gang rape—the condition of all prostituted women. And they were turned into necrophiliac pornography—no one knows how many were murdered.

But the Japanese didn't make movies, put a woman's violation into a permanence beyond her own will to remember or not. They didn't pass her on—on tape—to laughing groups of boys to be enjoyed again and more, in peacetime, too. Piece-time.

This matters to women. The shame of rape—including in Asian and Muslim societies—pales next to the shame of being made into filmed pornography: the violation of *you* becoming a male legacy, a documentary record of being split open in the deepest humiliation; the pornography of you outliving you.

Can't we care about this? Can't we stand up for the rights of women—in Bosnia, in Croatia, and here, too—by repudiating this pornography of genocide? Or will the Serbian military be able to put U.S. dollars in the bank: the spoils of war, profits made from our appetite for the filmed remains of raped women?

BEAVER TALKS

1

I did not hesitate to let it be known of me, that the white man who expected to succeed in whipping, must also succeed in killing me.

—Frederick Douglass,
Narrative of the Life of Frederick Douglass,
An American Slave Written by Himself

In 1838, at the age of twenty-one, Frederick Douglass became a runaway slave, a hunted fugitive. Though later renowned as a powerful political orator, he spoke his first public words with trepidation at an abolitionist meeting—a meeting of white people—in Massachusetts in 1841. Abolitionist leader William Lloyd Garrison recalled the event:

He came forward to the platform with a hesitancy and embarrassment, necessarily the attendants of a sensitive mind in such a novel position. After apologizing for his ignorance, and reminding the audience that slavery was a poor school for the human intellect and heart, he proceeded to narrate some of the facts in his own history as a slave. . . . As soon as he had taken his seat, filled with hope and admiration, I rose . . . [and] . . . reminded the audience of the peril which surrounded this self-emancipated young man at the North,—even in Massachusetts, on the soil of the Pilgrim Fathers, among the descendants of revolutionary sires; and I appealed to them, whether they would ever allow him to be carried back into slavery—law or no law, constitution or no constitution.[1]

Always in danger as a fugitive, Douglass became an organizer for the abolitionists; the editor of his own newspaper, which advocated both abolition and women's rights; a station chief for the underground railroad; a close comrade of John Brown's; and the only person willing, at the Seneca Falls Convention in 1848, to second Elizabeth Cady Stanton's resolution demanding the vote for women. To me, he has been a political hero: someone whose passion for human rights was both visionary and rooted in action; whose risk was real, not rhetorical; whose endurance in pursuing equality set a standard for political honor. In his writings, which were as eloquent as his orations, his repudiation of subjugation was uncompromising. His political intelligence, which was both analytical and strategic, was suffused with emotion: indignation at human pain, grief at degradation, anguish over suffering, fury at apathy and collusion. He hated oppression. He had an empathy for those hurt by inequality that crossed lines of race, gender, and class because it was an empathy animated by his own experience—his own experience of humiliation and his own experience of dignity.

To put it simply, Frederick Douglass was a serious man—a man serious in the pursuit of freedom. Well, you see the problem. Surely it is self-evident. What can any such thing have to do with us—with women in our time? Imagine—in present time—a woman saying, and meaning, that a man who expected to succeed in whipping, must also succeed in killing her. Suppose there were a politics of liberation premised on that assertion—an assertion not of ideology but of deep and stubborn outrage at being misused, a resolute assertion, a serious assertion by serious women. What are serious women; are there any; isn't seriousness about freedom by women for women grotesquely comic; we don't want to be laughed at, do we? What would this politics of liberation be like? Where would we find it? What would we have to do? Would we have to do something other than dress for success? Would we have to stop the

people who are hurting us from hurting us? Not debate them; stop
them. Would we have to stop slavery? Not discuss it; stop it. Would we
have to stop pretending that our rights are protected in this society?
Would we have to be so grandiose, so arrogant, so unfeminine as to believe that the streets we walk on, the homes we live in, the beds we sleep
in are *ours*—belong to us—really belong to us: we decide what is right
and what is wrong and if something hurts us, it stops. It is, of course,
gauche to be too sincere about these things, and it is downright ridiculous to be serious. Intelligent people are well mannered and moderate,
even in pursuing freedom. Smart women whisper and say please.

Now imagine Cherry Tart or Bunny or Pet or Beaver saying, and
meaning, that a man who expected to succeed in whipping must also
succeed in killing her. She says it; she means it. It is not a pornographic
scenario in which she is the dummy forced by the pimp-ventriloquist
to say the ubiquitous no-that-means-yes. It is not the usual sexual
provocation created by pornographers using a woman's body, the sub-
text of which is: I refuse to be whipped so whip me harder, whip me
more; I refuse to be whipped, what I really want is for you to kill me;
whip me, then kill me; kill me, then whip me; whatever you want,
however you want it—was it good for you? Instead, the piece on the
page or in the film steps down and steps out: I'm real, she says. Like
Frederick Douglass, she will be hesitant and embarrassed. She will feel
ignorant. She will tell a first-person story about her own experience in
prostitution, in pornography, as a victim of incest, as a victim of rape,
as someone who has been beaten or tortured, as someone who has
been bought and sold. She may not remind her audience that sexual
servitude is a poor school for the human intellect and heart—sexually
violated, often since childhood, she may not know the value of her
human intellect or her human heart—and the audience cannot be
counted on to know that she deserved better than she got. Will there
be someone there to implore the audience to help her escape the
pornography—law or no law, Constitution or no Constitution; will
the audience understand that as long as the pornography of her exists
she is a captive of it, a fugitive from it? Will the audience be willing to

fight for her freedom by fighting against the pornography of her, because, as Linda Marchiano said of *Deep Throat,* "every time someone
watches that film, they are watching me being raped"[2]? Will the audience understand that she is standing in for those who didn't get away;
will the audience understand that those who didn't get away were
someone—each one was someone? Will the audience understand what
stepping down from the page or out of the film cost her—what it took
for her to survive, for her to escape, for her to dare to speak now about
what happened to her then?

"I'm an incest survivor, ex-pornography model, and ex-prostitute,"
the woman says. "My incest story begins before preschool and ends
many years later—this was with my father. I was also molested by an
uncle and a minister . . . my father forced me to perform sexual acts
with men at a stag party when I was a teen-ager. . . . My father was my
pimp in pornography. There were three occasions from ages nine to sixteen when he forced me to be a pornography model . . . in Nebraska, so,
yes, it does happen here."[3]

I was thirteen when I was forced into prostitution and pornography,
the woman says. I was drugged, raped, gang-raped, imprisoned, beaten,
sold from one pimp to another, photographed by pimps, photographed
by tricks; I was used in pornography and they used pornography on me;
"[t]hey knew a child's face when they looked into it. It was clear that I
was not acting of my own free will. I was always covered with welts and
bruises. . . . It was even clearer that I was sexually inexperienced. I literally didn't know what to do. So they showed me pornography to teach
me about sex and then they would ignore my tears as they positioned
my body like the women in the pictures and used me."[4]

"As I speak about pornography, here, today," the woman says, "I am
talking about my life." I was raped by my uncle when I was ten, by my
stepbrother and stepfather by the time I was twelve. My stepbrother was
making pornography of me by the time I was fourteen. "I was not even
sixteen years old and my life reality consisted of sucking cocks, posing
nude, performing sexual acts and actively being repeatedly raped."[5]

These are the women in the pictures; they have stepped out, though the pictures may still exist. They have become very serious women; serious in the pursuit of freedom. There are many thousands of them in the United States, not all first put in pornography as children though most were sexually molested as children, raped or otherwise abused again later, eventually becoming homeless and poor. They are feminists in the antipornography movement, and they don't want to debate "free speech." Like Frederick Douglass, they are fugitives from the men who made a profit off of them. They live in jeopardy, always more or less in hiding. They organize to help others escape. They write—in blood, their own. They publish sometimes, including their own newsletters. They demonstrate; they resist; they disappear when the danger gets too close. The Constitution has nothing for them—no help, no protection, no dignity, no solace, no justice. The law has nothing for them—no recognition of the injuries done them by pornography, no reparations for what has been taken from them. They are real, and even though this society will do nothing for them, they are women who have resolved that the man who expects to succeed in whipping must also succeed in killing them. This changes the nature of the women's movement. It must stop slavery. The runaway slave is now part of it.

2

> One new indulgence was to go out evenings alone. This I worked out carefully in my mind, as not only a right but a duty. Why should a woman be deprived of her only free time, the time allotted to recreation? Why must she be dependent on some man, and thus forced to please him if she wished to go anywhere at night?
>
> A stalwart man once sharply contested my claim to this freedom to go alone. "Any true man," he said with fervor, "is always ready to go with a woman at night. He is her natural protector." "Against what?" I inquired. As a matter of fact, the thing a woman is most afraid to meet on a dark street is her natural protector. Singular.
>
> —Charlotte Perkins Gilman,
> *The Living of Charlotte Perkins Gilman: An Autobiography*

She was thirteen. She was at a Girl Scout camp in northern Wisconsin. She went for a long walk in the woods alone during the day. She had long blond hair. She saw three hunters reading magazines, talking, joking. One looked up and said: "There's a live one." She thought they meant a deer. She ducked and started to run away. They meant her. They chased her, caught her, dragged her back to where they were camped. The magazines were pornography of women she physically resembled: blond, childlike. They called her names from the pornography: Little Godiva, Golden Girl, also bitch and slut. They threatened to kill her. They made her undress. It was November and cold. One held a rifle to her head; another beat her breasts with his rifle. All three raped her—penile penetration into the vagina. The third one couldn't get hard at first so he demanded a blow job. She didn't know what that was. The third man forced his penis into her mouth; one of the others cocked the trigger on his rifle. She was told she had better do it right. She tried. When they were done with her they kicked her: they kicked her naked body and they kicked leaves and pine needles on her. "[T]hey told me that if I wanted more, that I could come back the next day."6

She was sexually abused when she was three by a boy who was fourteen—it was a "game" he had learned from pornography. "[I]t seems really bizarre to me to use the word 'boy' because the only memory I have of this person is as a three year old. And as a three year old he seemed like a really big man." When she was a young adult she was drugged by men who made and sold pornography. She remembers flashing lights, being forced onto a stage, being undressed by two men and sexually touched by a third. Men were waving money at her: "one of them shoved it in my stomach and essentially punched me. I kept wondering how it was possible that they couldn't see that I didn't want to be there, that I wasn't there willingly."7

She had a boyfriend. She was twenty-one. One night he went to a stag party and watched pornography films. He called her up to ask if he could have sex with her. She felt obligated to make him happy. "I also felt that the refusal would be indicative of sexual quote unquote hang-ups on my part and that I was not quote unquote liberal enough. When he arrived, he informed me that the other men at the party were envious that he had a girlfriend to fuck. They wanted to fuck too after watching the pornography. He informed me of this as he was taking his coat off." He had her perform oral sex on him: "I did not do this of my own volition. He put his genitals in my face and he said 'Take it all.'" He fucked her. The whole encounter took about five minutes. Then he dressed and went back to the party. "I felt ashamed and numb and I also felt very used."[8]

She was seventeen, he was nineteen. He was an art student. He used her body for photography assignments by putting her body in contorted positions and telling her rape stories to get the expression he wanted on her face: fear. About a year later he had an assignment to do body casts in plaster. He couldn't get models because the plaster was heavy and caused fainting. She was a premed student. She tried to explain to him how deleterious the effects of the plaster were. "When you put plaster on your body, it sets up, it draws the blood to the skin and the more area it covers on your body, the more blood is drawn to your skin. You become dizzy and nauseous and sick to your stomach and finally faint." He needed his work to be exhibited, so he needed her to model. She tried. She couldn't stand the heat and the weight of the plaster. "He wanted me to be in poses where I had to hold my hands up over my head, and they would be numb and they would fall. He eventually tied my hands over my head." They got married. During the course of their marriage he began to consume more and more pornography. He would read excerpts to her from the magazines about group sex, wife swapping, anal intercourse, and bondage. They would go to pornography films and wet T-shirt contests with friends. "I felt devastated and disgusted watching it. I was told by those men that if I wasn't as smart as I was and if I would be more sexually liberated and more sexy that I would get along a lot better in the world and that they and a lot of other men would like me more. About this time I started feeling very terrified. I realized that this wasn't a joke anymore." She asked her mother for help but was told that divorce was a disgrace and it was her responsibility to make the marriage work. He brought his friends home to act out the scenarios from the pornography. She found the group sex humiliating and disgusting, and to prevent it she agreed to act out the pornography in private with her husband. She began feeling suicidal. He was transferred to an Asian country in connection with his job. The pornography in the country where they now lived was more violent. He took her to live sex shows where women had sex with animals, especially snakes. Increasingly, when she was asleep he would force intercourse on her. Then he started traveling a lot, and she used his absence to learn karate. "One night when I was in one of those pornographic institutions, I was sitting with a couple of people that I had known, watching the women on stage and watching the different transactions and the sales of the women and the different acts going on, and I realized that my life wasn't any different than these women except that it was done in the name of marriage. I could see how I was being seasoned to the use of pornography and I could see what was coming next. I could see more violence and I could see more humiliation and I knew at that point I was either going to die from it, I was going to kill myself, or I was going to leave. And I was feeling strong enough that I left. . . . Pornography is not a fantasy, it was my life, reality."[9]

At the time she made this statement, she couldn't have been older than twenty-two. She was terrified that the people would be identifiable, and so she spoke in only the most general terms, never specifying their relationship to her. She said she had lived in a house with a divorced woman, that woman's children, and the ex-husband, who refused to leave. She had lived there for eighteen years. During that time, "the woman was regularly raped by this man. He would bring pornographic magazines, books, and paraphernalia into the bedroom with him and tell her that if she did not perform the sexual acts that were being done in the 'dirty' books and magazines he would beat and kill her. I know about this because my bedroom was right next to hers. I could hear everything they said. I could hear her screams and cries. In addition, since I did most of the cleaning in the house, I would often come across the books, magazines, and paraphernalia that were in the bedroom and other rooms of the house. . . . Not only did I suffer through the torture of listening to the rapes and tortures of a woman, but I could see what grotesque acts this man was performing on her from the pictures in the pornographic materials. I was also able to see the systematic destruction of a human being taking place before my eyes. At the time I lived with the woman, I was completely helpless, powerless in regard to helping this woman and her children in getting away from this man." As a child, she was told by the man that if she ever told or tried to run away he would break her arms and legs and cut up her face. He whipped her with belts and electrical cords. He made her pull her pants down to beat her. "I was touched and grabbed where I did not want him to touch me." She was also locked in dark closets and in the basement for long periods of time.[10]

She was raped by two men. They were acting out the pornographic video game "Custer's Revenge." She was American Indian; they were white. "They held me down and as one was running the tip of his knife across my face and throat he said, 'Do you want to play Custer's Last Stand? It's great. You lose but you don't care, do you? You like a little pain, don't you, squaw.' They both laughed and then he said, 'There is a lot of cock in Custer's Last Stand. You should be grateful, squaw, that all-Amerikan boys like us want you. Maybe we will tie you to a tree and start a fire around you.' "[11]

Her name is Jayne Stamen. She is currently in jail. In 1986, she hired three men to beat up her husband. She wanted him to know what a beating felt like. He died. She was charged with second-degree murder; convicted of first-degree manslaughter; sentenced to eight-and-a-half to twenty-five years. She was also convicted of criminal solicitation: in 1984 she asked some men to kill her husband for her, then reneged; she was sentenced on the criminal solicitation charge to two-and-a-third to seven years. The sentences are to run consecutively. She was tortured in her marriage by a man consumed by acting out pornography. He tied her up when he raped her; he broke bones; he forced anal intercourse; he beat her mercilessly; he penetrated her vagina with objects, "his rifle, or a long-necked wine decanter, or twelve-inch artificial rubber penises." He shaved the hair off her pubic area because he wanted, in his words, to "screw a baby's cunt." He slept with a rifle and kept a knife by the bed; he would threaten to cut her face with the knife if she didn't act out the pornography, and he would use the knife again if she wasn't showing pleasure. He called her all the names: whore, slut, cunt, bitch. "He used to jerk himself off on my chest while I was sleeping, or I would get woke up with him coming in my face and then he'd urinate on me." She tried to escape several times. He came after her armed with his rifle. She became addicted to alcohol and pills. "The papers stated that I didn't report [the violence] to the police. I did have the police at my home on several occasions. Twice on Long Island was for the gun threats, and once in Starrett City was also for the gun. The rest of the times were for the beatings and throwing me out of the house. A few times the police helped me get away from him with my clothes and the boys. I went home to my mom's. [He came after her with a rifle.] I went to the doctor's and hospitals on several occasions, too, but I could not tell the truth on how I 'hurt myself.' I always covered up for him, as I knew my life depended on that." The judge wouldn't admit testimony on the torture because he said the husband wasn't on trial. The defense lawyer said in private that he thought she probably enjoyed the abusive sex. Jayne's case will be appealed, but she may well have to stay in jail at Bedford Hills, a New York State prison for women, for the duration of the appeal because Women Against Pornography, a group that established the Defense Fund for Jayne Stamen, has not been able to raise bail money for her. Neither have I or others who care. It isn't chic to help such women; they aren't the Black Panthers. Ironically, there are many women—and recently a teen-age girl, a victim of incest—who have hired others to kill the men—husbands, fathers—who were torturing them because they could not bear to do it themselves. Or the woman pours gasoline on the bed when he sleeps and lights the fire. Jayne didn't hire the men to kill her husband; the real question may be, why not? why didn't she? Women don't understand self-defense the way men do—perhaps because sexual abuse destroys the self. We don't feel we have a right to kill just because we are being beaten, raped, tortured, and terrorized. We are hurt for a long time before we fight back. Then, usually, we are punished: "I have lived in a prison for ten years, meaning my marriage," says Jayne Stamen, ". . . and now they have me in a real prison."12

I've quoted from statements, all made in public forums, by women I know well (except for Jayne Stamen; I've talked with her but I haven't met her). I can vouch for them; I know the stories are true. The women who made these particular statements are only a few of the thousands of women I have met, talked with, questioned: women who have been hurt by pornography. The women are real to me. I know what they look like standing tall; I've seen the fear; I've watched them remember; I've talked with them about other things, all sorts of things: intellectual issues, the weather, politics, school, children, cooking. I have some idea of their aspirations as individuals, the ones they lost during the course of sexual abuse, the ones they cherish now. I know them. Each one, for me, has a face, a voice, a whole life behind her face and her voice. Each is more eloquent and more hurt than I know how to convey. Since 1974, when my book *Woman Hating* was first published, women have been seeking me out to tell me that they have been hurt by pornography; they have told me how they have been hurt in detail, how much, how long, by how many. They thought I might believe them, initially, I think, because I took pornography seriously in *Woman Hating*. I said it was cruel, violent, basic to the way our culture sees and treats women—and I said the hate in it was real. Well, they knew that the hate in it was real because they had been sexually assaulted by that hate. One does not make the first tentative efforts to communicate about this abuse to those who will almost certainly ridicule one. Some women took a chance on me; and it was a chance, because I often did not want to listen. I had my limits and my reasons, like everyone else. For many years, I heard the same stories I have tried to encapsulate here: the same stories, sometimes more complicated, sometimes more savage, from thousands of women, most of whom hadn't dared to tell anyone. No part of the country was exempt; no age group; no racial or ethnic group; no "life-style" however "normal" or "alternative." The statements I have paraphrased here are not special: not more sadistic, not chosen by me because they are particularly sickening or offensive. In fact, they are not particularly sickening or offensive. They simply are what happens to women who are brutalized by the use of pornography on them.

Such first-person stories from women are dismissed by defenders of pornography as "anecdotal"; they misuse the word to make it denote a story, probably fictive, that is small, trivial, inconsequential, proof only of some defect in the woman herself—the story tells us nothing about pornography but it tells us all we need to know about the woman. She's probably lying; maybe she really liked it; and if it did happen, how could anyone (sometimes referred to as "a smart girl like you") be stupid enough, simple-minded enough, to think that pornography had anything to do with it? Wasn't there, as one grinning adversary always asks, also coffee in the house? The coffee, he suggests, is more likely to be a factor in the abuse than the pornography—after all, the bad effects of coffee have been proven in the laboratory. What does one do when women's lives are worth so little—worth arrogant, self-satisfied ridicule and nothing else, not even the appearance, however false, of charity or concern? Alas, one answers: the man (the husband, the boyfriend, the rapist, the torturer—you or your colleague or your best friend or your buddy) wasn't reading the coffee label when he tied the knots; the directions he followed are found in pornography, and, frankly, they are not found anywhere else. The first-person stories are human experience, raw and true, not mediated by dogma or ideology *or* social convention; "human" is the trick word in the sentence. If one values women as human beings, one cannot turn away or refuse to hear so that one can refuse to care without bearing responsibility for the refusal. One cannot turn one's back on the women or on the burden of memory they carry. If one values women as human beings, one will not turn one's back on the women who are being hurt today and the women who will be hurt tomorrow.

Most of what we know about the experience of punishment, the experience of torture, the experience of socially sanctioned sadism, comes from the first-person testimony of individuals—"anecdotal" material. We have the first-person stories of Frederick Douglass and Sojourner Truth, of Primo Levi and Elie Wiesel, of Nadezhda Mandelstam and

Aleksandr Solzhenitsyn. Others in the same or different circumstances of torture and terror have spoken out to bear witness. Often, they were not believed. They were shamed, not honored. We smelled the humiliation, the degradation, on them; we turned away. At the same time, their stories were too horrible, too impossible, too unpleasant; their stories indicted those who stood by and did nothing—most of us, most of the time. Respectfully, I suggest that the women who have experienced the sadism of pornography on their bodies—the women in the pornography and the women on whom the pornography is used—are also survivors; they bear witness, now, for themselves, on behalf of others. "Survivors," wrote Terrence Des Pres, "are not individuals in the bourgeois sense. They are living remnants of the general struggle, and certainly they know it."[13] Of these women hurt by pornography, we must say that they know it now. Before, each was alone, unspeakably alone, isolated in terror and humiliated even by the will to live—it was the will to live, after all, that carried each woman from rape to rape, from beating to beating. Each had never heard another's voice saying the words of what had happened, telling the same story; because it is the same story, over and over—and none of those who escaped, survived, endured, are individuals in the bourgeois sense. These women will not abandon the meaning of their own experience. That meaning is: pornography is the orchestrated destruction of women's bodies and souls; rape, battery, incest, and prostitution animate it; dehumanization and sadism characterize it; it is war on women, serial assaults on dignity, identity, and human worth; it is tyranny. Each woman who has survived knows from the experience of her own life that pornography is captivity—the woman trapped in the picture used on the woman trapped wherever he's got her.

3

The burden of proof will be on those of us who have been victimized. If I [any woman] am able to prove that the picture you are holding, the one where the knife is stuffed up my vagina, was taken when my pimp forced me at gunpoint and

photographed it without my consent, if my existence is proved
real, I am coming to take what is mine. If I can prove that the
movie you are looking at called *Black Bondage*, the one where
my black skin is synonymous with filth and my bondage and
my slavery is encouraged, caused me harm and discrimination,
if my existence is proved real, I am coming to take what is
mine. Whether you like it or not, the time is coming when you
will have to get your fantasy *off my ass.*

—Therese Stanton,
"Fighting for Our Existence"
in *Changing Men*, No. 15, fall 1985

In the fall of 1983, something changed. The speech of women hurt by
pornography became public and real. It, they, began to exist in the
sphere of public reality. Constitutional lawyer Catharine A. MacKinnon
and I were hired by the City of Minneapolis to draft an amendment to
the city's civil rights law: an amendment that would recognize pornography as a violation of the civil rights of women, as a form of sex discrimination, an abuse of human rights. We were also asked to organize
hearings that would provide a legislative record showing the need for
such a law. Essentially, the legislators needed to know that these violations were systematic and pervasive in the population they represented,
not rare, peculiar anomalies.

The years of listening to the private stories had been years of despair
for me. It was hopeless. I could not help. There was no help. I listened;
I went on my way; nothing changed. Now, all the years of listening were
knowledge, real knowledge that could be mined: a resource, not a burden and a curse. I knew how women were hurt by pornography. My
knowledge was concrete, not abstract: I knew the ways it was used; I
knew how it was made; I knew the scenes of exploitation and abuse in
real life—the lives of prostitutes, daughters, girlfriends, wives; I knew
the words the women said when they dared to whisper what had happened to them; I could hear their voices in my mind, in my heart. I
didn't know that there were such women all around me, everywhere, in
Minneapolis that fall. I was heartbroken as women I knew came for-

ward to testify: though I listened with an outer detachment to the sto-ries of rape, incest, prostitution, battery, and torture, each in the service of pornography, inside I wanted to die.

The women who came forward to testify at the hearings held by the Minneapolis City Council on December 12 and 13, 1983, gave their names and specified the area of the city in which they lived. They spoke on the record before a governmental body in the city where they lived; there they were, for family, neighbors, friends, employers, teachers, and strangers to see, to remember. They described in detail sexual abuse through pornography as it had happened to them. They were ques-tioned on their testimony by Catharine MacKinnon and myself and also by members of the city council and sometimes the city attorney. There were photographers and television cameras. There were a couple of hundred people in the room. There was no safety, no privacy, no re-treat, no protection; only a net of validation provided by the testimony of experts—clinical psychologists, prosecutors, experimental psycholo-gists, social scientists, experts in sexual abuse from rape crisis centers and battered women's shelters, and those who worked with sex offend-ers. The testimony of these experts was not abstract or theoretical; it brought the lives of more women, more children, into the room: more rape, more violation through pornography. They too were talking about real people who had been hurt, sometimes killed; they had seen, known, treated, interviewed, numbers of them. A new social truth emerged, one that had been buried in fear, shame, and the silence of the socially pow-erless: no woman hurt by pornography was alone—she never had been; no woman hurt by pornography would ever be alone again because each was—truly—a "living remnant of the general struggle." What the sur-vivors said was speech; the pornography had been, throughout their lives, a means of actively suppressing their speech. They had been turned into pornography in life and made mute; terrorized by it and made mute. Now the mute spoke; the socially invisible were seen; the women were real; they mattered. This speech—their speech—was new in the world of public discourse, and it was made possible by the devel-opment of a law that some called censorship. The women came forward because they thought that the new civil rights law recognized what had happened to them, gave them recourse and redress, enhanced their civil dignity and human worth. The law itself gave them *existence*. I am real; they believed me; I count; social policy at last will take my life into account, validate my worth—me, the woman who was forced to fuck a dog; me, the woman he urinated on; me, the woman he tied up for his friends to use; me, the woman he masturbated in; me, the woman he branded or maimed; me, the woman he prostituted; me, the woman they gang-raped.

The law was passed twice in Minneapolis in 1983 and 1984 by two different city councils; it was vetoed each time by the same mayor, a man active in Amnesty International, opposing torture outside of Minneapolis. The law was passed in 1984 in Indianapolis with a redrafted definition that targeted violent pornography—the kind "everyone" opposes. The city was sued for passing it; the courts found it unconstitutional. The appeals judge said that pornography did all the harm we claimed—it promoted insult and injury, rape and assault, even caused women to have lower wages—and that these effects proved its power as speech; therefore, it had to be protected. In 1985, the law was put on the ballot by popular petition in Cambridge, Massachusetts. The city council refused to allow it on the ballot; we had to sue for ballot access; the civil liberties people opposed our having that access; we won the court case and the city was ordered to put the law on the ballot. We got 42 percent of the vote, a higher percentage than feminists got on the first women's suffrage referendum. In 1988, the law was on the ballot in Bellingham, Washington, in the presidential election; we got 62 percent of the vote. The city had tried to keep us off the ballot; again we had to get a court order to gain ballot access. The City of Bellingham was sued by the ACLU in federal court for having the law, however unwillingly; a federal district judge found the law unconstitutional, simply reiterating the previous appeals court decision in the Indianapolis case—indeed, there was a statement that the harms of pornography were recognized and not in dispute.

We have not been able to get the courts to confront a real woman plaintiff suing a real pornographer for depriving her of real rights through sexual exploitation or sexual abuse. This is because the challenges to the civil rights law have been abstract arguments about speech, as if women's lives are abstract, as if the harms are abstract, conceded but not real. The women trapped in the pictures continue to be perceived as the free speech of the pimps who exploit them. No judge seems willing to look such a woman, three-dimensional and breathing, in the face and tell her that the pimp's use of her is his constitutionally protected right of speech; that he has a right to express himself by violating her. The women on whom the pornography is used in assault remain invisible and speechless in these court cases. No judge has had to try to sleep at night having heard a real woman's voice describing what happened to her, the incest, the rape, the gang rape, the battery, the forced prostitution. Keeping these women silent in courts of law is the main strategy of the free speech lawyers who defend the pornography industry. Hey, they love literature; they deplore sexism. If some women get hurt, that's the price we pay for freedom. Who are the "we"? What is the "freedom"? These speech-loving lawyers keep the women from speaking in court so that no judge will actually be able to listen to them.

Women continue speaking out in public forums, even though we are formally and purposefully silenced in actual courts of law. Hearings were held by a subcommittee of the Senate Judiciary Committee on the effects of pornography on women and children; the Attorney General's Commission on Pornography listened to the testimony of women hurt by pornography; women are demanding to speak at conferences, debates, on television, radio. This civil rights law is taught in law schools all over the country; it is written about in law journals, often favorably; increasingly, it has academic support; and its passage has been cited as precedent in at least one judicial decision finding that pornography in the workplace can be legally recognized as sexual harassment. The time of silence—at least the time of absolute silence—is over. And the civil rights law developed in Minneapolis has had an impact around the world. It is on the agenda of legislators in England, Ireland, West Germany, New Zealand, Tasmania, and Canada; it is on the agenda of political activists all over the world.

The law itself is civil, not criminal. It allows people who have been hurt by pornography to sue for sex discrimination. Under this law, it is sex discrimination to coerce, intimidate, or fraudulently induce anyone into pornography; it is sex discrimination to force pornography on a person in any place of employment, education, home, or any public place; it is sex discrimination to assault, physically attack, or injure any person in a way that is directly caused by a specific piece of pornography—the pornographers share responsibility for the assault; in the Bellingham version, it is also sex discrimination to defame any person through the unauthorized use in pornography of their name, image, and/or recognizable personal likeness; and it is sex discrimination to produce, sell, exhibit, or distribute pornography—to traffic in the exploitation of women, to traffic in material that provably causes aggression against and lower civil status for women in society.

The law's definition of pornography is concrete, not abstract. Pornography is defined as the graphic, sexually explicit subordination of women in pictures and/or words that also includes women presented dehumanized as sexual objects, things, or commodities; or women presented as sexual objects who enjoy pain or humiliation; or women presented as sexual objects who experience sexual pleasure in being raped; or women presented as sexual objects tied up or cut up or mutilated or bruised or physically hurt; or women presented in postures or positions of sexual submission, servility, or display; or women's body parts—including but not limited to vaginas, breasts, buttocks—exhibited such that women are reduced to those parts; or women presented as whores by nature; or women presented being penetrated by objects or animals; or women presented in scenarios of degradation, injury, torture, shown as filthy or inferior, bleeding, bruised, or hurt in a context that makes these conditions sexual. If men, children, or transsexuals are used in any of the same ways, the material also meets the definition of pornography.

For women hurt by pornography, this law simply describes reality; it is a map of a real world. Because the law allows them to sue those who have imposed this reality on them—especially the makers, sellers, exhibitors, and distributors of pornography—they have a way of redraw-

ing the map. The courts now protect the pornography; they recognize
the harm to women in judicial decisions—or they use words that say
they recognize the harm—and then tell women that the Constitution
protects the harm; profit is real to them and they make sure the pimps
stay rich, even as women and their children are this country's poor. The
civil rights law is designed to confront both the courts and the pornographers with a demand for substantive, not theoretical, equality. This
law says: we have the right to stop them from doing this to us because
we are human beings. "If my existence is proved real, I am coming to
take what is mine," Therese Stanton wrote for every woman who wants
to use this law. How terrifying that thought must be to those who have
been using women with impunity.

Initially an amendment to a city ordinance, this law has had a global
impact because: (1) it tells the truth about what pornography is and
does; (2) it tells the truth about how women are exploited and hurt by
the use of pornography; (3) it seeks to expand the speech of women by
taking the pornographers' gags out of our mouths; (4) it seeks to expand
the speech and enhance the civil status of women by giving us the courts
as a forum in which we will have standing and authority; (5) it is a
mechanism for redistributing power, taking it from pimps, giving it to
those they have been exploiting for profit, injuring for pleasure; (6) it
says that women matter, including the women in the pornography. This
law and the political vision and experience that inform it are not going
to go away. We are going to stop the pornographers. We are going to
claim our human dignity under law. One ex-prostitute, who is an organizer for the passage of this civil rights law, wrote: "Confronting how
I've been hurt is the hardest thing that I've ever had to do in my life. A
hard life, if I may say so."[14] She is right. Confronting the pornographers
is easier—their threats, their violence, their power. Confronting the
courts is easier—their indifference, their contempt for women, their
plain stupidity. Confronting the status quo is easier. Patience is easier
and so is every form of political activism, however dangerous. Beaver is
real, all right. A serious woman—formidable even—she is coming to
take what is hers.

4

> That same night [July 20, 1944, the attempt by the generals to
> assassinate Hitler] he [Goebbels] turned his house into "a
> prison, headquarters and court rolled into one"; Goebbels him-
> self headed a commission of investigation; and he and Himmler
> cross-examined the arrested generals throughout the night.
> Those condemned, then or thereafter, were executed with re-
> volting cruelty. They were hanged from meat-hooks and slowly
> strangled. Goebbels ordered a film to be made of their trial and
> execution: it was to be shown, *in terrorem* to Wehrmacht audi-
> ences. However, the reaction of the first audience was so hostile
> that it had to be suppressed.
>
> —Hugh Trevor-Roper,
> in his introduction to *Final Entries 1945: The Diaries of Joseph Goebbels*

As far as I can determine, Goebbels's film of the generals slowly, horribly
dying—their innards caving in from the force of gravity on their hung
bodies, the slow strangulation pushing out their tongues and eyes and
causing erection (which strangulation invariably does in the male)—was
the first snuff film. The master of hate propaganda didn't get it right
though—a rare lapse. Audiences became physically sick. These were
Nazi audiences watching Nazi generals, men of power, the society's pa-
triarchs, so white they were Aryan; rulers, not slaves. It only works when
the torture is done on those who have been dehumanized, made inferior—not just in the eyes of the beholder but in his real world. Goebbels
started out with cartoons of Jews before the Nazis came to power; he
could have moved on to the films made in Dachau in 1942, for instance, of "the reactions of the men placed in the Luftwaffe's low-pres-
sure chambers"[15]; desensitizing his Nazi audiences to the humiliation,
the torture, of Jews, he could have made a film that would have
worked—of Jews hanging from meat hooks, slowly strangled. But never
of power, never of those who were the same, never of those who had
been fully human to the audience the day before, never of those who
had been respected. Never.

Des Pres says it is easier to kill if "the victim exhibits self-disgust; if he cannot lift his eyes for humiliation, or if lifted they show only emptiness. . . ."[16] There is some pornography in which women are that abject, that easy to kill, that close to being dead already. There is quite a lot of it; and it is highly prized, expensive. There is still more pornography in which the woman wets her lips and pushes out her ass and says hurt me. She is painted so that the man cannot miss the mark: her lips are bright red so that he can find the way into her throat; her vaginal lips are pink or purple so that he can't miss; her anus is darkened while her buttocks are flooded with light. Her eyes glisten. She smiles. Sticking knives up her own vagina, she smiles. She comes. The Jews didn't do it to themselves and they didn't orgasm. In contemporary Amerikan pornography, of course, the Jews do do it to themselves—they, usually female, seek out the Nazis, go voluntarily to concentration camps, beg a domineering Nazi to hurt them, cut them, burn them—and they do climax, stupendously, to both sadism and death. But in life, the Jews didn't orgasm. Of course, neither do women; not in life. But no one, not even Goebbels, said the Jews liked it. The society agreed that the Jews deserved it, but not that they wanted it and not that it gave them sexual pleasure. There were no photographs from Ravensbrück concentration camp of the prostitutes who were incarcerated there along with other women gasping for breath in pleasure; the gypsies didn't orgasm either. There were no photographs—real or simulated—of the Jews smiling and waving the Nazis closer, getting on the trains with their hands happily fingering their exposed genitals or using Nazi guns, swastikas, or Iron Crosses for sexual penetration. Such behaviors would not have been credible even in a society that believed the Jews were both subhuman and intensely sexual in the racist sense—the men rapists, the women whores. The questions now really are: why is pornography credible in our society? how can anyone believe it? And then: how subhuman would women have to be for the pornography to be true? To the men who use pornography, how subhuman are women? If men believe the pornography because it makes them come—them, not the women—what is sex to men and how will women survive it?

Pornography: Men Possessing Women—written from 1977 through

1980, published in 1981 after two separate publishers reneged on contractual agreements to publish it (and a dozen more refused outright), out of print in the United States for the last several years—takes power, sadism, and dehumanization seriously. I am one of those serious women. This book asks how power, sadism, and dehumanization work in pornography—against women, for men—to establish the sexual and social subordination of women to men. This book is distinguished from most other books on pornography by its bedrock conviction that the power is real, the cruelty is real, the sadism is real, the subordination is real: the political crime against women is real. This book says that power used to destroy women is atrocity. *Pornography: Men Possessing Women* is not, and was never intended to be, an effete intellectual exercise. I want real change, an end to the social power of men over women; more starkly, his boot off my neck. In this book, I wanted to dissect male dominance; do an autopsy on it, but it wasn't dead. Instead, there were artifacts—films, photographs, books—an archive of evidence and documentation of crimes against women. This was a living archive, commercially alive, carnivorous in its use of women, saturating the environment of daily life, explosive and expanding, vital because it was synonymous with sex for the men who made it and the men who used it—men so arrogant in their power over us that they published the pictures of what they did to us, how they used us, expecting submission from us, compliance; we were supposed to follow the orders implicit in the pictures. Instead, some of us understood that we could look at those pictures and see them—see the men. Know thyself, if you are lucky enough to have a self that hasn't been destroyed by rape in its many forms; and then, know the bastard on top of you. This book is about him, the collective him: who he is; what he wants; what he needs (the key to both his rage and his political vulnerability); how he's diddling you and why it feels so bad and hurts so much; what's keeping him in place on you; why he won't move off of you; what it's going to take to blow him loose. A different kind of blow job. Is he scared? You bet.

Pornography: Men Possessing Women also puts pornography, finally, into its appropriate context. A system of dominance and submission, pornography has the weight and significance of any other historically real torture or punishment of a group of people because of a condition of birth; it has the weight and significance of any other historically real exile of human beings from human dignity, the purging of them from a shared community of care and rights and respect. Pornography happens. It is not outside the world of material reality because it happens to women, and it is not outside the world of material reality because it makes men come. The man's ejaculation is real. The woman on whom his semen is spread, a typical use in pornography, is real. Men characterize pornography as something mental because their minds, their thoughts, their dreams, their fantasies, are more real to them than women's bodies or lives; in fact, men have used their social power to characterize a $10-billion-a-year trade in women as fantasy. This is a spectacular example of how those in power cannibalize not only people but language. "We do not know," wrote George Steiner, "whether the study of the humanities, of the noblest that has been said and thought, can do very much to humanize. We do not know; and surely there is something rather terrible in our doubt whether the study and delight a man finds in Shakespeare make him any less capable of organizing a concentration camp."[17] As long as language is a weapon of power—used to destroy the expressive abilities of the powerless by destroying their sense of reality—we do know. Beaver knows.

Some have said that pornography is a superficial target; but, truly, this is wrong. Pornography incarnates male supremacy. It is the DNA of male dominance. Every rule of sexual abuse, every nuance of sexual sadism, every highway and byway of sexual exploitation, is encoded in it. It's what men want us to be, think we are, make us into; how men use us; not because biologically they are men but because this is how their social power is organized. From the perspective of the political activist, pornography is the blueprint of male supremacy; it shows how male supremacy is built. The political activist needs to know the blueprint. In cultural terms, pornography is the fundamentalism of male dominance.

Its absolutism on women and sexuality, its dogma, is merciless. Women are consigned to rape and prostitution; heretics are disappeared and destroyed. Pornography is the essential sexuality of male power: of hate, of ownership, of hierarchy; of sadism, of dominance. The premises of pornography are controlling in every rape and every rape case, whenever a woman is battered or prostituted, in incest, including in incest that occurs before a child can even speak, and in murder—murders of women by husbands, lovers, and serial killers. If this is superficial, what's deep?

5

When I first wrote *Pornography,* I was going to use these lines from Elizabeth Barrett Browning's letters as an epigraph: "If a woman ignores these wrongs, then may women as a sex continue to suffer them; there is no help for any of us—let us be dumb and die."[18] I changed my mind, because I decided that no woman deserved what pornography does to women: no woman, however stupid or evil, treacherous or cowardly, venal or corrupt; no woman. I also decided that even if some women did, I didn't. I also remembered the brave women, the women who had survived, escaped; in the late 1970s, they were still silent, but I had heard them. I don't want them, ever, to be dumb and die; and certainly not because some other woman somewhere is a coward or a fool or a cynic or a kapo. There are women who will defend pornography, who don't give a damn. There are women who will use pornography, including on other women. There are women who will work for pornographers—not as so-called models but as managers, lawyers, publicists, and paid writers of "opinion" and "journalism." There are women of every kind, all the time; there are always women who will ignore egregious wrongs. My aspirations for dignity and equality do not hinge on perfection in myself or in any other woman; only on the humanity we share, fragile as that appears to be. I understand Elizabeth Barrett Browning's desperation and the rage behind it, but I'm removing her curse. No woman's betrayal will make us dumb and dead—no more and never again. Beaver's endured too much to turn back now.

NOTES

1. William Lloyd Garrison, Preface, *Narrative of the Life of Frederick Douglass, An American Slave Written by Himself,* Frederick Douglass, ed. Benjamin Quarles (Cambridge, Mass.: The Belknap Press of Harvard University Press, 1960), p. 5.

2. Public Hearings on Ordinances to Add Pornography as Discrimination Against Women, Minneapolis City Council, Government Operations Committee, December 12 and 13, 1983, in transcript, p. 16.

3. Name withheld, manuscript.

4. Sarah Wynter, pseudonym, manuscript, June 19, 1985.

5. Name withheld, manuscript; also testimony before the Subcommittee on Juvenile Justice of the Committee on the Judiciary, United States Senate, September 12, 1984.

6. See Public Hearings, Minneapolis, pp. 38–39.

7. See Public Hearings, Minneapolis, pp. 39–41.

8. See Public Hearings, Minneapolis, p. 41.

9. See Public Hearings, Minneapolis, pp. 42–46.

10. See Public Hearings, Minneapolis, pp. 65–66.

11. See Public Hearings, Minneapolis, pp. 66–67.

12. Direct quotations are from the Statement of Jayne Stamen, issued by Women Against Pornography, February 14, 1988.

13. Terrence Des Pres, *The Survivor: An Anatomy of Life in the Death Camps* (New York: Pocket Books, 1977), p. 39.

14. Toby Summer, pseudonym, "Women, Lesbians and Prostitution: A Working-class Dyke Speaks Out Against Buying Women for Sex," *Lesbian Ethics,* vol. 2, no. 3, summer 1987, p. 37.

15. Roger Manvell and Heinrich Fraenkel, *Himmler* (New York: G. P. Putnam's Sons, 1965), p. 105.

16. Des Pres, *The Survivor,* p. 68.

17. George Steiner, *Language and Silence* (New York: Atheneum, 1977), pp. 65–66.

18. Elizabeth Barrett Browning, *Letters of Elizabeth Barrett Browning* in Mary Daly, *Gyn/Ecology: The Metaethics of Radical Feminism* (Boston: Beacon Press, 1978), p. 153.

RESISTANCE

MASS MURDER IN MONTRÉAL

The Sexual Politics of Killing Women

I t is very hard to think of an adequate way to mourn, but we know that tears are not adequate. We know how to cry. The question is: how do we fight back?

We might have wanted to claim the benefits of liberal feminism. We might have wanted to say, "Look at us—aren't we wonderful? Do you know how many women are now in law schools? Do you know how many women are now on construction sites?" Well, not enough. But in the last year, since these fourteen women were murdered,* feminists cannot stand up with any sense of pride and say: "Look at what we have done." We stand today with grief and terror and rage. There is no liberal feminist credit to claim. We want to say: "They were in that school because of us. You see, we broke down the barriers." That is now a two-edged sword. Yes, they were in the school because of us; we did break down the barriers. And this man, who was not crazy, who was political in his thinking and in his action, understood the meaning of those barriers coming down, and he committed a political act so that we would retreat, so that new barriers could be built, and so that women would not have the heart or courage or patience or endurance to keep breaking barriers.

---

*Fourteen women students were murdered on December 6, 1989, at the École Polytechnique, the Université de Montréal's engineering school.

105

We have been asked by many people to accept that women are making progress, because one sees our presence in these places where we weren't before. And those of us who are berated for being radicals have been saying: "That is not the way we measure progress. We count the number of rapes. We count the women who are being battered. We keep track of the children who are being raped by their fathers. We count the dead. And when those numbers start to change in a way that is meaningful, we will then talk to you about whether or not we can measure progress."

All of the accomplishments of feminism—for which, by the way, we are not often thanked (and that is why we rush in to claim anything we can)—have been made not always with deep politeness, but they have been made with extraordinary patience and self-restraint, by which I mean: we have not used guns. We have used words. We have marched saying words. And we are punished for achieving everything we achieve; we are punished for every statement we make; we are punished for every act toward self-determination. Every assertion of dignity is punished either socially by the great media out there—when they choose to recognize us, it is usually through ridicule and contempt—or by the men around us, who are the foot soldiers in this very real war in which the violence is almost exclusively on one side. The purpose of the punishment is very clear, whether the punishment itself is an act of forced sex or being beaten or being insulted with words or being harassed walking down the street or being sexually harassed in your place of work: "Get inside. Shut your mouth. Do what I tell you." Which is usually reduceable to: "Clean the house and open your legs." Many of us have said no. We say it in different ways. We say it at different times. But we say no and we've said it loudly enough and collectively enough that it has begun to resonate in the public sphere. No, we will not. No.

There is an answer to our no. A semiautomatic gun is one answer. There are also knives. This is not a pleasant conversation that we're having.

The press, the establishment politicians, and the social pundits are using differences between this mass murder and the usual patterns of violence against women to confuse the issues, as if the differences are what matter and not what is the same. We know what is the same. So, first, let us talk analytically about the differences, instead of just letting them manipulate the differences to make this slaughter into an event that simply will never be replicated in all the history of the world.

Women, as you know, are usually killed in our own homes, in what is called private, because a man and a woman together are not considered a *social* unit. It is him, he is the human being. She is his subordinate. The privacy is his, and in it he can do what he wants to her. We are usually hurt without the scrutiny of cameras and announcements. We are usually hurt by men we know and especially by men with whom we have been intimate, by which I mean sexually involved. In the society in which we live, intercourse is a phenomenon of ownership of women. Men who have had sex with women believe or feel or think—whatever the right word is—that that woman, then, in some way, belongs to them. And, indeed, all of the euphemisms for sexual intercourse in English express ownership: *possession*—I possessed her; the verb *to have*—I had her; *take*—I took her; sex as *conquest*—I conquered her; *violation*—I violated her. All of these words and expressions are used as synonyms for sexual intercourse. None of these words are the so-called dirty words.

Women are usually killed in isolation, not in a public place. Women are usually killed simply for being women, not for being feminists. The women who are most often killed by strangers are women who live out on the streets—women in prostitution or homeless women. This population of women is overwhelmingly characterized by being doubly disenfranchised, which is to say that they come from racially stigmatized groups. They are impoverished even by the standards of women, and I think that it is really a mistake to say that they are being hurt by strangers, because in fact, when you look at the transaction, what happens to prostitutes on the streets is a form of date rape—or date death, really. A man buys a date and he hurts or kills the woman. A significant number of those women who are killed are called "Jane Doe." No one knows where Jane Doe came from. No one knows who her people are. There is no place for her. She has no home in which to be killed.

It used to be that women were sexual chattel under the law, so that the man had the backing of the state. Now, men exercise their sense of possession and ownership in a more laissez-faire manner. They bear more personal responsibility for making sure that you stay subordinate. It's hard on them: you know how rebellious you are, and they have to work twenty-four hours a day at this, which can't be easy. That is what you are reading in the newspapers even as men write about these murders—that they, the men, are suffering. But not enough. Not yet.

One of the differences in the way Marc Lépine killed these women is that when women are killed, it is almost never called murder. There are many euphemisms: "it was a family fight," "father kills wife and children." We're told that there has been a "domestic tragedy" instead of a mass murder. Marc Lépine was a mass murderer. This was not some little family soap opera in which one man has killed several people and what those people have in common is a shared powerlessness in relation to him and the fact that, as far as society is concerned, he owns them or has an implicit right to own them.

We are frequently told that the man has been under terrible stress. He's been having a terrible time. It's very pathetic and pitiful—for him. We are also told that his wife provoked it. And when prostitutes are raped or killed, the policy of the police in the United States has been not to begin to take the murders seriously until the number of corpses are in the double digits. That has been official state policy.

These women were murdered—because they were women but also because they were engineering students; because they were learning a male science; because they wanted sacred male knowledge. They were trespassing on sacred male ground. They wanted to be engineers, and that was taken to be a militant act of aggression on their part.

What is the same in their deaths is that Marc Lépine, along with other men who hurt or kill women, cannot, could not, coexist outside a context in which women were completely submissive. He couldn't tolerate it. And when men can't stand something, they do something about it. And here is the deepest criticism of us: when we can't stand something, we often don't. Marc Lépine felt he had a right to do what he did. He said: "Life does not bring me joy." The boy was looking for joy; he wanted to bring the fun back into his life. But there is a precondition for joy in masculine terms, and that precondition is that women are in their place, a subordinate place. You can't have a lot of fun in the world as a man if women anywhere in your perception are getting out of control.

I have seen a lot of the press up here say the equivalent of "I don't want to be associated with Marc Lépine." Well, yes, it is true that not every man picks up a semiautomatic gun, but a lot of them don't have to, because they have pens. And a lot of them don't have to, because they exercise destructive, annihilating power in other ways over women. They destroy women body and soul, but yes, the shells are allowed to keep walking around. The shells are useful. Remember the part about lying down and spreading your legs. You don't have to have a heart. You don't have to have a spirit. Marc Lépine reacted the way that white people in the Amerikan South reacted when the "Whites Only" signs started coming down—that is to say, with violence. And feminists are the active agents of change. We're the people who are responsible for polluting his environment. We have done that—by introducing women into the professions, into working-class jobs from which women were excluded, and by introducing women into history. I hope you have read Marc Lépine's letter, which was just recently published [released by the police to the press one year after the murders], in which he said that war is a male territory, part of masculine heroism, male identity, and even the suggestion that women had behaved heroically in a situation of war was a deep political insult to him. This is a masculinity that is based on the erasure of women, metaphorically and literally, and what I want you to note about it is its extraordinary cowardice, its unbelievable cowardice. In the massacre of fourteen women, the cowardice is clear, but the cowardice is clear in every act of rape as well. In the United States, of the rapes that are reported, 43 percent are pair or gang rapes. Of that, 27 percent are committed by three or more men; 16 percent by two men. We are living in the world as it is not because men are physically stronger than we are but because they gang up to attack us and hurt us. In every act of brutality toward us, what we see is a coward. The husband who batters his wife needs the support of the state to keep doing it. And he gets it—he gets the compliance of the society; he gets reinforcement from the media that tell him battery is really a sexy thing to do; he gets his $10-billion-a-year pornography industry in which women are the raw material bought and sold for him, so that he can have some of that joy Marc Lépine talked about. The men who use women as prostitutes are also big, bad, and brave. They take women who have been sexually molested as children, who are poor, who are homeless, who have no help or solace in this society, and they use them. If you look at male violence against women, what you will see is the cowardice of that violence.

The way men use women in prostitution is a lot like gang rape, in the sense that what men do to women they do for the sake of each other: "I am a man, another man was here before me, another man will be here after me, he and I have masculinity in common because we both use her—she is simply the vehicle by which I experience our collective superiority to anyone who is like her. I own her because I have bought her. I own her because I have bought her—both the wife and the prostitute; I am morally superior to her because I have bought her; she belongs to me and her behavior is mine to control."

I saw a sociologist on television last night, a male sociologist, perfectly fine guy. In his learned opinion, which was exceptionally erudite, the massacre was the "first"—and I wrote it down because I didn't want to exaggerate—"the first political act against women." The courts don't commit political acts against women when they are organized to support the rapists and the batterers, no; nor when they take women's children away from them, and, as is happening in the United States, give them to fathers who are raping them. That's not political. Nothing that has ever happened to us before is political. We are supposed to believe that we have our private lives and, well, a good man is hard to find. But you just keep searching and searching and eventually, hopefully before you are brain-dead from being beaten, you will find him. That's not political; it's personal, which is why everyone talks about psychologists. They are here to convince you that this is personal, not political. And the authorities here in Montréal are trying to convince you that if you organize politically against male violence, you will be responsible for making men angrier. On every television show, in every newspaper, at the forum last night at which city officials spoke and answered questions, we were told: "Men haven't really gotten used to these new roles for women. That's why they're hurting women."

Well, men used to have the legal right to beat their wives, so why were they doing it then? Something has changed, but their behavior has stayed the same. They beat their wives when the state said they could beat their wives, and now that the law has changed, they beat their wives.

I think that what all these male authorities are trying to say is this: "We don't understand why he killed them, because he hadn't fucked them. If he had fucked them, we would understand it. And it would have something to do with us. It would be private—it would be none of your business. But we would understand it. But when a man kills a woman with whom he doesn't have that relationship, he's crazy. Not stressed; *crazy.*"

Male control of women through law and through the church has broken down considerably. Now, that's the kind of statement one can make as long as one doesn't say, "We did it." But we did it. The reason we are not chattel in marriage is that we changed those damn laws. We have created a rebellion of women in marriage. There are women who do not accept that marriage means that men have bought sexual access. We changed that; we did that. So, what do men do if they don't have the law that they had before, the police that go with the law that they had before, the power of the church that they had before? Well, let me tell you: a $10-billion-a-year pornography industry in the United States turns each man into his own state, his own church, and tells him how to control and hurt women. Systems of power are capable of reorganizing themselves, and the fact that things look different does not mean that the hierarchy has changed. It's the hierarchy we have to look at, not the fact that some social patterns of behavior are different. We have to look at who is on top and who is on the bottom, and then, if we have heart enough to do it, we have to look at what he is doing to her while he is on top and she is on the bottom.

I am astonished, of course, that these intelligent people who keep this machine going don't understand why we recognize in this massacre something familiar instead of something completely anomalous. What we recognize as being familiar is the hate that is in the act, the hate for women, the bitterness and resentment against women who are not being sexually submissive—at that moment at least—and the rage, his rage toward us. I doubt that there are any women in this room who don't recognize from our own lives those elements in men, and we see it in this act, and therefore this act seems familiar, not bizarre and entirely unique.

Some of the women who were murdered may have been feminists and some not. Women do not get the right to say, "I am, I am." We are all just the same, one way or another. We can look at this and we can understand that the men around us will widely experience any act of dignity on our part as an act of feminism, whether it is or it is not; any act of stepping outside the circle of submission as an act of feminism, whether it is or it is not. I want us to understand that as well as Marc Lépine did.

There are two usual strategies for dealing with a dead woman when she has been murdered by a man. One is the one you are seeing here, which is: we look at the man and we socially create sympathy for him. The other is that we look at the woman or women and we find out what's wrong with her or them. Maybe if three women had been killed, we would be reading about all the terrible things they had done—by the age of twenty-one. And the media would be trying to convince the public-at-large that the victims deserved what happened to them because, after all, were they virgins? How many men had they been with? This is the way murdered women are usually treated. But because of the rootedness of these women in this community, because of the social power of their families, because of the fact that, with respect to other people, they themselves are part of an elite, these women are not being treated this way—yet. The newspapers won't do it. Books by misogynist men will. Our intrepid investigative reporter or sociologist or psychologist will go out there and find the men who know the real dirt and publish a book. This is not over yet.

I would like to say something that I find very difficult to say. It is not a cheap remark. I think that one of the most important commitments that anyone can make to life or to feminism is to make sure that you deserve your death if you die at the hands of a misogynist, that you have done everything that he in his mind accuses you of, that every act of treason he is killing you for is one you have committed. Like many women, I have a long history of violence against me, and I say, to my increasing shame, that everyone who has hurt me is still walking around. They're fine. Nothing has happened to them. And when I look at my own life, I think about the difference between being beaten because I didn't clean the refrigerator and having my life threatened because I am fighting the pornographers. There is a better and a worse, and it is better to encounter anything when you have made a choice that puts you where you want to be, fighting for your own freedom and fighting for the freedom of the women around you. Feminists should remember that while we often don't take ourselves very seriously, the men around us often do. I think that the way we can honor these women who were executed, for crimes that they may or may not have committed—which is to say, for political crimes—is to commit every crime for which they were executed, crimes against male supremacy, crimes against the right to rape, crimes against the male ownership of women, crimes against the male monopoly of public space and public discourse. We have to stop men from hurting women in everyday life, in ordinary life, in the home, in the bed, in the street, and in the engineering school. We have to take public power away from men whether they like it or not and no matter what they do. If we have to fight back with arms, then we have to fight back with arms. One way or another we have to disarm men. We have to be the women who stand between men and the women they want to hurt. We have to end the impunity of men, which is what they have, for hurting women in all the ways they systematically do hurt us.

The feminist is the woman who is there not because she is his woman, but because she is the sister of the woman he is being a weapon against. Feminism exists so that no woman ever has to face her oppressor in a vacuum, alone. It exists to break down the privacy in which men rape, beat, and kill women. What I am saying is that every one of us has the responsibility to be the woman Marc Lépine wanted to murder. We need to live with that honor, that courage. We need to put fear aside. We need to endure. We need to create. We need to resist, and we need to stop dedicating the other 364 days of the year to forgetting everything we know. We need to remember every day, not only on December 6. We need to consecrate our lives to what we know and to our resistance to the male power used against us.

TERROR, TORTURE, AND RESISTANCE

We're here because of an emergency. You all know that. We want to speak about the progress we've made, but we know that women are not any safer from rape now than when we started out. I'm glad that the Canadian Mental Health Association is concerned with our health—because I for one am sick to death. I am sick from the numbers of women who are being brutalized and raped and sodomized, who are being killed, who are missing, who in a women's culture of non-violence don't hurt the people who are hurting us. We take our own lives. We commit suicide.

So many women I have known have spent every day of their lives fighting to stay alive, because of the despair they carry around with them from the sexual abuse that they have experienced in their lives. And these are brave, creative women. These are women who thought that they had a right to dignity, to individuality, to freedom—but in fact they couldn't walk down a city block in freedom. Many of them were raped as children in their own homes, by relatives—by fathers, uncles, brothers—before they were "women." Many of them were beaten by the men who loved them—their husbands, lovers. Many of them were tortured by those men. When you look at what happened to these women, you want to say, "Amnesty International, where are you?"—because the prisons for women are our homes. We live under martial law. We live in a rape culture. Men have to be sent to prison to live in a culture that is as rapist as the normal home in North America. We live under what amounts to a military curfew, enforced by rapists. We say we're free citizens in a free society. But we lie. We lie about it every day.

We survive through amnesia, by being unable to remember what happened to us. We survive by not remembering the name of the woman who was in the newspaper yesterday, who was walking somewhere and was missing. What was her name? There are too many of them. I am sick to death of not being able to remember the names. There's one name especially I can never remember: the woman who was gang-raped on the pool table in New Bedford, Massachusetts, by four men while everyone else in the bar stood and watched and cheered. That woman died in an automobile accident, the kind the police will always call suicide, within one year after the rape trial. Three months before this woman was raped on that pool table, *Hustler* ran a spread of a woman being gang-raped on a pool table. Everything that was done to the woman in the pornography was done to that woman, in that bar, that night. After the New Bedford gang rape, *Hustler* ran a photograph of a woman in a pornographic pose, sitting on a pool table, depicted like a postcard, saying, "Welcome to New Bedford." The rape trial was televised in the United States. The ratings beat out the soap operas. People watched it as entertainment every day. The woman was driven out of town, even though the rapists were convicted. Within one year she was dead and no matter how hard I try, I can't remember her name. Hollywood made a movie called *The Accused*, a brilliant, incredible movie in which Jodie Foster, through her artistry, shows us that a woman is a human being. It takes two hours to establish for a mainstream audience that in fact that's true, so that at the point when we reach the gang-rape scene, we understand that someone has been hurt in a way that goes beyond the sum of the physical brutalities that were done to her. The Hollywood version had a happy ending. The voyeurs were convicted of having incited the rape, and the woman triumphed. I sat in the theater thinking, *But she's dead. What's her name? Why can't I remember her name?*

And then there are the women whose names I do remember: for instance, Jennifer Levin, a woman who was murdered in New York in Central Park by a man who had been her lover. And the reason I know her name is that when she was murdered by this lover of hers, the New York tabloid press put her name on the front page in headlines to say what a slut she was. Now, I didn't buy any of those papers; it's just that I couldn't leave my house and not read the headlines. So the boy goes to trial—a white boy, an upper-class boy, wealthy. It gets called "the preppie murder case." And we hear for the first time about something called the rough-sex defense. It goes as follows: "She wanted to have really rough, painful, humiliating sex. She was an aggressive bitch and she tried to tie him up. And she hurt him, and he got so upset that in trying to free himself, he accidentally strangled her, with her bra." In this scenario, the way women are treated when women are raped is suddenly the way women are treated when women are murdered: she provoked it. She wanted it. She liked it and she got what she deserved. When the head of our sex-crimes unit, Linda Fairstein, tried to get a conviction of this man, Robert Chambers, for murder, she had a problem: she couldn't find a motive. She didn't think that she could convince the jury that there was any reason for Robert Chambers to kill Jennifer Levin. Of course, there wasn't any reason, except that he wanted to—and he could. He plea-bargained, so the jury decision never came in. Most of us thought he was going to be acquitted. After he plea-bargained, videos were shown on television of Mr. Chambers at sex parties making fun of strangling the woman—sitting naked, surrounded by women, reenacting the murder and laughing about it. We live in a world where men kill women and the motives are not personal at all. As any woman in this room who has ever been beaten or raped knows, it is one of the most impersonal experiences you will ever have. You are a married woman. You live with a man. You think that he knows you and you know him. But when he begins to hurt you, he does it because you're a woman—not because you're whoever you are.

I want us to stop lying. I think that we tell a lot of lies to get through every day, and I want us to stop. One of the lies we tell is that this kind of woman hating is not as pernicious, as lethal, as sadistic, as vicious as other kinds of hatred that are directed against people because of a condition of birth. We have recognized some of the historical atrocities that have occurred. We say to ourselves, this isn't the same. I'm Andrea. I'm Jane. I'm me. But everyone has said that. Every Jew pushed onto a train said, "But why are you doing this? I'm me." The Nazis didn't have a personal motive that could be understood in those terms.

We are in a situation of emergency. You know that. There is no longer the belief on any woman's part that she will be exempt whatever her politics, whatever her class, whatever her race, whatever her profession. Only liars and deniers count on not being raped, beaten, used, forced—let alone having freedom. We have a right to freedom.

What happens when you're walking down that street? You can't get lost in thought, can you? You better know who's around you at every moment. We live in a police state where every man is deputized. I want us to stop smiling. I want us to stop saying we're fine. I want us to stop saying that this can be fixed after it happens. We may be able to use whatever it is we learn from being hurt, but can it be fixed? No. It cannot be fixed. So the question is, How do we stop it from happening?

We have had a brilliant movement that has saved many lives. I, especially, thank and honor those of you who work in rape crisis centers and in battered women's shelters. I wish to hell you had been there during some earlier parts of my life. Anyone currently in her forties could not have had the help you provide. But we have to change our focus: we have to stop it from happening. Otherwise we accept as our condition that the rape of women and brutality toward women are normal, and the question is how to regulate it, how to reduce it. Maybe men could go to more hockey games than they go to now—you know, have other outlets, diversions?

I'm here to say that the war against women is a real war. There's nothing abstract about it. This is a war in which his fist is in your face. We walk around saying, "It didn't happen today" or "It hasn't happened yet" or "I've been lucky for the last three months" or "Oh, I found a good one now. Nice one, he won't hurt me too much. He may insult me a lot, but he won't hurt me." Maybe it's true and maybe it isn't—but we have to find out how to stop men from hurting women at all, under any circumstances.

You know that most women are hurt in their homes. You know that most women who are murdered are killed in their homes by intimates, not by strangers. A political movement, as I understand it, exists to change the way social reality is organized. That means we need to understand everything about the way this system works. Every woman who has had experience with sexual violence of any kind has not just pain, and not just hurt, but knowledge—knowledge of male supremacy, knowledge of what it is, knowledge of what it feels like—and can begin to think strategically about how to stop it. We are living under a reign of terror. I want us to stop accepting that that's normal. And the only way that we can stop accepting that that's normal is if we refuse to have amnesia every day of our lives—if we remember what we know about the world we live in and get up in the morning determined to do something about it.

We need to understand how male violence works. That's one of the reasons that studying pornography and fighting the pornography industry are so important—because that's the Pentagon, the war room. Pornographers train the soldiers; then the soldiers go out and do the actions on us. We're the population that the war is against. This has been a terrible war. Our resistance has not been serious; it has not been enough. The minute we think we might have a right to do something about that pornography shop—legal or illegal—we stop thinking. We don't believe we have any legal right to do much about it, let alone an illegal right. Inside us, this worthlessness that we carry around—which is the main consequence of the fear that we live with—makes us subscribe, in terms of our behavior, to the system that says that the life of the man who wants to hurt us is worth more than ours. We accept it. A lot of our ability to survive is based on forgetting it as much as we can. I understand that I am talking to women who spend more time than most women with the reality of sexual abuse. If the premise is that the freedom of women matters and that the equality of women matters, then "education" is not enough. You know that men are educated. They know rape and battery are wrong.

The rapist still knows more about rape than we do. He's keeping secrets from us; we're not keeping secrets from him. The pimps know how to manipulate and sell women. They're not stupid men. I challenge the notion that rape and prostitution and other vicious violations of women's rights are abnormal and that the regular, sanctioned male use of women in intercourse is unrelated to the "excesses" that we seem to be just falling over all the time. We women who want to be hurt so much, it's actually us provoking it all. When a woman has been raped and goes into court, why is it that the judges' premises are the same as pornographers'? Intercourse has been a material way of owning women. This is real, this is concrete. We know it; most of us have experienced it. I'm talking about history, and I'm talking about sexuality not as an idea in your head but as what happens to a woman when she is in bed with a man. If we are not willing to look at intercourse as a political institution—directly related to the ways in which we are socialized to accept our inferior status, and one of the ways in which we are controlled—we are not ever going to get to the roots of the ways in which male dominance works in our lives.

The basic premise about women is that we are born to be fucked. That is it. Now, that means a lot of things. For a lot of years it meant that marriage was outright ownership of a woman's body and intercourse was a right of marriage. That meant that intercourse was per se an act of force, because the power of the state mandated that the woman accept intercourse. She belonged to the man. The cultural remnant of this is that in our society, men experience intercourse as possession of women. The culture talks about intercourse as conquest—women surrendering, women being taken. This is a paradigm for rape, not a paradigm for reciprocity, equality, mutuality, or freedom. When the premise is that women exist on earth in order to be sexually available to men for intercourse, it means that our very bodies are seen as having boundaries that have less integrity than male bodies do. Men have orifices; men can be penetrated. The point of homophobia is to direct men toward women, to punish men for not using women. Homophobia is an acknowledgment of how aggressive and how dangerous men know male sexuality can be for women. When a woman goes into court and she says, "I've been raped," the judge, the defense lawyer, the press, and many other people say: no, you had intercourse. And she says, "No, I was raped." And they say a little bit of force is fine. It's still true. It hasn't changed. When you look at male domination as a social system, what you see is that it is organized to make certain that women are sexually available for men. That is its basic premise. We have a choice, and the choice is not in the political science books. The universities are not trying to work out this level of choice for us. The question is, What comes first, men's need to get laid or women's dignity? And I am telling you that you cannot separate the so-called abuses of women from the so-called normal uses of women. The history of women in the world as sexual chattel makes it impossible to do that.

There are other implications—because as sex is currently socialized and existing in our society, men cannot have sex with women who are their equals. They're incapable of it. That's what objectification is about. In order to get a response from men, one has to be the right kind of thing. Now, think about what that means: the woman polices herself. She makes decisions that make her freedom impossible, because if she is going to live, if she is going to make a living, she is going to have to be the kind of object to which the man will respond in a way that is important to him, in a way that is sexual. Sexual harassment on the job is not some kind of accident. The fact that women are migrants in the workplace is not an accident. When you enter into the sexual agreement to be a thing, you then narrow your own possibilities for freedom. You then accept, as a basic premise of your life, that you will be available, not challenge his sexual hegemony, not demand equality in intimacy. After all, you've already given up your own body, to the plastic surgeon or to the lover or voyeur. The women, the mothers, who bound their daughters' feet so that their daughters' feet were three inches long—crippled—did it because that was the standard of beauty. If a woman wanted to eat, a man had to find her beautiful. If that meant she couldn't walk for the rest of her life, it was a trade-off that had to be made. It was Let's Make a Deal. And we women are still playing Let's Make a Deal. Instead of deciding what we want, what we need, we have a second-class standard for our own freedom. We're afraid, not because we're cowards—goddammit, we are not cowards; we are brave people—but instead of fighting the system that forces us to make these deals, we use our bravery to sustain ourselves when we make one. When we make a choice it has got to be a choice rooted in equality—not in the fact that every woman is still one man away from welfare.

In the United States, violence against women is a major pastime. It is a sport, an amusement, a mainstream cultural entertainment. It is real and it is pervasive. It is epidemic. It's very hard to make anyone notice it because there is so much of it. In the United States we have had thirty years of the total saturation of the society with pornography. In this thirty years, we have had many people who have wanted us to study the problem. We have had many people who have wanted us to debate the issues. We have studied, we have debated, we have done it all. There has been the development in the United States of a very major population of men called serial killers—men who rape and kill mostly women, sometimes children. They usually mutilate the bodies. Sometimes they have sex before. Sometimes they have sex after. Now, we can say it's a power trip, but the fact of the matter is that for them, that's the way they have sex: by mutilating and hurting and killing us. We have in the United States a continuing epidemic of murders of women. We have huge missing pieces of our populations in cities. In Kansas City, the police say that since 1977, sixty women have been killed. Three quarters of them have been black. They've been women in prostitution. They have been mutilated, or left in what the police and the media—the euphemisms are extraordinary—call suggestive positions. One of the patterns of serial killers is that they do to their victims the things they have seen in pornography, and they leave their victims posed as pornography. Pornography is involved in the biographies of all serial killers. Sometimes they use it to stalk their victim, sometimes they use it to plan their crime. Sometimes they use it to rev themselves up to commit the acts. Yet people keep insisting that there must be something in the air or in the water. How is it that all these guys get these ideas to do all these things? What could it be? Let's go on an egg hunt and try to find it. Well, the fact of the matter is, it's in the pornography being sold everywhere. Pornography says go get them, do this to them, it's fun. The pornography says they'll like it, too. That's the truth, and society has to stay organized so that there are enough women to provide the raw material for that pornography.

The conditions that provide the raw material are poverty, usually incestuous child abuse, and homelessness. We didn't have that knowledge before; we do now. What happens to women? How does it happen? We now know a lot. It is time to begin to act on what we know. We know that pornography causes sexual abuse. We know that in the United States the average age of rapists is going down. It's now boys in their young teen-age years who are committing a preponderance of first assaults against young girls. There are young boys who stick things in infants and kill them. When asked why they did it that way, they say they've seen it in pornography. There are young boys who take guns and try to put them in women's vaginas. Where did they see it? Where did they learn it? Ask them. Ask the ones who have been put in jail, in places for juvenile sex offenders. They will tell you, "I saw it in pornography." Now, what makes somebody want to do it may be different than how he learns to do it. But the fact of the matter is that if you live in a society that is saturated with this kind of woman hating, you live in a society that has marked you as a target for rape, for battery, for prostitution, or for death. These are, in my view, the facts.

I want you to talk about the violence against women, and you're here to talk about healing. I wish that you could raise the dead. That is what I would like to see. This is a political point. One of the reasons that the Right reaches so many women is that the Right has a transcendent god who says I will heal all your hurt and all your pain and all your wounds: "I died for you. I will heal you." Feminists do not have a transcendent god who can heal that way. We have ideas about fairness and justice and equality. And we have to find ways to make them real. We don't have magic. We don't have supernatural powers. And we can't keep sticking together women who have been broken into little pieces. Fighting back is as close to healing as we are going to come. It is important to understand that we will live with a fair amount of pain for most of our lives. If your first priority is to live a painless life, you will not be able to help yourself or other women. What matters is to be a warrior. Having a sense of honor about political struggle is healing. Discipline is necessary. Actions against men who hurt women must be real. We need to win. We are in a war. We have not been fighting back. We need to win this war. We need a political resistance. We need it aboveground. We need it with our law-makers, with our government officials. We need it with our professional women. We need it aboveground. We need it underground too.

Everything that didn't happen to you—and I apply this to myself; it's part of the way that I survive—is a little slack in your leash. You weren't raped when you were three, or you weren't raped when you were ten, or you weren't battered, or you weren't in prostitution—whatever it is that you managed to miss is the measure of your freedom and strength, and the measure of what you owe to other women. I'm not asking you to be martyrs; I'm asking you to give up your lies. I'm asking you to live your lives, honorably and with dignity. I'm asking you to fight. I'm asking you to do things for women that women do all the time in political struggle for men. Women put our bodies on the line in political strug-gles in which both sexes are involved, but we do not do it for women. I'm not asking you to get caught; I'm asking you to escape. I'm asking you to run for your life. If you need to run through a brick wall, run through it. If you get some bruises on your arms, it's better than having him give the bruises to you because you were standing still. None of us has the right to stand still.

I ask you to consider addressing the pornography issue in social pol-icy terms, which I believe means passing some version of the civil rights law that we developed in Minneapolis. Obscenity laws say that women's bodies are dirty—that's what they're based on. Criminal laws do not stop the pornography industry. The business can go on; somebody else can manage it. Instead we must make men accountable for the ways in which women are exploited in pornography, recognize it as a form of sex discrimination, understand that it destroys women's chances in life, and say, "You are going to pay a penalty. We're going to take your money away from you. We're going to find a way to hurt you back. No more free ride for you, Mr. Pimp. You're going to pay a price."

I think it's very important that rape, battery, and prostitution be recognized legally as violations of the civil rights of women, as human rights violations of the greatest magnitude. It's important that we construct a legal system that acknowledges our dignity by acknowledging our wholeness as human beings.

I am asking you to retaliate against rapists, to organize against rapists. We know who the rapists are. We know because they do it to us. He did it to me; he did it to my best friend. We know who he is. We know that it happened: when, where, and how. I'm asking you to take rape seriously. If the law won't do anything, you must do something.

I'm asking you to close down the pornography outlets wherever you can and to stop the distribution wherever you can, in whatever way you can.

I am asking you to stop passing: stop having feminism be part of a secret life. I am asking you not to apologize to anyone for standing up for women.

I am asking you to organize political support for women who kill men who have been hurting them. They have been isolated and alone. This is a political issue. They're being punished, because at some moment in their lives, they resisted a domination that they were expected to accept. They stand there in jail for us, for every one of us who got away without having to pull the trigger, for every one of us who lived to tell about getting away without having the trigger pulled on us.

I am asking you to stop men who beat women. Get them jailed or get them killed, but stop them. Men who rape make a choice to rape. And men who beat women make a choice to beat women. And we women now have choices that we have to make to fight back.

I am asking you to look at every single political possibility for fighting back—instead of saying, "I asked him, I told him, but he just wouldn't stop." We need to find ways to do it together. But we need to do it.

PORNOGRAPHY HAPPENS

For twenty years, people that you know and people that you do not know inside the women's movement, with its great grassroots breadth and strength, have been trying to communicate something very simple: pornography happens. It happens. Lawyers, call it what you want—call it speech, call it act, call it conduct. Catharine A. MacKinnon and I called it a practice when we described it in the antipornography civil rights ordinance that we drafted for the City of Minneapolis in 1983; but the point is that it happens. It happens to women, in real life. Women's lives are made two-dimensional and dead. We are flattened on the page or on the screen. Our vaginal lips are painted purple for the consumer to clue him in as to where to focus his attention such as it is. Our rectums are highlighted so that he knows where to push. Our mouths are used and our throats are used for deep penetration.

I am describing a process of dehumanization, a concrete means of changing someone into some thing. We are not talking about violence yet; we are nowhere near violence.

Dehumanization is real. It happens in real life; it happens to stigmatized people. It has happened to us, to women. We say that women are objectified. We hope that people will think that we are very smart when we use a long word. But being turned into an object is a real event; and

126

the pornographic object is a particular kind of object. It is a target. You are turned into a target. And red or purple marks the spot where he's supposed to get you.

This object wants it. She is the only object with a will that says, hurt me. A car does not say, bang me up. But she, this nonhuman thing, says hurt me—and the more you hurt me, the more I will like it.

When we look at her, that purple painted thing, when we look at her vagina, when we look at her rectum, when we look at her mouth, when we look at her throat, those of us who know her and those of us who have been her still can barely remember that she is a human being.

In pornography we literally see the will of women as men want to experience it. This will is expressed through concrete scenarios, the ways in which women's bodies are positioned and used. We see, for instance, that the object wants to be penetrated; and so there is a motif in pornography of self-penetration. A woman takes some thing and she sticks it up herself. There is pornography in which pregnant women for some reason take hoses and stick the hoses up themselves. This is not a human being. One cannot look at such a photograph and say, This is a human being, she has rights, she has freedom, she has dignity, she is someone. One cannot. That is what pornography *does* to women.

We talk about fetishism in sex.* Psychologists have always made that mean, for example, a man who ejaculates to or on a shoe. The shoe can be posed as it were on a table far from the man. He is sexually excited; he masturbates, maybe rubs up against the shoe; he has sex "with" the shoe. In pornography, that is what happens to a woman's body: she is

---

*"The word *fetish* comes from the Portuguese *feitiço*, which means 'charm' or 'made thing.' A fetish is a magical, symbolic object. Its first meaning is religious: the magical object is regarded with irrational, extreme, extravagant trust or reverence (to paraphrase Merriam-Webster). In sexual meaning, the magic of the fetish is in its power to cause and sustain penile erection. . . .

"No sense of her own purpose can supersede, finally, the male's sense of her purpose: to be that thing that enables him to experience raw phallic power. In pornography, his sense of purpose is fully realized. She is the pinup, the centerfold, the poster, the postcard, the dirty picture, naked, half-dressed, laid out, legs spread, breasts or ass protruding. She is the thing

(continued)

turned into a sexual fetish and the lover, the consumer, ejaculates on her. In the pornography itself, he does ejaculate *on* her. It is a convention of pornography that the sperm is on her, not in her. It marks the spot, what he owns and how he owns it. The ejaculation on her is a way of saying (through showing) that she is contaminated with his dirt; that she is dirty. This is the pornographer's discourse, not mine; the Marquis de Sade always refers to ejaculate as pollution.

Pornographers use every attribute any woman has. They sexualize it. They find a way to dehumanize it. This is done in concrete ways so that, for instance, in pornography the skin of black women is taken to be a sexual organ, female of course, despised, needing punishment. The skin itself is the fetish, the charmed object; the skin is the place where the violation is acted out—through verbal insult (dirty words directed at the skin) and sexualized assault (hitting, whipping, cutting, spitting on, bondage including rope burns, biting, masturbating on, ejaculating on).

In pornography, this fetishizing of the female body, its sexualization and dehumanization, is always concrete and specific; it is never abstract and conceptual. That is why all these debates on the subject of pornography have such a bizarre quality to them. Those of us who know that pornography hurts women, and care, talk about women's real lives, insults and assaults that really happen to real women in real life—the women in the pornography and the women on whom the pornography is used. Those who argue for pornography, especially on the ground of freedom of speech, insist that pornography is a species of idea, thought, fantasy, situated inside the physical brain, the mind, of the consumer no less.

In fact we are told all the time that pornography is really about ideas.

---

she is supposed to be: the thing that makes him erect. In literary and cinematic pornography, she is taught to be that thing: raped, beaten, bound, used, until she recognizes her true nature and purpose and complies—happily, greedily, begging for more. She is used until she knows only that she is a thing to be used. This knowledge is her authentic erotic sensibility: her erotic destiny. . . ." Dworkin, *Pornography: Men Possessing Women* (New York: E. P. Dutton, 1989), pp. 123, 128.

See Andrea Dworkin, "Objects," in *Pornography: Men Possessing Women* (New York: E. P. Dutton, 1989), pp. 101–28.

Well, a rectum doesn't have an idea, and a vagina doesn't have an idea, and the mouths of women in pornography do not express ideas; and when a woman has a penis thrust down to the bottom of her throat, as in the film *Deep Throat*, that throat is not part of a human being who is involved in discussing ideas. I am talking now about pornography without visible violence. I am talking about the cruelty of dehumanizing someone who has a right to more.

In pornography, everything means something. I have talked to you about the skin of black women. The skin of white women has a meaning in pornography. In a white-supremacist society, the skin of white women is supposed to indicate privilege. Being white is as good as it gets. What, then, does it mean that pornography is filled with white women? It means that when one takes a woman who is at the zenith of the hierarchy in racial terms and one asks her, What do you want?, she, who supposedly has some freedom and some choices, says, I want to be used. She says, use me, hurt me, exploit me, that is what I want. The society tells us that she is a standard, a standard of beauty, a standard of womanhood and femininity. But, in fact, she is a standard of compliance. She is a standard of submission. She is a standard *for* oppression, its emblem; she models oppression, she incarnates it; which is to say that she does what she needs to do in order to stay alive, the configuration of her conformity predetermined by the men who like to ejaculate on her white skin. She is for sale. And so what is her white skin worth? It makes her price a little higher.

When we talk about pornography that objectifies women, we are talking about the sexualization of insult, of humiliation; I insist that we are also talking about the sexualization of cruelty. And this is what I want to say to you—that there is cruelty that does not have in it overt violence.

There is cruelty that says to you, you are worth nothing in human terms. There is cruelty that says you exist in order for him to wipe his penis on you, that's who you are, that's what you are for. I say that dehumanizing someone is cruel; and that it does not have to be violent in order for it to be cruel.

Things are done to women day in and day out that would be construed to be violent if they were done in another context, not sexualized,
to a man; women are pushed, shoved, felt up, called dirty names, have
their passage physically blocked on the street or in the office; women
simply move on, move through, unless the man escalates the violence to
what the larger patriarchal world takes to be real violence: ax murder;
sadistic stranger rape or gang rape; serial killing not of prostitutes. The
touching, the pushing, the physical blockades—these same invasions
done to men would be comprehended as attacks. Done to women, people seem to think it's bad but it's okay, it's bad but it's all right, it's bad
but, hey, that's the way things are; *don't make a federal case out of it.* It occurs to me that we have to deal here—at the heart of the double standard—with the impact of orgasm on our perception of what hatred is
and is not.

Men use sex to hurt us. An argument can be made that men have to
hurt us, diminish us, in order to be able to have sex with us—break
down barriers to our bodies, aggress, be invasive, push a little, shove a
little, express verbal or physical hostility or condescension. An argument
can be made that in order for men to have sexual pleasure with women,
we have to be inferior and dehumanized, which means controlled,
which means less autonomous, less free, less real.

I am struck by how hate speech, racist hate speech, becomes more
sexually explicit as it becomes more virulent—how its meaning becomes more sexualized, as if the sex is required to carry the hostility. In
the history of anti-Semitism, by the time one gets to Hitler's ascendance
to power in the Weimar Republic, one is looking at anti-Semitic hate
speech that is indistinguishable from pornography*—and it is not only
actively published and distributed, it is openly displayed. What does

---

Der Stürmer is the outstanding example of anti-Semitic propaganda that reached the
threshold of pornography while advocating race-hate. Founded in 1923 by Julius Streicher,
a rabid anti-Semite who joined forces with Hitler in 1921 after an independent run as a
Jew-hating rabble-rouser, *Der Stürmer* had Hitler's strong support, from the years of struggle
(as the Nazis called them) through Hitler's reign, the years of persecution and annihilation.
As late as 1942, Joseph Goebbels, minister of propaganda, wrote in his diary: "The Führer

that orgasm do? That orgasm says, I am real and the lower creature, that thing, is not, and if the annihilation of that thing brings me pleasure, that is the way life should be; the racist hierarchy becomes a sexually charged ideal. There is a sense of biological inevitability that comes from the intensity of a sexual response derived from contempt; there is biological urgency, excitement, anger, irritation, a tension that is satisfied in humiliating and belittling the inferior one, in words, in acts.†

We wonder, with a tendentious ignorance, how it is that people believe bizarre and transparently false philosophies of biological superiority. One answer is that when racist ideologies are sexualized, turned into concrete scenarios of dominance and submission such that they give people sexual pleasure, the sexual feelings in themselves make the ideologies seem biologically true and inevitable. The feelings seem to be natural; no argument changes the feelings; and the ideologies, then, also seem to be based in nature. People defend the sexual feelings by defending the ideologies. They say: my feelings are natural so if I have an orgasm from hurting you, or feel excited just by thinking about it, you are my natural partner in these feelings and events—your natural

---

sent word to me that he does not desire the circulation of the *Stürmer* to be reduced or that it stop publishing all together. . . . I, too, believe that our propaganda on the Jewish question must continue undiminished" (cited in Telford Taylor, *The Anatomy of the Nuremberg Trials* [New York: Alfred A. Knopf, 1992], p. 377).

†Tried at Nuremberg, Streicher was convicted of crimes against humanity and hanged on October 16, 1946. On his way to the hanging scaffolding he shouted "Heil Hitler!" and on it he shouted the bizarre—but in the circumstances clearly anti-Semitic—words, "Purim festival, 1946."

In his fascinating recent account of the Nuremberg trials, Telford Taylor, who was one of the prosecutors for the United States, suggests that Streicher was wrongly sentenced to death because "there was no accusation that Streicher himself had participated in any violence against Jews, so the sole (and difficult) legal issue was whether or not 'incitement' was a sufficient basis for his conviction" (Taylor, p. 376). This is a distinctly U.S.-based revisionism in keeping with the increasing fanaticism of First Amendment free speech absolutism. In Nuremberg, a relationship between sexualized hate propaganda and genocide was demonstrated. Many Western democracies responded by criminalizing the kind of hate speech, or incitement to genocide, in which Streicher engaged, indeed, at which he excelled. The United States has apparently, as a matter of law and public policy, decided to masturbate to it.

role is whatever intensifies my sexual arousal, which I experience as self-importance, or potency; you are nothing but you are *my* nothing, which makes me someone; using you is my right because being someone means that I have the power—the social power, the economic power, the imperial sovereignty—to do to you or with you what I want.

This phenomenon of feeling superior through a sexually reified racism is always sadistic; its purpose is always to hurt. Sadism is a dynamic in every expression of hate speech. In the use of a racial epithet directed at a person, for instance, there is a desire to hurt—to intimidate, to humiliate; there is an underlying dimension of pushing someone down, subordinating them, making them less. When that hate speech becomes fully sexualized—for instance, in the systematic reality of the pornography industry—and a whole class of people exists in order to provide sexual pleasure and a synonymous sense of superiority to another group, in this case men, when that happens, we dare not tolerate that being called freedom.

The problem for women is that being hurt is ordinary. It happens every day, all the time, somewhere to someone, in every neighborhood, on every street, in intimacy, in crowds; women are being hurt. We count ourselves lucky when we are only being humiliated and insulted. We count ourselves goddamn lucky when whatever happens falls short of rape. Those who have been beaten in marriage (a euphemism for torture) also have a sense of what luck is. We are always happy when something less bad happens than what we had thought possible or even likely, and we tell ourselves that if we do not settle for the less bad there is something wrong with us. It is time for us to stop that.

When one thinks about women's ordinary lives and the lives of children, especially female children, it is very hard not to think that one is looking at atrocity—if one's eyes are open. We have to accept that we are looking at ordinary life; the hurt is not exceptional; rather, it is systematic and it is real. Our culture accepts it, defends it, punishes us for resisting it. The hurt, the pushing down, the sexualized cruelty are intended; they are not accidents or mistakes.

Pornography plays a big part in normalizing the ways in which we are demeaned and attacked, in how humiliating and insulting us is made to look natural and inevitable.

I would like you especially to think about these things. Number one: pornographers use our bodies as their language. Anything they say, they have to use us to say. They do not have that right. They must not have that right. Number two: constitutionally protecting pornography as if it were speech means that there is a new way in which we are legally chattel. If the Constitution protects pornography as speech, our bodies then belong to the pimps who need to use us to say something. They, the humans, have a human right of speech and the dignity of constitutional protection; we, chattel now, moveable property, are their ciphers, their semantic symbols, the pieces they arrange in order to communicate. We are recognized only as the discourse of a pimp. The Constitution is on the side it has always been on: the side of the profit-making property owner even when his property is a person defined as property because of the collusion between law and money, law and power. The Constitution is not ours unless it works for us, especially in providing refuge from exploiters and momentum toward human dignity. Number three: pornography uses those who in the United States were left out of the Constitution. Pornography uses white women, who were chattel. Pornography uses African-American women, who were slaves. Pornography uses stigmatized men; for instance, African-American men, who were slaves, are often sexualized by contemporary pornographers as animalistic rapists. Pornography is not made up of old white men. It isn't. Nobody comes on them. They are doing this to us; or protecting those who do this to us. They do benefit from it; and we do have to stop them.

Think about how marriage controlled women, how women were property under the law; this did not begin to change until the early years of the twentieth century. Think about the control the church had over women. Think about what a resistance has been going on, and all the trouble you have made for these men who took for granted that you belonged to them. And think about pornography as a new institution of social control, a democratic use of terrorism against all women, a way of saying publicly to every woman who walks down the street: avert your eyes (a sign of second-class citizenship), look down, bitch, because when you look up you're going to see a picture of yourself being hung, you're going to see your legs spread open.

Pornography tells us that the will of women is to be used. And I just want to say that the antipornography civil rights ordinance that Catharine MacKinnon and I developed in Minneapolis says that the will of women is *not* to be used; the Ordinance repudiates the premises of the pornography; its eventual use will show in the affirmative that women want equality.

Please note that the Ordinance was developed in Minneapolis, and that its twin city, St. Paul, passed a strong city ordinance against hate crimes; the courts struck down both. I want you to understand that there are some serious pornographers in Minneapolis and some serious racists in St. Paul and some serious citizens in both cities who want the pornography and the racism to stop. The Ordinance that Catharine and I drafted came out of that political culture, a grassroots, participatory political culture that did not want to tolerate either kind of cruelty toward people.

In the fall of 1983, Catharine and I were asked by a group of neighborhood activists to testify at a local zoning committee meeting. The group represented an area of Minneapolis that was primarily African-American, with a small poor-white population. The city council kept zoning pornography *into* their neighborhood. For seven years they had been fighting a host of zoning laws and zoning strategies that allowed pornography to destroy the quality of life around them. The city could write off their neighborhood and others like it because they mostly were not white and they mostly were poor; the pornography was purposefully put in such places and kept out of wealthier, whiter neighborhoods.

These activists came to us and said: we know now that the issue here is woman hating. That is virtually a direct quote: we know now that the issue here is woman hating. And we want to do something about it. What can we do?

They knew what to do. They organized MacKinnon and me, that's for sure; and they organized Minneapolis. The whole city was organized on a grassroots level to stand against the woman hating in pornography. That was our mandate when we drafted the antipornography civil rights law; and constituencies of poor people, people of color, were organized in behalf of the lives of women in those communities. A city in the United States was organized by an ever expanding feminist wave of political workers that brought in working-class women, current and former prostitutes, academics, out and visible lesbians, students, and, inter alia, a small army of sexual abuse victims to demand passage of an amendment to the municipal civil rights law that recognized pornography as sex discrimination, as a violation of the civil rights of women. This amendment, which MacKinnon and I later redrafted to be a free-standing statute, is commonly called "the Ordinance."

The Ordinance got the massive, committed, excited support it did because it is fair, because it is honest, and because it is on the side of those who have been disenfranchised and oppressed. People mobilized—not from the top down but from the bottom up—to support the Ordinance because it does stand directly in the way of the woman hating in pornography: the bigotry, the hostility, the aggression that exploit and target women. It does this by changing our perceptions of the will of women. It destroys the authority of the pornographers on that subject by putting a law, dignity, real power, meaningful citizenship in the hands of the women they hurt. No matter how she is despised in the pornography or by the pornographers and their clients, she is respected by this law. Using the Ordinance, women get to say to the pimps and the johns: we are not your colony; you do not own us as if we were territory; my will as expressed through my use of this Ordinance is, I don't want it, I don't like it, pain hurts, coercion isn't sexy, I resist being someone else's speech, I reject subordination, I speak, I speak for myself now, I am going into court to speak—to you; and you will listen.

We wanted a law that repudiates what happens to women when pornography happens to women. In general, the legal system's misogyny mimics the pornographers'; abstractly we can call it gender bias, but the legal system incorporates an almost visceral hatred of women's bodies, as if we exist to provoke assaults, like them, lie about them—and are not really injured by them. I have a character in *Mercy*—named Andrea—who says that you have to be clean to go before the law.* Now, no women are clean, or clean enough. That is what we find out every time we try to prosecute a rape; we're not clean.

But certainly the women who have been turned into pornography are not clean, and the women being sold on street corners are not clean, and the women who are being battered and pornographized in their homes are not clean. When a woman uses this Ordinance—if a woman ever gets a chance to use this Ordinance—she will not need to be clean to say, with dignity and authority, I am someone, therefore I resist.

When the Minneapolis City Council passed this Ordinance they said, women are someone, women matter, women want to fight back, we will give them what they want. The Minneapolis City Council had an idea of the will of women that contradicted the pornographers'; they got that different idea from the women who came to testify for the Ordinance, especially those who had grounds to use the Ordinance. The Ordinance's clarity and authority derive from the flesh-and-blood experiences of women who want to use it: women whose lives have been savaged by pornography. The Ordinance expresses their will to resist, and the enormous strength, translated into a legal right, of their capacity to endure, to survive.

The woman using the Ordinance will be saying, I am someone who has endured, I have survived, I matter, I know a lot, and what I know matters; it matters, and it is going to matter here in court, you pimp, because I am going to use what I know against you; and you, Mr. Con-

---

*". . . and even if there's laws by the time they have hurt you you are too dirty for the law; the law needs clean ones but they dirty you up so the law won't take you; there's no crimes they committed that are crimes in the general perception because we don't count as to crimes as I have discovered time and time again as I try to think if what he did that hurt me so bad was a crime to anyone or was anything you could tell someone about so they would care; for you; about you; so you was human." (See Dworkin, *Mercy* [London: Secker & Warburg, 1990], pp. 303–4.)

sumer, I know about you, and I am going to use what I know even about you, even when you are my teacher, my father, my lawyer, my doctor, my brother, my priest. I am going to use what I know.

It was not a surprise to Catharine MacKinnon and myself when, after the Ordinance was passed, the newspapers said—ah-ha, it was a right-wing, fundamentalist achievement. They were saying to us, to MacKinnon and me, you are no one, you can't exist, it could not have been *your* idea. And it was not a surprise to us when people believed it. We did not like it, but it was not a surprise.

And when the court said to the injured women who wanted to use the Ordinance, you are no one, the pimp is someone, he matters, we are going to protect him, it was not a surprise. And when the court said, the consumer is someone, none of you women are anyone no matter how much you have been hurt but he is someone and we are here for him, that was not a surprise. And it was not a surprise when the court said to women: when you assert your right to equality you are expressing an opinion, a point of view, which we should be debating in the famous marketplace of ideas, not legislating; when you claim you were injured—that rape, that beating, that kidnapping—you have a viewpoint about it, but in and of itself the injury does not signify. And it was not a surprise when the court said that there was a direct relationship between pornography as defined in the Ordinance and injuries to women, including rape and battery, but that relationship does not matter because the court has a viewpoint, which happens to be the same as the pornographers': you women are not worth anything except what we pay for you in that famous free marketplace where we take your actual corporeal reality to be an idea.

None of this was a surprise. Every little tiny bit of it was an outrage.

We wrote the Ordinance for the women who had been raped and beaten and prostituted in and because of pornography. They wanted to use it to say, I am someone and I am going to win. We are part of them, we have lived lives as women, we are not exempt or separate from any of this. We wrote the Ordinance in behalf of our own lives, too.

I want to ask you to make certain that women will have a right and a chance to go into a U.S. court of law and say: this is what the pornographers did to me, this is what they took from me and I am taking it back, I am someone, I resist, I am in this court because I resist, I reject their power, their arrogance, their cold-blooded, cold-hearted malice, and I am going to win.

You here today have to make that possible. It has been ten years now. It has been ten years. Count the number of women who have been hurt in those ten years. Count how many of us have been lucky enough to be only insulted and humiliated. Count. We cannot wait another ten years; we need you, we need you now—please, organize.

PROSTITUTION
AND MALE SUPREMACY

I'm very honored to be here with my friends and my peers, my sisters in this movement.

I also feel an awful lot of conflict about being here, because it is very hard to think about talking about prostitution in an academic setting.

The assumptions of academia can barely begin to imagine the reality of life for women in prostitution. Academic life is premised on the notion that there is a tomorrow and a next day and a next day; or that someone can come inside from the cold for time to study; or that there is some kind of discourse of ideas and a year of freedom in which you can have disagreements that will not cost you your life. These are premises that those who are students here or who teach here act on every day. They are antithetical to the lives of women who are in prostitution or who have been in prostitution.

If you have been in prostitution, you do not have tomorrow in your mind, because tomorrow is a very long time away. You cannot assume that you will live from minute to minute. You cannot and you do not. If you do, then you are stupid, and to be stupid in the world of prostitution is to be hurt, is to be dead. No woman who is prostituted can afford to be that stupid, such that she would actually believe that tomorrow will come.

I cannot reconcile these different premises. I can only say that the premises of the prostituted woman are my premises. They are the ones that I act from. They are the ones that my work has been based on all of these years. I cannot accept—because I cannot believe—the premises of the feminism that comes out of the academy: the feminism that says we will hear all these sides year after year, and then, someday, in the future, by some process that we have not yet found, we will decide what is right and what is true. That does not make sense to me. I understand that to many of you it does make sense. I am talking across the biggest cultural divide in my own life. I have been trying to talk across it for twenty years with what I would consider marginal success.

I want to bring us back to basics. Prostitution: what is it? It is the use of a woman's body for sex by a man, he pays money, he does what he wants. The minute you move away from what it really is, you move away from prostitution into the world of ideas. You will feel better; you will have a better time; it is more fun; there is plenty to discuss, but you will be discussing ideas, not prostitution. Prostitution is not an idea. It is the mouth, the vagina, the rectum, penetrated usually by a penis, sometimes hands, sometimes objects, by one man and then another and then another and then another and then another. That's what it is.

I ask you to think about your own bodies—if you can do so outside the world that the pornographers have created in your minds, the flat, dead, floating mouths and vaginas and anuses of women. I ask you to think concretely about your own bodies used that way. How sexy is it? Is it fun? The people who defend prostitution and pornography want you to feel a kinky little thrill every time you think of something being stuck into a woman. I want you to feel the delicate tissues in her body that are being misused. I want you to feel what it feels like when it happens over and over and over and over and over and over and over again: because that is what prostitution is. The repetition will kill you, even if the man doesn't.

Which is why—from the perspective of a woman in prostitution or a woman who has been in prostitution—the distinctions other people make between whether the event took place in the Plaza Hotel or somewhere more inelegant are not the distinctions that matter. These are irreconcilable perceptions, with irreconcilable premises. Of course the circumstances must matter, you say. No, they do not, because we are talking about the use of the mouth, the vagina, and the rectum. The circumstances don't mitigate or modify what prostitution is.

And so, many of us are saying that prostitution is intrinsically abusive. Let me be clear. I am talking to you about prostitution per se, without more violence, without extra violence, without a woman being hit, without a woman being pushed. Prostitution in and of itself is an abuse of a woman's body. Those of us who say this are accused of being simpleminded. But prostitution is very simple. And if you are not simpleminded, you will never understand it. The more complex you manage to be, the further away from the reality you will be—the safer you will be, the happier you will be, the more fun you will have discussing the issue of prostitution. In prostitution, no woman stays whole. It is impossible to use a human body in the way women's bodies are used in prostitution and to have a whole human being at the end of it, or in the middle of it, or close to the beginning of it. And no woman gets whole again later, after. Women who have been abused in prostitution have some choices to make. You have seen very brave women here make some very important choices: to use what they know; to try to communicate to you what they know. But nobody gets whole, because too much is taken away when the invasion is inside you, when the brutality is inside your skin. We try so hard to communicate, all of us to each other, the pain. We plead, we make analogies. The only analogy I can think of concerning prostitution is that it is more like gang rape than it is like anything else.

Oh, you say, gang rape is completely different. An innocent woman is walking down the street and she is taken by surprise. Every woman is that same innocent woman. Every woman is taken by surprise. In a prostitute's life, she is taken by surprise over and over again. The gang rape is punctuated by a money exchange. That's all. That's the only difference. But money has a magical quality, doesn't it? You give a woman money and whatever it is that you did to her she wanted, she deserved.

Now, we understand about male labor. We understand that men do things they do not like to do in order to earn a wage. When men do alienating labor in a factory we do not say that the money transforms the experience for them such that they loved it, had a good time, and in fact, aspired to nothing else. We look at the boredom, the dead-endedness; we say, surely the quality of a man's life should be better than that.

The magical function of money is gendered; that is to say, women are not supposed to have money, because when women have money, presumably women can make choices, and one of the choices that women can make is not to be with men. And if women make the choice not to be with men, men will then be deprived of the sex that men feel they have a right to. And if it is required that a whole class of people be treated with cruelty and indignity and humiliation, put into a condition of servitude, so that men can have the sex that they think they have a right to, then that is what will happen. That is the essence and the meaning of male dominance. Male dominance is a political system.

It is always extraordinary, when looking at this money exchange, to understand that in most people's minds the money is worth more than the woman is. The $10, the $30, the $50 is worth much more than her whole life. The money is real, more real than she is. With the money he can buy a human life and erase its importance from every aspect of civil and social consciousness and conscience and society, from the protections of law, from any right of citizenship, from any concept of human dignity and human sovereignty. For fifty fucking dollars any man can do that. If you were going to think of a way to punish women for being women, poverty would be enough. Poverty is hard. It hurts. The bitches would be sorry they're women. It's hard to be hungry. It's hard not to have a nice place to live in. You feel real desperate. Poverty is very punishing. But poverty isn't enough, because poverty alone does not provide a pool of women for men to fuck on demand. Poverty is insufficient to create that pool of women, no matter how hungry women get. So, in different cultures, societies are organized differently to get the same result: not only are women poor, but the only thing of value a woman has is her so-called sexuality, which, along with her body, has been turned into a sellable commodity. Her so-called sexuality becomes the only thing that matters; her body becomes the only thing that anyone wants to buy. An assumption then can be made: if she is poor and needs money, she will be selling sex. The assumption may be wrong. The assumption does not create the pool of women who are prostituted. It takes more than that. In our society, for instance, in the population of women who are prostituted now, we have women who are poor, who have come from poor families; they are also victims of child sexual abuse, especially incest; and they have become homeless.

Incest is boot camp. Incest is where you send the girl to learn how to do it. So you don't, obviously, have to send her anywhere, she's already there and she's got nowhere else to go. She's trained. And the training is specific and it is important: not to have any real boundaries to her own body; to know that she's valued only for sex; to learn about men what the offender, the sex offender, is teaching her. But even that is not enough, because then she runs away and she is out on the streets and homeless. For most women, some version of all these kinds of destitution needs to occur.

I have thought a lot in the last couple of years about the meaning of homelessness for women. I think that it is, in a literal sense, a precondition, along with incest and poverty in the United States, to create a population of women who can be prostituted. But it has a wider meaning, too. Think about where any woman really has a home. No child is safe in a society in which one out of three girls is going to be sexually abused before she is eighteen.[1] No wife is safe in a society in which recent figures appear to say that one out of two married women has been or is being beaten.[2] We are the homemakers; we make these homes but we have no right to them. I think that we have been wrong to say that prostitution is a metaphor for what happens to all women. I think that homelessness really is that metaphor. I think that women are dispossessed of a place to live that is safe, that belongs to the woman herself, a place in which she has not just sovereignty over her own body but sovereignty over her actual social life, whether it is life in a family or among friends. In prostitution, a woman remains homeless.

But there is something very specific about the condition of prostitution that I would like to try to talk about with you.

I want to emphasize that in these conversations, these discussions about prostitution, we are all looking for language. We are all trying to find ways to say what we know and also to find out what we don't know. There is a middle-class presumption that one knows everything worth knowing. It is the presumption of most prostituted women that one knows nothing worth knowing. In fact, neither premise is true. What matters here is to try to learn what the prostituted woman knows, because it is of immense value. It is true and it has been hidden. It has been hidden for a political reason: to know it is to come closer to knowing how to undo the system of male dominance that is sitting on top of all of us.

I think that prostitutes experience a specific inferiority. Women in general are considered to be dirty. Most of us experience this as a metaphor, and, yes, when things get very bad, when terrible things happen, when a woman is raped, when a woman is battered, yes, then you recognize that underneath your middle-class life there are assumptions that because you are a woman you are dirty. But a prostitute lives the literal reality of being the dirty woman. There is no metaphor. She is the woman covered in dirt, which is to say that every man who has ever been on top of her has left a piece of himself behind; and she is also the woman who has a purely sexual function under male dominance so that to the extent people believe that sex is dirty, people believe that prostituted women are dirt.

The prostituted woman is, however, not static in this dirtiness. She's contagious. She's contagious because man after man after man comes on her and then he goes away. For instance, in discussions of AIDS, the prostituted woman is seen as the source of the infection. That is a specific example. In general, the prostituted woman is seen as the generative source of everything that is bad and wrong and rotten with sex, with the man, with women. She is seen as someone who is deserving of punishment, not just because of what she "does"—and I put *does* in quotes, since mostly it is done to her—but because of what she is.

She is, of course, the ultimate anonymous woman. Men love it. While she is on her twenty-fourth false name—dolly, baby, cutie, cherry tart, whatever all the pornographers are cooking up this week as a marketing device—her namelessness says to the man, she's nobody real, I don't have to deal with her, she doesn't have a last name at all, I don't have to remember who she is, she's not somebody specific to me, she's a generic embodiment of woman. She is perceived as, treated as—and I want you to remember this, this is real—vaginal slime. She is dirty; a lot of men have been there. A lot of semen, a lot of vaginal lubricant. This is visceral, this is real, this is what happens. Her anus is often torn from the anal intercourse, it bleeds. Her mouth is a receptacle for semen, that is how she is perceived and treated. All women are considered dirty because of menstrual blood but she bleeds other times, other places. She bleeds because she's been hurt, she bleeds and she's got bruises on her.

When men use women in prostitution, they are expressing a pure hatred for the female body. It is as pure as anything on this earth ever is or ever has been. It is a contempt so deep, so deep, that a whole human life is reduced to a few sexual orifices, and he can do anything he wants. Other women at this conference have told you that. I want you to understand, believe them. It's true. He can do anything he wants. She has nowhere to go. There is no cop to complain to; the cop may well be the guy who is doing it. The lawyer that she goes to will want payment in kind. When she needs medical help, it turns out he's just another john. Do you understand? She is literally nothing. Now, many of us have experiences in which we feel like nothing, or we know that someone considers us to be nothing or less than nothing, worthless, but for a woman in prostitution, this is the experience of life every day, day in and day out.

He, meanwhile, the champion here, the hero, the man, he's busy bonding with other men through the use of her body. One of the reasons he is there is because some man has been there before him and some man will be there after him. This is not theory. When you live it, you see that it is true. Men use women's bodies in prostitution and in gang rape to communicate with each other, to express what they have in common. And what they have in common is that they are not her. So she becomes the vehicle of his masculinity and his homoeroticism, and he uses the words to tell her that. He shares the sexuality of the words, as well as the acts, directed at her, with other men. All of those dirty words are just the words that he uses to tell her what she is. (And from the point of view of any woman who has been prostituted—if she were to express that point of view, which it is likely she will not—the fight that male artists wage for the right to use dirty words is one of the sicker and meaner jokes on the face of this earth, because there is no law, no rule, no etiquette, no courtesy that stops any man from using every single one of those words on any prostituted woman; and the words have the sting that they are supposed to have because in fact they are describing her.) She's expendable. Funny, she has no name. She is a mouth, a vagina, and an anus—who needs her in particular when there are so many others? When she dies, who misses her? Who mourns her? She's missing—does anybody go look for her? I mean, who is she? She is no one. Not metaphorically no one. Literally, no one.

Now, in the history of genocide, for instance, the Nazis referred to the Jews as lice and, they said, we are going to exterminate them.[3] In the history of the slaughter of the indigenous people of the Americas, those who made policy said, they're lice, kill them.[4] Catharine MacKinnon talked earlier about gender cleansing: murdering prostitutes. She is right. Prostituted women are women who are there, available for the gynocidal kill. And prostituted women are being killed every single day, and we don't think we're facing anything resembling an emergency. Why should we? They're no one. When a man kills a prostitute, he feels righteous. It is a righteous kill. He has just gotten rid of a piece of dirt, and the society tells him he is right.

There is also a specific kind of dehumanization experienced by women who are prostituted. Yes, all women experience being objects, being treated like objects. But prostituted women are treated like a certain kind of object, which is to say, a target. A target isn't any old object. You might take pretty good care of some objects that you have around the house. But a target you go after. You put the dart in the hole. That's what the prostitute is for. What that should tell you is how much aggression goes into what a man does when he seeks out, finds, and uses a prostituted woman.

One of the conflicts that I feel about talking here, being here, is that I am afraid that anything I say that is even slightly abstract will immediately move everyone's mind off of the fundamental issue. And the fundamental issue is what is done to women who are in prostitution, what exactly prostitution is. But I have to risk that because I want to say to you that you can't think about prostitution unless you are willing to think about the man who needs to fuck the prostitute. Who is he? What is he doing? What does he want? What does he need?

He is everyone. I want you to take one hour, on Monday. I want you to walk through your school, and I want you to look at every man. I want you to take his clothes off with your eyes. I want you to see him with a stiff prick. I want you in your mind to put him on top of a woman with money on the table next to them. Everyone. The dean of this law school, the professors, the male students, everyone. If you are going to the emergency room, I want you to do it. If you have a heart attack, I want you to do it with the intern who is taking care of you. Because this is the world that prostituted women live in. It is a world in which no matter what happens to you, there is another man who wants a piece of you. And if you need something from him, you have to give him that piece.

Men who use prostitutes think they are real big and real brave. They're very proud of themselves—they brag a lot. They write novels, they write songs, they write laws—productive folk—and they have a sense that they are very adventurous and heroic, and why do they think that? Because they are predators who go out and hump women—they rub up against a woman who's dirty and they live to tell about it. Goddamn it. They live to tell about it. Unfortunately. Virtually all the time, no matter what they have done, no matter what harm they have done to her—they live to tell about it, sing about it, write about it, make television shows about it, make movies about it. I would like to say to you that these men are cowards, that these men are brutes, that these men are fools, that these men are able to do what they do because they have the power of men as a class behind them, which they get because men use force against women. If you want a definition of what a coward is, it's needing to push a whole class of people down so that you can walk on top of them. Societies are organized so that men have the power they need, to use women the way that they want to. Societies can be organized in different ways and still create a population of women who are prostituted. For instance, in the United States the women are poor, mostly incest victims, homeless. In parts of Asia, they are sold into slavery at the age of six months because they are females. It does not have to be done the same way in every place to be the same thing.

Male dominance means that the society creates a pool of prostitutes by any means necessary so that men have what men need to stay on top, to feel big, literally, metaphorically, in every way; and yet men are our standard for being human. We say we want to be human. We say that we want them to treat us like human beings. In a male-dominant society, men are the human beings. I want to point out to you that we use the word *human* metaphorically. We are not talking about how men act. We are talking about an idea, a dream, a vision that we have of what a human being is. We are saying that we do not want them stepping on top of us; we are also saying implicitly that they are not a good enough standard for what being human is because look at what they are doing to us. We cannot want to be like them because being like them means using people the way that they use people—for the sake of establishing one's importance or one's identity. I am saying that in part men are mythological figures to us when we talk about them as human beings. We are not talking about how men really behave. We are talking about the mythology of men as arbiters of civilization. This political movement involves understanding that the human qualities that we want in life with each other are not qualities that characterize the way men really behave.

What prostitution does in a society of male dominance is that it establishes a social bottom beneath which there is no bottom. It is the bottom. Prostituted women are all on the bottom. And all men are above it. They may not be above it much but even men who are prostituted are above the bottom that is set by prostituted women and girls. Every man in this society benefits from the fact that women are prostituted whether or not every man uses a woman in prostitution. This should not have to be said but it has to be said: prostitution comes from male dominance, not from female nature. It is a political reality that exists because one group of people has and maintains power over another group of people. I underline that because I want to say to you that male domination is cruel. I want to say to you that male domination must be destroyed. Male domination needs to be ended, not simply reformed, not made a little nicer, and not made a little nicer for some women. We need to look at the role of men—really look at it, study it, understand it—in keeping women poor, in keeping women homeless, in keeping girls raped, which is to say, in creating prostitutes, a population of women who will be used in prostitution. We need to look at the role of men in romanticizing prostitution, in making its cost to women culturally invisible, in using the power of this society, the economic power, the cultural power, the social power, to create silence, to create silence among those who have been hurt, the silence of the women who have been used.

We need to look at the role of men in creating a hatred of women, in creating prejudice against women, in using the culture to support, promote, advocate, celebrate aggression against women. We need to look at the role of men in creating a political idea of freedom that only they can actually have. What is freedom? Two thousand years of discourse and somehow it manages to leave us out. It is an amazingly self-serving monologue that they have had going here. We need to look at the role of men in creating political systems that subordinate women; and that means that we have to look at the role of men in creating prostitution, in protecting prostitution—how law enforcement does it, how journalism does it, how lawyers do it, how artists do it. We need to know the ways in which all those men use prostitutes and in doing so destroy the human dignity of the women.

The cure to this problem is political. That means taking power away from men. This is real stuff; it is serious stuff. They have too much of it.

They do not use it right. They are bullies. They do not have a right to what they have; and that means it has to be taken away from them. We have to take the power that they have to use us away from them. We have to take the power that they have to hurt us away from them. We have to take their money away from them. They have too much of it. Any man who has enough money to spend degrading a woman's life in prostitution has too much money. He does not need what he's got in his pocket. But there is a woman who does.

We need to take away their social dominance—over us. We live in a tyranny of liars and hypocrites and sadists.

Now, it will cost you to fight them. They have to be taken off of women, do you understand me? They need to be lifted up and off. What is intractable about prostitution is male dominance. And it is male dominance that has to be ended so that women will not be prostituted.

You, you—you have to weaken and destroy every institution that is part of how men rule over women. And don't ask if you should. The question is how, not if. How? Do one thing, rather than spend your lives debating if you should do this or if you should do that and do they really deserve it and is it really fair? Fair? Is it really fair? Darlings, we could get the machine guns out tonight. Fair? We break our own hearts with these questions. Is it fair? Don't respect their laws. No. Don't respect their laws. Women need to be making laws. I hope that Catharine MacKinnon and I have set an example. We have tried to. There is no reason for any woman, any woman in the world, to be basically performing fellatio on the current legal system. But mostly that is what one is in law school to learn how to do.

What I hope you will take away from here is this: that any vestige of sex hierarchy, any, will mean that some women somewhere are being prostituted. If you look around you and you see male supremacy, you know that somewhere where you cannot see, a woman is being prostituted, because every hierarchy needs a bottom and prostitution is the bottom of male dominance. So when you accommodate, when you compromise, when you turn a blind eye, you are collaborating. Yes, I know that your life is also at stake but yes you are collaborating, both things are true, in the destruction of another woman's life.

I am asking you to make yourselves enemies of male dominance, because it has to be destroyed for the crime of prostitution to end—the crime against the woman, the human rights crime of prostitution: and everything else is beside the point, a lie, an excuse, an apology, a justification, and all the abstract words are lies, justice, liberty, equality, they are lies. As long as women are being prostituted they are lies. You can tell the lie and in this institution you will be taught how to tell the lie; or you can use your lives to dismantle the system that creates and then protects this abuse. You, a well-trained person, can stand with the abuser or with the rebel, the resister, the revolutionary. You can stand with the sister he is doing it to; and if you are very brave you can try to stand between them so that he has to get through you to get to her. That, by the way, is the meaning of the often misused word *choice*. These are choices. I am asking you to make a choice.

NOTES

1. Diana E. H. Russell, *Sexual Exploitation: Rape, Child Sexual Abuse, and Workplace Harassment* (Beverly Hills, CA: Sage Publications, 1984), pp. 193–94.
2. Nancy Gibbs, "Til Death Do Us Part," *Time*, January 18, 1993, pp. 38, 41.
3. For example, Heinrich Himmler observed that "anti-Semitism is exactly the same as delousing." See Robert Jay Lifton, *The Nazi Doctors: Medical Killing and the Psychology of Genocide* (New York: Basic Books, Inc., Publishers, 1986), p. 477, citing Hans Buchheim, "Command and Compliance," in *Anatomy of the SS State*, Krausnick et al., eds. (New York: Walker & Company, 1968), p. 338.
4. David E. Stannard, *American Holocaust: Columbus and the Conquest of the New World* (New York: Oxford University Press, 1992), p. 131.

FREEDOM NOW

Ending Violence Against Women

The first thing I want to do is to thank you for being there for so many women who have nowhere to go, no one to help, who live in communities in which people deny what is happening in the apartment right next to them, in the house down the street. I thank you for being there for women who need help.

When we talk about battery we are not talking about something that only happens to a few women; we're talking about something that happens to as many as half the married women in the United States. It is staggering to understand that the place where a woman is most at jeopardy is in fact her own home. Four thousand women a year in the United States are killed in their own homes, not by strangers who break in, but by men who presumably love them. It is urgent to understand what is "normal" about battery, why it doesn't seem—to the husband, often to the wife, to the neighbors, to the families—that something unbelievably disastrous and terrible is happening when a woman is being beaten.

When I say that battery is "normal," I mean that battery expresses a lot of attitudes and opinions that people, including women, have about women. It also expresses a power relationship between men and women that is taken to be not only commonplace but correct—the right relationship, in which it's appropriate that men have power and certain kinds of control over women's lives—especially women they are married to, women they live with, women with whom they are "intimate."

I come from a time when there was no recognition at all that a woman who was being beaten, tortured—on the verge of being murdered—needed help. For those of you who remember, remember now; for those of you who never knew, try to imagine: it was her fault; she deserved it; she brought it on herself. If she weren't bad, it wouldn't be happening. And as far as she knew, it wasn't happening to anybody else in the world; she was the only one, the only one being treated this way by her husband—because we didn't talk about battery; battery did not have a social existence; it was a private, secret nightmare for women who had nowhere to turn. And when women asked for help, they were told, "It's your fault. Look to yourself. What are you doing wrong? Do it right. Well, of course he got angry; you didn't do the laundry right—he works hard all day. Well, he's very upset; there's a recession on. Well, of course when he comes home at night he doesn't want his peas on *that* side of the plate; of course not—fool. And his response may or may not have been a little bit excessive; but hey, he's under a lot of pressure." I want to remind you what the experience of battery is, because we become callous to it. Being battered is being hit. It is being hit a lot. It is being hit so that you hurt. It is being hit so that sometimes the bruises show, and sometimes they don't; and sometimes it is being hit by someone who is very skilled and really knows how to hit. He has learned through hitting other women; he has learned by practicing on the woman he's hitting now. Women are battered by policemen who are trained in how the human body responds to pain; by doctors who know where the kidney is and where the spleen is.

But being battered is also being a captive. When you look at what happens to women in battery, the only other place where you can see the same kind of systematic physical and psychological injuries is in prisons in which people are tortured. Almost everything that we now know about how to help people who have been tortured in prisons under situations of political repression comes from what we have learned by studying what is done to battered women—because in the home the situation is virtually the same. Now, why should it be that in a home, a woman is a prisoner, a captive, in a nightmare she can't get out of?

There are a lot of reasons: some of them are economic, some of them are social, some of them have to do with the inability of the neighbors to hear the scream. A lot of reasons have to do with fear of the man who's hurting the woman. Hey, you don't want him coming after *you*. Better you should not know what is happening to her. And before the existence of the battered-women's movement, when she would turn to other people and ask for help, not only was it her fault, but most of the time they would deny that it was even happening. Surely she was misunderstanding, misinterpreting, misrepresenting, misexpressing, making a terrible mistake. And the terrible mistake was not that she was with the man who was hurting her; it was that she was complaining about it.

When you are battered, over time, you are physically tortured. I am not speaking in hyperbole. I don't mean that you're hurt very, very badly. I don't mean that it's a very bad thing that you're being hurt, although it is a very bad thing. I mean that batterers purposefully, seriously torture the women that they're hurting. They do it physically. Sometimes they use degrees of force so unconscionable as to be impossible to believe: for instance, hitting a woman with a big wooden beam; using knives on a woman; using a baseball bat on a woman. Sometimes the woman is tied up and tortured and it is called sex when she is hurt. She is often sleep deprived, purposefully, the way she would be if she were in a prison. He takes her life and he messes with it in order to fracture it, to break it into little pieces so that she has no life left. The effects of sleep deprivation on prisoners who are being tortured are not any different than the effects of sleep deprivation on battered women.

What does it mean to have a life as a sovereign human being when your body belongs to someone else, such that you cannot get a night's sleep? Your perceptions become distorted. You ask for help and you're told that your perceptions are distorted. You say, "Right, I haven't slept." Some of it is purposeful: a woman is let to sleep for twenty minutes, then twenty minutes, then twenty minutes, then twenty minutes—each piece of sleep interrupted by some kind of an assault, sometimes for weeks, for months.

The power of the batterer is in his fists, it's in his money, it's in his social power, but it is also in his apparent irrationality. It is in the fact that the woman who is being hurt cannot anticipate what he will do next to her; what he will do next to someone else—to a child, to a dog, to a cat, to whatever she loves, whomever she loves. What he will do next she doesn't know. If she stands up to him, she will be hurt. If she submits to him, she will still be hurt.

When you live in a world that's governed by laws you don't understand and can't understand, you can be destroyed mentally by that world. No human being can live being subjected to the irrational hatred of another person in intimacy, in their private life. It's hard enough if you must deal with prejudice in the social world, on the street; it's hard enough if you're going to be beaten up because your skin is the wrong color, because you have the wrong-sexed partner by your side. But when in your intimate life you are going to be hurt and you don't know why, and you don't know when, and you don't know how—you only know if not today then tomorrow—it will drive you mad. And then they will say, "Ah-ha, you see, she was mad."

The fear that the battered woman experiences is beyond the power of any language I have to express to you. It is a fear of a recrimination that is total—the man controls the total universe of the woman. It has to do with every little detail of her life. It is a punishment for anything at any time, and therefore, one lives in an ocean of fear; one swims and swims and swims and thinks, *So what if I keep swimming? When will this stop? God, help me, let me, die.* That is what happens to battered women who do not get away. They pray to die—because it seems peaceful and it seems better. And it probably is better.

There is an extraordinary humiliation in being battered, in not being able to stand up as a simple human being with dignity: one believes that one has done something wrong or it would not be happening. A woman is told all her life that she is responsible for the behaviors of the men around her, so when this is happening to her, she believes—no matter what her ideology, no matter how militantly feminist or deeply religious she is—"It's my fault. I did it."

There's also something deeper: a shame—a kind of shame that I believe only people in captivity can feel—when you are forced to do things that are incredibly degrading to you; to follow the orders of somebody else, for instance, just because he gives them, just because you are afraid. You experience within yourself a lack of self-respect so bottomless that there is no self to respect.

This all happens in a situation of intimacy. This happens not because the Nazis have marched into town and taken over your home. It doesn't happen because there's a plundering horde coming from somewhere else. It happens with someone, presumably, that you're with because you care about him; you love; maybe you decided to have children together; maybe you had a feeling of friendship for him; but you're with him for reasons of intimacy—he matters to you. And partly you're there because you think that he cares about you.

We have a skewed standard for loving and caring for women. We have a double standard: a man can show how much he cares by being violent. See, he's jealous; he cares. A woman shows how much she cares by how much she's willing to be hurt, by how much she will take, how much she will endure, how suicidal she's prepared to be.

In all these years I have thought and talked to other women about battery, having experienced it, there is one form of blame I think we deserve: Christians call it the sin of pride. The pride is that we believe that for the sake of love we can endure anything. And we make a stand—because of pride—to endure anything. We cannot. We must not. We should not. Our shoulders do not have to carry that weight. We do not bear the burden of all the love in the world, such that we are annihilated, for the sake of somebody else's life, or for the more selfish sake of proving that we're really good women; really good, honest, loving mates; that really "we didn't deserve it—look, we're still here. Yes, he did something terrible; but look, here we are, prepared still to love him."

There is an ideology to romance that says the use of force is an expression of strong feeling for a woman: when a man uses various gradations of force against her, what he's doing is expressing his deep desire for her. Most of us have been taught that, in one form or another. Some of us have learned it through our religions; some of us have learned it through popular culture; some of us have seen *Gone With the Wind* four thousand times. It is everywhere. We measure his desire by what he's willing to do to her, and we celebrate the force that he's willing to show; then, when she shows up as a pile of bleeding bones in a hospital emergency room, we say, "Oh, that wasn't so romantic after all." No, it wasn't. And it wasn't from the beginning. That's what we have to understand: it wasn't romantic from the very start, when it just looked like "he really wants her a lot."

There is in romance, in sexual relations, an implicit, purposeful, systematic sense of ownership—of how men own women. Sexuality can be an expression of that; it can be an expression of physical ownership of women. In the experience of being battered, the husband is doing the same things a torturer would do, the same things an assassin would do—but he's the husband. We're not allowed to say bad things about him. We're not even allowed to say bad things about him when he is actively brutalizing a woman. And when he does it in front of our eyes, we turn around, most of us, and walk away—and then, it's not that we say nothing: we say bad things—but we say them about her.

It is easy to say that men beat women in order to express domination, to exercise control; these are easy sentences to say. But I need to ask you to think about what they really mean. We're talking about people who live together; we're talking about twenty-four hours a day; we're talking about the woman's body; we're talking about control of every function of her body; we're talking about how she dresses; we're talking about how she walks; we're talking about whether she uses the toothpaste from the middle or the bottom, about how much toilet paper she uses. In intimate relations, we are talking about every aspect of behavior that an adult should decide for herself.

Women who are battered are under a curfew. The curfew is imposed by a policeman who is the husband. Adult human beings decide who their friends are; they decide who they want to talk to; they decide which books they want to read and which movies they want to go see. If they want to go see a movie and their partner doesn't and they decide to go alone, that's what they do. That's what being an adult is in the most ordinary sense, but most women don't exercise those simplest expressions of freedom. It's not just because we're afraid to go out after dark because of the men we are *not* married to—although we have reason enough for that.

When political people talk about male supremacy, we talk about it in large ways: patterns of violence against women; female poverty and its meaning in a woman's life. But when we talk about battery, we have to remember that we are talking about every aspect of a human life, every single day, all the time. The problem of human freedom has never been considered from the point of view of a woman's life. Thomas Jefferson did not consider this problem of freedom; our Constitution does not address it. When the Constitution was written, women were chattel; most African-American women and men were slaves. There isn't any system of government anywhere in the world predicated on the notion that if a woman isn't free, no one is free. There isn't any political science anywhere in the world that says, in a way that matters, the primary concern about human freedom has to be about the lives of women and children because they're the ones who haven't had freedom.

When we talk about what men do to women, many of us are treated, of course, as if we are making it up. We're not making it up. We're careful not to exaggerate it. If we know that one out of two women is being beaten but we can only prove that in some cities in the country one out of twenty-five women is being beaten, that's what we say: one out of twenty-five.* Yet whatever it is we say, legal and social authorities come back and say, "That doesn't happen." When the women's movement first started talking about battered women, we were told, "That doesn't happen"—by law enforcement people, by the FBI, by sociologists who now make all their money getting grants to study battery—yes, they discovered that it happens. And now the U.S. Justice Department re-

---

*I am thinking of Del Martin's pioneering 1976 book *Battered Women* (San Francisco New Glide Publishers), in which she gives a random sample of battery statistics from different U.S. cities.

ports that most violent acts against women are committed by someone known to them.* This violence includes battery, aggravated assault, sexual assault, and homicide. We were right.

And we were right for a very simple reason: we listened to the people to whom it happened; we listened to women; we believed what women said. We know that when you see a situation of terror and you hear about it over and over again, it's not likely that each woman is making it up. It is likely that there are systematic characteristics of this terror that we can look at and understand. When we said women were being raped, we were told that wasn't true—every now and then there might be a psychotic killer—but hey, not very often. And in fact, approximately one out of three women in the United States is in some way sexually abused before she becomes an adult. So we have the experiences of women, and we take them seriously.

We also have history—which is actually not a matter of opinion. Women were legally property; we were legally chattel; white women were legally chattel in the United States. White women, the racially superior women in a racist country, were at the top of the pile, and belonged to the men who owned them. They didn't own the clothes on their back; guardianship of their children passed to another male if the husband died; intercourse was a right of marriage.

The woman, if she was married, wasn't just owned as a piece of property. Slavery is a crucial phenomenon in this country, and the experiences of African-American women in relation to marriage were different (and heartbreaking), because the slave owner owned both man and woman. But if we take what we consider the "normative" experience— the white experience—then what we see is that empirically and paradigmatically women as a class, including slave women, were owned not just outside but inside. The right of sexual access to us is part of the way we were owned. The children that we had were owned as property by the man who owned us.

---

*Ronet Bachman, U.S. Department of Justice, Bureau of Justice Statistics, *Violence Against Women: A National Crime Victimization Survey Report* (Washington, D.C.: January 1994).

Now, the reason that this remains important—even though it has changed somewhat—is that laws about marital rape have not changed enough. When a woman was owned in marriage, intercourse was a male right because the husband owned the woman, she was his wife, he had a sexual right to her. He couldn't rape her because intercourse and punishment of her, called "chastisement," were his legal rights.

When we take a stand and say, "If you force a woman to have sex inside marriage, that is rape," we are saying you cannot own a woman in marriage. You do not own her body; you don't own it outside, and you don't own it inside. That is an urgent political stand for us to take, against the possession that husbands have over wives, the entitlement, the sense of "I have a right to do to her what I want to do—leave me alone, why are you bothering me? This isn't your business. If I hurt her, I hurt her. It's like my car: if I want to drive my car into a brick wall, I drive it into a brick wall, what business is that of yours?" That attitude used to be grounded in law. We now have a little distance from that, but not enough. When we look at male culture and what men say about women, and when we talk to battered women, we can say that when men have sex with women they feel a sense of entitlement, ownership, and superiority that goes beyond what any adult human being has a right to feel about another adult human being.

This movement has got to take a stand and say that men do not have sexual rights to women's bodies. And this movement has to understand— when you see women who are hurt coming to you and you're thinking, *This is so irrational, so insane; why is this happening, what is driving this man?*—part of what is driving him is that he has had intimate sexual relations with this woman and from his point of view she belongs to him. If you want to get in the way of that, you do so at threat to yourself.

It is a big mistake to think that you can do anything about battery if you will not look at the common, ordinary assumption in it about men and women: that a man experiences a right of sexual possession over a woman. He has a long historical reason for feeling it, and he really believes it to be true. We are changing that, and the change means that there is a lot of social conflict. A lot of men are angry. A lot of women are afraid.

But it is going to change—it has to change. If it doesn't, men will continue to batter women because they will continue to feel that they have the right, an implicit, God-given right, to own that person over there, because of the sexual relationship that the man had with the woman.

Battered women do run away. They run away and they go back. And they run away and they go back. And they run away and they go back. There didn't used to be shelters anywhere. Anyone who wanted to help a battered woman was going to have to deal with the anger of the man. Because there's now some state support for shelters, the state stands a little bit between the man and whoever is helping the woman—but not between the man and the woman.

I want to explain something to you about the experience of running away so that maybe, for those of you who find it bewildering, you will have some idea of what it means to run away and then decide to go back. Most women have the idea that a house, when they get married and they live in it—they clean it and they take care of it and they buy pretty things for it and fix it up—is their home. They have this dumb idea. And it's amazing how much human beings want a home to live in. So a woman, "a homemaker," makes a home—where she and her husband and their children will live together. She may also be "working"; she may not be.

In this time of social transition, we're talking about so many experiences that are changing—that's the good part. The hard part is to try to keep track of the ways in which they're changing so that we know what's happening around us. Of course she works, she works all the time. She may be doing paid labor outside the home. Regardless, she thinks she has a home. And when she runs away she has reached the point of deciding—understanding, believing—that she cannot stay one more second. She may run away because a particular outburst of violence has been too terrible to stand. She may be very badly hurt when she runs away. She may run away because she's had a period of peace, and she feels stronger and she thinks she can run away—but most women leave at moments of high desperation, at moments when the husband goes for the children, at moments when she believes she's going to be killed.

And then she gets out there and, still, even with the battered women's movement, still, there's no place for women to go in this country.

I come from New York City; it's a big city. Two years ago, the police got a quarter of a million phone calls—just phone calls, just to the police, that a woman was being beaten. There were in New York City 429 beds for women who were being battered. Most places in the country are not better off than that.

So she runs away, and she's desperate, and she's probably just been hurt. She may have children. She may have money, she may not; but even if she has money, she won't have access to it. The money might be in the bank, but within twenty-four hours it's his not hers. He's not desperate and bleeding. He knows what to do. She gets out there, and there are a whole lot of other men on the street. She's vulnerable; and she doesn't have money. And one way or another, they come after her; they come after her to pick her up; they come after her to flirt; they come after her to help her—meaning, usually, an exchange of something she needs for something they want.

When she leaves this home that she thought she had, she goes out into a land with predators in it—who are glad she's there, because she is vulnerable. And when she's out there, she starts remembering that she had a home. And she starts thinking that she has a right to have a home. She may even get angry at the man who hurt her, and took her home away from her. And somehow or another she will, in her mind, find a rationale for reclaiming the home that she believes she has a right to.

But there's nothing straightforward in society for her to do. She can't go to a court and say, "Look, I am a homemaker; I made the home. I would like to live there. You see, I bought the curtains, cleaned the floors, cooked the food." She is suddenly homeless. And the power, the desire, the feeling of having a right to be there is very often what sends women back into trying to make deals with the batterer. She has to say, "I'm sorry I left." She has to say, "It was my fault; I didn't mean it." She has to say, "You were right." And if she says all of those things convincingly enough, and if he wants her to come back, whatever his reasons, she will then have a home.

But what will have happened to her? She will have had the experience of submission, real submission—humiliation: "I am down on my knees, please take me back." And "Please take me back" sometimes just means "Let me inside. I need a place to live; and you're my best chance, please take me back." We see women entering into bargains in which, basically, they are giving up any possibility of physical safety in order to have a place to live, in order to have food on the table for their children. It's not just the money deal; it's not just the economic deal; it's that we do have a right to a home—don't we?

When is there a time in an adult woman's life that this society says: a woman without a man has a right to a home on her own terms—she has a right to live in some kind of dignity with some kind of safety. The problem of battery can't be solved if we don't understand that a woman in this society actually does have a right to have a home. We're homeless people unless we enter into a relationship with a man for a home. I am not speaking about not entering into relationships with men; I am saying that those relationships need to be relationships chosen in real freedom.

When a woman runs away from battery, she finds out that she wanted to be hurt all along. This may be the most shocking news she'll ever get in her life. If she goes to a therapist, the therapist is likely to tell her, even today, that she did the things she did in order to be hurt. Her priest, her minister, her rabbi are likely to tell her the same thing. Her family doctor is likely to tell her the same thing. One hopes no one at the shelter will tell her the same thing, but there are cases in which that has happened. This is an all-pervasive ideology about women: that what makes us distinct from other people is that we really crave this brutal kind of attention from men, and we provoke it because we're looking for pain.

And there's an underlying philosophy here that says that women are basically masochistic, that the masochism is sexual—and part of what that means is that when men hurt us, it's not really the same kind of problem as if a man were to kidnap a man and hurt him. No one says, when a man hurts another man, that the second man enjoyed it. No one says it was a sexual experience for him. No one says that something in his nature craved it—otherwise, why would he have been a drunken fool in that bar, and said the things that he said to the first man? No matter what men do to provoke violence, no one says it's in the nature of men to provoke violence. No matter how much male-on-male violence we see in our society, no one says, "God, how come these men like not just beating up other people; they like being beat up?" But with women, whenever we're hurt, there's an explanation already in place: we wanted it.

Now, part of what this does is to make us second-class, because it means that there's a different standard of what's appropriate for women. There's a different standard of dignity. For instance, a man and woman are married and she's hit the first time—not the fourteenth time—and she goes to her family and she says, "He hit me." Do they say, "Move out. Your rights have been violated"? They are not likely to. The advice that she will get is that it's her role and her nature both to take care of him and, implicitly, to accept the pain. It's bad advice. She should move out the first time.

The issue here is the rights of human beings. And if you understand that women are human beings you must ask: what is the right and honorable and proper way for this person to be treated by that person? When feminists ask precisely that question, we're told we don't pay any attention to the realities of gender. Well, we pay a hell of a lot of attention to gender; that's why we look at rape and battery and try to do something about them—because these are crimes against human beings that happen because of gender prejudice—because of a prejudice against women, a hatred of women—that we do not deserve, that we have not earned, that no one has a right to act out on us. But we internalize that hatred and we settle for second-best because we know we can't have day-to-day real equality. And we try to cut our losses, and we cut our deals, and we do the best that we can, and women keep getting beaten.

People in the battered-women's movement, feminists, have been very reluctant to say that we are talking about rape within marriage when we talk about women having sex with their husbands inside a marriage in which there is violence, and the kind of emotional abuse that goes with the violence. It is my opinion that when a woman is being brutalized, being hit, being tortured, being intimidated—that then when the man has sex with her he is raping her. She is in a continuous situation of force. The fact that the force was not applied at the moment before intercourse does not mean that the intercourse was engaged in freely. In this circumstance, freedom is a sick joke, and so is the notion of consent. There is no freedom when a woman is living in a situation in which, day in and day out, her bread and her water are intimidation, brutality, and pain.

I would like to see us stop trying to be so damn civil to the people who are hurting us. I would like for us to stop thinking we need to prove anything to them. They need to prove to *us* that they can respect our lives enough to make social policy that stops battery. And as long as battery is going on, the woman who is being battered is also being raped. That is the truth from my point of view, and I would like to see us not gloss it over, because every time we do, we tell a lie about what is happening to the woman. And we also make stronger the unspoken assumptions that the sex may be fine, but the battery is something different. The battery is not something different. Possession is the way they're related.

Twenty years ago, in 1972, I made an escape (not from the home in which I was battered, I had done that already—and still found an assassin husband ready to beat me up every time I turned the corner). I escaped in the middle of the night, and I ran away to a different country. Had I not, I don't believe I would be alive. Current research shows that battered women are in more danger when they leave than when they're actually in the batterer's home—in more danger of being killed. If there is a no-win situation, that's it. Escape only means continuing to live a life in which someone wants to hurt you. And the only time you get any relief from living that life is if he finds another woman he wants to hurt. There's not a lot of solace in that.

What do we do about the batterers? This question is an urgent one. You pull them off of one woman, they find another woman. There aren't individual solutions to this problem, although every woman's life saved is a victory of sorts. What I'm trying to say is that escape is always only partial. Women who have been battered often remain hunted. It's not just that we stay frightened, which we do; it's not just that we have nightmares, which we do; it's not just that we have flashbacks in which everything is real and happening right now instead of in the past, which we do. It's that he's out there. He is somewhere. He is hurting someone. And if he's not, it's sort of an accident. It's for some reason that doesn't have anything to do with justice. You may have gotten away, but you didn't get justice. You may have gotten away, but you didn't get freedom. Because he's out there.

I ask myself the question, What is freedom for a battered woman? Initially, it's just not being hit. It's anything that will stop you from being hit. That's incredible freedom: you go through a day and nobody hits you. You go through two days and nobody hits you. You go through a week and you haven't been hit and you can barely believe it. But then you want to walk down the street and you don't know where he is. Are you free? No, you're not free. We cannot talk about what freedom is for women without talking about what freedom is for battered women. To me, that means that every woman who is or has been battered has to have in our society a real right of sovereignty over her body. There have to be boundaries that she can set and that everyone else is legally bound to respect. If they don't, they will be punished. No exceptions. No bullshit.

A woman has a right to safety—in real life, not abstractly. A lot has to change before safety is possible. All the implicit assumptions about women's inferiority have to change.

Women will never be free unless we are not any longer treated as objects, which includes sexual objects. We are human beings; we are the center of our own lives. We are not things for men to act out on. We will never be free unless we stop the notion that violence is okay. It's not okay. Nobody has a right to control another human being through violence. We cannot continue to sanction violence as a way of life—for both victim and executioner. Women are not ever going to be free unless all the institutions that support hurting women end—including the use of pornography by men, such that the hurting of women becomes a form of sexual entertainment; including the exploitation of women in prostitution, such that men have a right to lease women's bodies for sexual release whenever they want; and including incest, now the reigning model of male–female relations.

We have to deal with the sexualization of children in our society. As women have rebelled and aspired—however much we think we failed—to some kind of social equality, men have looked for sex objects who will fit a sexual paradigm based on inequality. The question is, Can men have sex with equals? The answer may well be no. If the answer is no, the men have to change or we have to give up equality. I think we should decide not to give up equality.

Another thing that has to change is that all the people who can't hear the screams have got to start being able to hear them. Those who can't see the bruises on women standing in front of them have to be able to see them. They also have to have something they can do about it, and somewhere they can go when they hear, when they see.

Think about the legal and social meaning of privacy, the sense in which a man's home is his castle. Privacy for men is often power over women and children. Women need to be arguing for equality, not for privacy. For those of you who are involved in the prochoice struggle, think about the way privacy has been the basis for arguing for our rights over our body. When we argue for privacy, we collude in protecting the privacy of men in their homes who hurt women and children. We need to pursue a different strategy in relation to getting and keeping the abortion right.

I know many of you do not agree—you are not prochoice—but what I am talking about here is that every single issue has to be thought through in terms of what it means about male dominance over women and children. Does it reinforce the power of men in the home over women and children?

Strong women are also victims of battery; smart women, weak women, stupid women. There is nothing about being victimized that says anything at all about the character of the woman to whom it happens. We have a right to resist unfairness, and this is a political struggle. If we do not deal with the things that give men their social and economic power over women, we cannot stop battery from happening. We can take care of one injured woman after another, but we can't otherwise stop her from being beaten. And surely those of you who have seen the injuries would rather stop the injuries from happening than simply take care of woman after woman after woman who's been hurt.

I want us to use our capacity to bear pain—which in women is quite highly developed—in the pursuit of political change. I want us to take all that concern that we have about being made outsiders—being pushed into exile because we don't conform—and use it politically.

And finally I want to say that what's urgent is to make the war against women visible. When it's invisible we can't fight it, and when it's invisible every single woman is isolated in the trauma of what is happening to her. She has no way out, and she has no way to become whole again. But standing together, and seeing the connections in the various kinds of violence against women—and in the exploitation that is not overtly violent—we can go up against the power of the batterer, the legal system that still protects him, and the society that gives him privileges over us.

But the woman has to win. We have to win. Our lives are at stake here. There is a great sadness in escape without freedom. But it is very much better than not escaping at all. And the happiness that a battered woman feels in being able to live an individual life and make her own decisions, from the largest to the smallest—in feeling the joy of self-determination—is overwhelming.

I thank you for every single day of your lives that you have done something to help any woman who's been battered. Speaking for so many women, I thank you from the bottom of my heart.

REMEMBER, RESIST, DO NOT COMPLY

I want us to think about how far we have come politically. I would say we have accomplished what is euphemistically called "breaking the silence." We have begun to speak about events, experiences, realities, truths not spoken about before; especially experiences that have happened to women and been hidden—experiences that the society has not named, that the politicians have not recognized; experiences that the law has not addressed from the point of view of those who have been hurt. But sometimes when we talk about "breaking the silence," people conceptualize "the silence" as being superficial, as if there is talk—chatter, really—and laid over the talk there is a superficial level of silence that has to do with manners or politeness. Women are indeed taught to be seen and not heard. But I am talking about a deep silence: a silence that goes to the heart of tyranny, its nature. There is a tyranny that preordains not only who can say what but what women especially can say. There is a tyranny that determines who cannot say anything, a tyranny in which people are kept from being able to say the most important things about what life is like for them. That is the kind of tyranny I mean.

The political systems that we live in are based on this deep silence. They are based on what we have not said. In particular, they are built on what women—women in every racial group, in every class, including the most privileged—have not said. The assumptions underlying our political systems are also based on what women have not said. Our ideas of democracy and equality—ideas that men have had, ideas that express what men think democracy and equality are—evolved absent the voices, the experiences, the lives, the realities of women. The principles of freedom that we hear enunciated as truisms are principles that were arrived at despite this deep silence: without our participation. We are all supposed to share and take for granted the commonplace ideas of social and civic fairness; but these commonplace ideas are based on our silence. What passes as normal in life is based on this same silence. Gender itself—what men are, what women are—is based on the forced silence of women; and beliefs about community—what a community is, what a community should be—are based on this silence. Societies have been organized to maintain the silence of women—which suggests that we cannot break this deep silence without changing the ways in which societies are organized.

We have made beginnings at breaking the deep silence. We have named force as such when it is used against us, although it once was called something else. It used to be a legal right, for instance, that men had in marriage. They could force their wives to have intercourse and it was not called force or rape; it was called desire or love. We have challenged the old ideology of sexual conquest as a natural game in which women are targets and men are conquering heroes; and we have said that the model itself is predatory and that those who act out its aggressive imperatives are predators, not lovers. We have said that. We have identified rape; we have identified incest; we have identified battery; we have identified prostitution; we have identified pornography—as crimes against women, as means of exploiting women, as ways of hurting women that are systematic and supported by the practices of the societies in which we live. We have identified sexual exploitation as abuse. We have identified objectification and turning women into commodities for sale as dehumanizing, deeply dehumanizing. We have identified objectification and sexual exploitation as mechanisms for creating inferiority, real inferiority: not an abstract concept but a life lived as an inferior person in a civil society. We have identified patterns of violence that take place in intimate relationships. We know now that most rape is not committed by the dangerous and predatory stranger but by the dangerous and predatory boyfriend, lover, friend, husband, neighbor, the man we are closest to, not the man who is farthest away.

And we have learned more about the stranger, too. We have learned more about the ways in which men who do not know us target us and hunt us down. We have refused to accept the presumption in this society that the victim is responsible for her own abuse. We have refused to agree that she provoked it, that she wanted it, that she liked it. These are the basic dogmas of pornography, which we have rejected. In rejecting pornography we have rejected the fundamentalism of male supremacy, which simply and unapologetically defines women as creatures, lower than human, who want to be hurt and injured and raped. We have changed laws so that, for instance, rape now can be prosecuted without the requirement of corroboration—there does not have to have been an eyewitness who saw the rape before a woman can press charges. There used to have to be one. A woman now does not have to fight nearly to the death in order to show that she resisted. If she was not sadistically injured—beaten black and blue, hit by a lead pipe, whatever—the presumption used to be that she consented. We have standardized the way in which evidence is collected in rape cases so that whether or not a prosecution can be brought does not depend on the whims or competence of investigating officers. We have not done any of this for battered women, though we have tried to provide some refuge, some shelter, an escape route. Nothing that we have done for women who have been raped or battered has helped women who have been prostituted.

We have changed social and legal recognition of who the perpetrator is. We have done that. We have challenged what appears to be the permanence of male dominance by destabilizing it, by refusing to accept it as reality, our reality. We have said no. No, it is not our reality.

And although we have provided services for rape victims, for battered women, we have never been able to provide enough. I suggest to you that if any society took seriously what it means to have half of its population raped, battered as often as women are in both the United States and Canada, we would be turning government buildings into shelters. We would be opening our churches to women and saying, "You own them. Live in them. Do what you want with them." We would be turning over our universities.

What remains to be done? To think about helping a rape victim is one thing; to think about ending rape is another. We need to end rape. We need to end incest. We need to end battery. We need to end prostitution and we need to end pornography. That means that we need to refuse to accept that these are natural phenomena that just happen because some guy is having a bad day.

In each country, male dominance is organized differently. In some countries, women have to deal with genital mutilation. In some countries, abortion is forced so that female fetuses are systematically aborted. In China, forced abortion is state-mandated. In India, a free-market economy forces masses of women to abort female fetuses and, failing that, to commit infanticide on female infants. Think about what policies on abortion mean for living, adult women: the meaning to their status. Notice that the Western concept of choice—crucial to us—does not cover the situation of women in either China or India. Each time we look at the status of women in a given country, we have to look at the ways in which male dominance is organized. In the United States, for instance, we have the growth of a population of serial killers. They are a subculture in my country. They are no longer lonely deviants. Law enforcement sources, always conservative, estimate that each and every day nearly 400 serial killers are active in the United States.

In my view, we need to concentrate on the perpetrators of crimes against women instead of asking ourselves over and over and over again, why did that happen to her? what's wrong with her? why did he pick her? Why should he hit or hurt anyone: what's wrong with him? He is the question. He is the problem. It is his violence that we find ourselves running from and hiding from and suffering from. The women's movement has to be willing to name the perpetrator, to name the oppressor. The women's movement has to refuse to exile women who have on them the stench of sexual abuse, the smell, the stigma, the sign. We need to refuse to exile women who have been hurt more than once: raped many times; beaten many times; not nice, not respectable; don't have nice homes. There is no women's movement if it does not include the women who are being hurt and the women who have the least. The women's movement has to take on the family systems in our countries: systems in which children are raped and tortured. The women's movement has to take on the battered women who have not escaped—and we have to ask ourselves why: not why didn't *they* escape, but why are we settling for the fact that they are still captives and prisoners.

We have to take on prostitution as an issue: not a debating issue; a life-and-death issue. Most prostituted women in the West are incest victims who ran away from home, who have been raped, who are pimped when they are still children—raped, homeless, poor, abandoned children. We have to take on poverty: not in the liberal sense of heartfelt concern but in the concrete sense, in the real world. We have to take on what it means to stand up for women who have nothing because when women have nothing, it's real nothing: no homes, no food, no shelter, often no ability to read. We have to stop trivializing injuries and insults to women the way our political systems do. As someone who has experienced battery and was then and is now a politically committed woman, I will tell you that the difference between being tortured because you have a political idea or commitment and being tortured because of your race or sex is the difference between having dignity of some kind and having no dignity at all. There is a difference.

We cannot change what is wrong with our feminism if we are willing to accept the prostitution of women. Prostitution is serial rape: the rapist changes but the raped woman stays the same; money washes the man's hands clean. In some countries women are sold into sexual slavery, often as children. In other countries—like Canada and the United States—prostitutes are created through child sexual abuse, especially incest, poverty, and homelessness. As long as there are consumers, in free-market economies prostitutes will be created; to create the necessary (desired) supply of prostitutes, children have to be raped, poor, homeless. We cannot accept this; we cannot accept prostitution.

We need to be able to prosecute marital rape with success: to get convictions. Successful prosecution of marital rape and eliminating prostitution challenge two ends of the same continuum. Do men own women or not? If men can buy and sell women on street corners, yes, they do own women. If men have a right to rape women in marriage—even an implicit right, because juries will not convict—yes, then men do own women. We are the ones who have to say—in words, in actions, in social policy, in law—no, men do not own women. In order to do that, we need political discipline. We need to take seriously the consequences of sexual abuse to us, to women. We need to understand what sexual abuse has done to us—why are we so damned hard to organize? We need to comprehend that sexual abuse has broken us into a million pieces and we carry those pieces bumping and crashing inside: we're broken rock inside; chaos; afraid and unsure when not cold and numb. We're heroes at endurance; but so far cowards at resistance.

There is a global trafficking in women; as long as women are being bought and sold in a global slave traffic we are not free. There is a pornography crisis in the United States. Women in the United States live in a society saturated with sexually brutal, exploitative material that says: rape her, beat her, hurt her, she will like it, it is fun for her. We need to put women first. Surely the freedom of women must mean more to us than the freedom of pimps. We need to do anything that will interrupt the colonizing of the female body. We need to refuse to accept the givens. We need to ask ourselves what political rights we need as women. Do not assume that in the eighteenth century male political thinkers answered that question and do not assume that when your own Charter* was rewritten in the twentieth century the question was answered. The question has not been answered. What laws do we need? What would freedom be for us? What principles are necessary for our well-being? Why are women being sold on street corners and tortured in their homes, in societies that claim to be based on freedom and justice? What actions must be taken? What will it cost us and why are we

---

*Canadian Charter of Rights and Freedoms, Part 1 of the Constitution Act of 1982.

too afraid to pay, and are the women who have gotten a little from the women's movement afraid that resistance or rebellion or even political inquiry will cost them the little they have gotten? Why are we still making deals with men one by one instead of collectively demanding what we need?

I am going to ask you to remember that as long as a woman is being bought and sold anywhere in the world, you are not free, nor are you safe. You too have a number; some day your turn will come. I'm going to ask you to remember the prostituted, the homeless, the battered, the raped, the tortured, the murdered, the raped-then-murdered, the murdered-then-raped; and I am going to ask you to remember the photographed, the ones that any or all of the above happened to and it was photographed and now the photographs are for sale in our free countries. I want you to think about those who have been hurt for the fun, the entertainment, the so-called speech of others; those who have been hurt for profit, for the financial benefit of pimps and entrepreneurs. I want you to remember the perpetrator and I am going to ask you to remember the victims: not just tonight but tomorrow and the next day. I want you to find a way to include them—the perpetrators and the victims—in what you do, how you think, how you act, what you care about, what your life means to you.

Now, I know, in this room, some of you are the women I have been talking about. I know that. People around you may not. I am going to ask you to use every single thing you can remember about what was done to you—how it was done, where, by whom, when, and, if you know, why—to begin to tear male dominance to pieces, to pull it apart, to vandalize it, to destabilize it, to mess it up, to get in its way, to fuck it up. I have to ask you to resist, not to comply, to destroy the power men have over women, to refuse to accept it, to abhor it, and to do whatever is necessary despite its cost to you to change it.

CONFRONTATIONS

RACE, SEX, AND SPEECH IN AMERIKA

AMERIKA NOW: THE ETERNAL PRESENT

The mental geography of Amerika is a landscape of forgetfulness, useful in a country saturated with sexual abuse; a flat nothingness—no history, no yesterday with facts and details; a desert lit up by the blinding glare of a relentless, empty optimism. The past is obliterated, because the past is burdened by bad news.

Slavery is a rumor, except that some black folk seem extremely pissed off about it. Rape is a lie, useful once for persecuting black men haunted by the rumor of slavery but now taken up with malignant intent by fanatic, angry women, traitors to forgetting. Free speech is bigger than a right; it is a theme park in which pimps and esteemed writers alternate "Discourse" with Spin-the-Bottle: one-handed art, one-handed sex—the sound of one hand typing. It's like a utopian summer camp for spoiled brats: once you enter Free Speech Park you can go on all the rides you want and nobody can stop you; so there.

My colleagues—writers and feminists—proudly call themselves First Amendment fundamentalists or absolutists, in self-proclaimed philosophical and pragmatic accord with those who learn rules by rote, recite dogma without deviation, and will not think. History moves and society

179

changes but forgetfulness is both blissful and patriotic. In Amerika, optimism and amnesia are forms of nationalism; and so is First Amendment fundamentalism—a happy loyalty to the status quo; we live in the best of all possible worlds. A country devoted to the eternal present is, of course, a perpetrator's dream come true; and Amerika does spawn perpetrators. Memory means accusation, recognition, discontent. In the Free Speech playground, one might rebel against being the pimp's ride, or even the esteemed writer's: don't fuck with me, one might say, spoiling the fun. The players, certain of their right to bang at will, might feel really bad: like, "censored."

At Amerika's best it produced Emerson, Whitman, Thoreau—they hated slavery; Elizabeth Cady Stanton, Susan B. Anthony, Margaret Fuller—they hated slavery; Frederick Douglass, Sojourner Truth, Harriet Tubman—they hated slavery. Each and every one of them embodied an honest Amerikan optimism in intellect and activism that was not based on forgetting. They thought; they acted; they were citizens no matter what the law said; and they did not hide from life, reality, and responsibility by hiding behind the law—oh, well, slavery is constitutional, enough said. They were also Victorians and moralists—current swearwords.

THE FOUNDING PATRIARCHS WERE TYRANTS

George Washington was the richest man in Amerika. He freed all his slaves when he died, unlike Thomas Jefferson, who did not.

James Madison made an annual profit of $257 on each slave he owned and spent $12 or $13 on maintenance.

In 1619, the first black slaves were imported and the Virginia House of Burgesses, the first representative assembly in Amerika, was established. The Virginia House set up a mechanism for recording and enforcing contracts, which made the exploitation of indentured servants easier and more secure, backed by local, not British, law and force.

By 1700, fifty Virginia families controlled most of the region's money and owned most of the land, slaves, indentured servants (to be precise:

owned the contracts of the indentured servants). The males of those families seemed to rotate being governor, advisers to the governor, and local magistrates.

In 1787, fifty-five white men met in Philadelphia to create a constitution, currently treated by both the political Right and Left as a divinely revealed text. Not much resembling Moses, most of them were lawyers; owned slaves and land or were rich from manufacturing or shipping (which implicated them in slave trafficking); owned white women—wives and daughters—who were not persons under the law. Half loaned money for profit. Forty had government bonds, thus a special interest in having a government that could redeem those bonds. Slaves, indentured servants, women, men who did not own property, and Indians were not invited to the party. It was a rich-white-guy thing.

The framers' idea was to form a republican central government that (1) could facilitate commerce among the states, internationally for the new union, and (if you are credulous) with the Indian nations; and (2) was too weak to interfere with slavery. Slavery was the basis for the agrarian economy of the South and the linchpin of what its ruling elite regarded as their "civilization." Slavery was still legal in the North, but the economy was industrial with a manufacturing and shipping base. This meant that the North profited handsomely from the transport and sale of kidnapped Africans.

The framers did protect slavery: outright in the body of the text ratified in 1787 for a twenty-year period and by creating a legal framework that kept the federal government anemic while giving the states virtually all the authority and powers of governance. The federal government had only the powers explicitly designated in the Constitution. For instance, it got to regulate commerce, create a navy, coin money, tax, go to war, all with the famous checks and balances that made each exercise purposefully difficult; and, with its two representative assemblies standing in for white men with money, the federal government could provide the appearance of democracy, though never the substance.

The Bill of Rights, which is the first ten amendments to the 1787 Constitution, was ratified in 1791 largely because the rabble, having defeated the British in the name of equality as well as independence, demanded a legal guarantee of democratic rights—as in "We hold these truths to be self-evident, that all men are created equal." The framers gave in after protracted and stubborn resistance. Not by accident, they saw to it that equality—as an idea, an ideal, a right, a principle, an element of liberty or law—disappeared from the Amerikan political vocabulary and was lost to constitutional law. But in fact the framers went even further: they created a trick bill of rights. Rather than guaranteeing democratic rights that were inalienable, inviolable, and affirmative—the states be damned—they used the Bill of Rights as yet another means of restricting federal power. No citizen had a straight-out right to speak, to assemble, to bear arms, such that the government was obligated to uphold the right for the sake of the citizen. The Bill of Rights applied only to the central government, not to the states; so that when the First Amendment said, "Congress shall make no law . . . ," only the United States Congress was restricted.

The problem—from the point of view of those who value rights—is both structural and purposeful. James Madison—brilliant and cunning, contemptuous of ordinary (not elite) men, and an enemy of direct democracy—engineered the faux Bill of Rights so that it gave *freedom from*, not *freedom to*. The Second Amendment right "to keep and bear arms" suggested that all those guns vouchsafed to white men could be mobilized by the states to fend off illegitimate federal power, which was the elite definition of tyranny. *Freedom from* protected an armed, landed, moneyed, white-male ruling class from the projected incursions of a potentially bigger power, a central government. Speech and guns need to be thought of as forms of wealth analogous to land, slaves, money, women. If you had them, the federal government could not interfere; if you did not, Madison's faux Bill of Rights did not give you the right to them.

The system appeared to work as a democracy for white men because land was bountiful and could be acquired: taken from Indians. There were many efforts to turn Indians into slaves, but these failed; so the white guys killed the Indians instead. At first the conflict might have passed for a classic imperialist war with two armed if unequal sides; but it soon became an intentional, organized genocide.

State governments maintained supremacy over the federal government, even after the Civil War. The Thirteenth, Fourteenth, and Fifteenth Amendments were designed to stop slavery—to supersede all state slave laws and to stop the actual practice—as well as to enfranchise men, not women, who had been slaves. Their enactment—in 1865, 1868, and 1870—amounted to a huge federal power grab, successful because the South lay ruined, in defeat. These amendments were victor's justice, the Union's dignifying its dead through, finally, abolition and a new assertion of domestic federal power. But the idea was still to restrict government, this time state government, not to give affirmative rights to citizens. Under the Fourteenth and Fifteenth Amendments, the state could not stand in the way of a black man's due process or voting rights, but a mob sure could. Only the Thirteenth Amendment, which prohibited "slavery" and "involuntary servitude," restricted both states and individual citizens.

Congress still represented white men; and the states were still able, despite these new amendments, to enact despotic laws that contravened every value symbolized by the Bill of Rights to Amerikans, who were dazzled by the symbolism but indifferent to the substance. Without fear of challenge, southern states created complicated Jim Crow laws, a legal system of apartheid, enforced by police power, state courts, force of arms, and vigilante terrorism. States were able to determine which citizens had which rights until the defeat of de jure (legal) segregation, which could not have been possible without a triumph of federal power and the near-total destruction of states' rights as such. Empirically speaking, this happened sometime in the mid-1960s. Even then, the authority of the federal government to pass the 1964 Civil Rights Act did not reside in the Bill of Rights—the government could not expand a right to speak or assemble to blacks, for instance, because no such right existed. The federal government's civil rights authority resided in the commerce clause of the U.S. Constitution, the so-called spending power of Congress (you take federal money, you do what the feds say), in the power of the federal government to organize its own agencies (e.g., to create a civil rights commission), and in the Fourteenth and Fifteenth Amendments. The segregationists tried to use the Bill of Rights (for instance, the First Amendment freedom of association right) as a shield; consequently the Bill of Rights had to be ignored—informally suspended, as it were—in order to enable the federal government to protect black lives and liberty: to extend the simplest rights of human civil society to blacks.

Women got the vote in 1920 by constitutional amendment, but it was not until 1971 that the U.S. Supreme Court deigned to recognize the civil existence of women by holding that, under the Fourteenth Amendment, Idaho could not favor males over women as administrators of wills and estates "solely on the basis of sex." Idaho, said the Supreme Court, had to have other good reasons, too. The decision (*Reed* v. *Reed*) is appallingly narrow and condescending; but sex discrimination became litigable and women litigious.

Fortunately in 1965, in *Griswold* v. *Connecticut*, the justices had found in the Bill of Rights "penumbras" (shadows) and "emanations" in the First, Third, Fourth, Fifth, and Ninth Amendments—take that, Madison, you old fart—allowing them to strike down a state law criminalizing contraception. The justices were specifically protecting marital privacy, gender-neutral, by giving it constitutional legitimacy. By 1973 the penumbras and emanations joined with the Fourteenth Amendment in *Roe* v. *Wade* to strike down a Texas law criminalizing abortion; but this time the privacy, gender-specific, "cannot be said to be absolute." His is; the married couple's (his) is; hers ain't.

So, every time African Americans or women have needed a right in order to exercise liberty, we have needed an affirmative right—backed up by federal power: the opposite of what the Bill of Rights allows. Each time, we go against the way the Constitution was framed and freedom was conceived. For blacks and women, the states have been the tyrant; but both groups have needed affirmative rights that no government could trump. And although I myself have never met a penumbra I didn't like, it is wrong for women to continue to live in the shadows—

of law or life. I want rights so affirmative they are lit up from inside: all
flame, all fire, no shadow, no faux.

For these reasons—and more—each time I hear a colleague—writer
or feminist—express adoration and obeisance to "the Founding Fathers"
and their sacred founding texts, I get physically ill. I've been fluish a lot
lately.

THOMAS JEFFERSON: PRIVACY, PROPERTY, AND MISOGYNY

In 1783 Thomas Jefferson wrote a model constitution for Virginia in
which he included a free speech clause: "Printing presses shall be subject
to no other restraint than liableness to legal prosecution for false facts
printed and published."

He meant printing presses, not satellites, video, or the Internet. Photography had not been invented yet; he did not take it into account.

Jefferson, though a lawyer and a politician, was not tricky like his
protégé James Madison. He respected language in a sincere and literary
way. "False facts" meant lies, inaccuracies, untruths.

The cruelty of contemporary media would not have surprised him,
but its invasiveness would have. Jack McLaughlin, who studied Jefferson's nearly lifelong preoccupation with designing and building Monticello, noted in *Jefferson and Monticello* that "[l]oss of control of his privacy was one of Jefferson's few real fears, so he took extraordinary efforts
to assure that this would not happen." It was not as if he were living in
a row house. His father, Peter, was a land speculator, owned 1,000 acres
outright in 1735, and was part of a company that had an 800,000-acre
land grant. Shadwell, where Jefferson was born in 1743, was built on
400 acres. When John Wayles, his wife's father, died, Jefferson got control of her inheritance of 135 slaves and 11,000 acres of land. Still, he
pulled down and rebuilt parts of Monticello to ensure privacy. In
Thomas Jefferson, Willard Sterne Randall summed up the conclusions of
many Jefferson biographers when he wrote that "Jefferson had a lifelong
aversion to revealing his personal life except to members of his own
family, and then only discreetly." Jefferson's sense of privacy—and his

entitlement to it—go to the heart of his conception of free speech: say what you want, standing on your land, not mine, and it had better be accurate, or the long arm of the law, indistinguishable from my own, will get you.

He was, like his peers, the head of a small empire, a feudal kingdom. He would not have given legal license to the camera to invade his domain. Limits to speech were implicit in his way of life, which is precisely what the Constitution and Bill of Rights were designed to protect. It was left to Tom Paine—not rich, not fortunate—to express the civic ethic that both men valued:

> Calumny is a species of treachery that ought to be punished so well as any other kind of treachery. It is a private vice productive of public evils; because it is possible to irritate men into disaffection by continual calumny who never intended to be disaffected.

Both Paine and Jefferson thought that a democratic republic was characterized by civil harmony and that verbal harassment based on lies or inaccuracies was a subversion of citizenship and civic society.

Jefferson's experience of speech included his own writing, his public speaking (which was timid and ineffective), and his love of books. During his lifetime he collected several libraries. Books were destroyed in a fire at Shadwell, the plantation on which he grew up. Later he sold a second collection at a low price to the United States government when the British burned the Library of Congress in the War of 1812. He was, in fact, so angry at the British that, according to historian Fawn Brodie, "he suggested paying incendiaries in London to set British buildings afire in return."

Though Jefferson died considerably in debt (and some of his slaves were sold to pay it off), he never stopped buying books in his lifetime. He wrote political essays, a model constitution, a book, and an autobiography. He kept journals and wrote thousands of letters (28,000 survive him). He wrote down every expenditure he made.

Jeffersonian free speech presumed privacy, literacy, bookishness, civility in public discourse, and a legal requirement of accuracy for publishers. It is an egregious mistake to think about the great and mesmerizing idea of free speech without remembering Jefferson's thousands of acres and many hundreds of books.

Jefferson's sense of self-sovereignty was not based on an abstract conception of man's worth or on childhood self-esteem. It came from his social and economic dominance over white women and his ownership of black slaves, male and female. His misogyny in particular seems related to issues of property.

His father, Peter, died owning sixty slaves when Thomas was fourteen. Not believing in primogeniture and entail, Peter did not leave all his wealth (land, slaves, money, horses, hogs) to Thomas, the eldest son, as was the custom. Instead Peter left Thomas's mother the use of all the land and capital until Thomas turned twenty-one, which Thomas seemed to resent deeply. Though Thomas himself did not believe in primogeniture and entail either, his antagonism to his mother became intense. Peter also left her lifetime use of one-third of his estate, which she would lose if she remarried. He left dowries and some land and slaves to his six daughters. Although the females did not actually own anything, Thomas's misogyny was ignited by Peter's delaying of his own outright ownership until he was twenty-one. When Shadwell burned down in 1770, Thomas mourned the loss of his books, a direct legacy from his father, but had no empathy for his mother. He used the occasion to move to Charlottesville while his mother and sisters lived in an overseer's shack; and he embarked on building Monticello for himself, as McLaughlin says, "motivated by a conscious desire to escape from the rule of his mother." In 1772 Jefferson married Martha Wayles and that year received a shipment of 280 African slaves. Martha's father, also a lawyer, was an extremely wealthy landowner and slave trafficker. After the death of his third wife, John Wayles took as his consort the slave Betty Hemings, who bore him many children, including Sally. When Wayles died, the same year Sally was born, Martha inherited as property her father's illicit mate and her own half-sister. Martha died in childbirth in 1782 at thirty-three.

As a young man, unmarried, Jefferson copied into his journals misogynist passages from Milton, Homer, Shakespeare, Pope, and now lesser known contemporary writers. In that same journal, according to Randall, "he fairly rants" against his mother. According to Brodie, "Later he confessed that when he suffered from insomnia as a young man, he would lie awake formulating 'a love and murder novel.'" In his later life he wrote to one of his daughters: "Nothing is more disgusting to our sex as a want of cleanliness and delicacy in yours," with detailed instructions as to how she should groom herself and dress. To another daughter on the occasion of her marriage he wrote: "The happiness of your life depends now on the continuing to please a single person. To this all other objects must be secondary, even your love to me."

When Jefferson was in revolutionary France as United States ambassador, he hated the politically committed women he met: "The tender breasts of ladies were not formed for political convulsions and the French ladies miscalculate much their own happiness when they wander from the field of their influence into that of politicks." He saw to it that his own legitimate daughters were well-educated but not for any public or political purpose. (He even had his teen-age slave Sally Hemings tutored in French and music.) While he publicly opposed slavery, the political disenfranchisement of his mother, wife, daughters, and sisters did not trouble him at all. He did not notice it. Instead, it seemed his daughters were educated for the purpose of intellectual and emotional intercourse with him. His letters to them are intimate and controlling, dictating every aspect of identity and behavior. His love is expressed with a sometimes seductive, sometimes overbearing intensity, but it is always conditional on obedience and compliance. "Keep my letters," he wrote his oldest daughter, "and read them at times, that you may always have present in your mind those things which will endear you to me." There is an incestuous quality to his intimacy and manipulation, further underscored by the callousness he felt to what would happen to them as adults when they were not his: "The chance that in marriage [my daughters] will draw a blockhead I calculate at about fourteen to one." Sally Hemings, of course, did not draw a blockhead: at the age of fourteen, not in marriage, she drew him.

SALLY HEMINGS, FOUNDING RAPE VICTIM

"For any slave child at Monticello," wrote Fawn Brodie, who in *Thomas Jefferson: An Intimate Biography* (1974) made the strong circumstantial case that Hemings was Jefferson's mate for thirty-eight years, "Jefferson was a kind of deity. Since her own father John Wayles had died in the year of her birth, Jefferson was perhaps as close to being a parental figure as anyone she had known." Brodie's sentimentality covers up the cruelty of both slavery and patriarchy: a master, an owner, a ruler was the reigning father figure. This, too, was what the Constitution and Bill of Rights were constructed to protect: the southern way of life—the white legitimate family who worshipped the deity through submission in manners and morals, and the secret black family, intimate and coerced.

It is, of course, considered rude and hyperbolic to call Jefferson a rapist. I call him that, with a sense of understatement. I think the emotional incest with his white daughters could be acted out with Sally Hemings and was. While the Bill of Rights when it was enacted kept the federal government from messing with Jefferson, it did nothing to keep Jefferson from messing with Sally.

The argument against characterizing Jefferson as a rapist is essentially this: Sally Hemings did not want freedom, and Jefferson exercised normative power for his rank in an ordinary way. Sally Hemings's lack of freedom cannot be denied; but romantics and patriots—and woman haters of both persuasions—want to believe that she would have chosen him if she could have; that in the realm of sex, for women, slavery and freedom have the same happy outcome, determined by nature, not oppression; that desire and force travel together, necessary and harmonious companions, each reinforcing the pull of the other. Epistemologies of desire aside, the culture works hard to make Sally responsible and Jefferson blameless.

The Merchant-Ivory film *Jefferson in Paris* (1995) continues a fictional tradition in which an adolescent Sally Hemings (played by Thandie Newton) sets her sights on the master (Nick Nolte) and virtually invades his chaste bed. In Barbara Chase-Riboud's 1979 novel, *Sally Hemings*, Sally describes the first time:

> I felt no fear, only an overwhelming tenderness. His presence for me was command enough; I took control of him. I bent forward and pressed a kiss on the trembling hands that encompassed mine, and the contact of my lips with his flesh was so violent that I lost all memory . . . I felt around me an exploding flower, not just of passion, but of long deprivation, a hunger for things forbidden, for darkness and unreason.

Jefferson calls out the name of "the other I so resembled . . . my half sister."

In keeping with conventional misogynist ideology, the slave is the master, even when the slave is a female child; and she is not bound by her legal status but by her sexual nature. Chase-Riboud uses her authority as an African-American woman and her considerable narrative skill to argue that Hemings repudiated legal freedom, which she had in France (where slavery was illegal), because sexual love made her a willing slave.

Steve Erickson, in his acclaimed 1993 novel, *Arc d'X*, makes desire a higher value than freedom by emphasizing and sexualizing Jefferson's coercion of Sally. Erickson's Jefferson is an erotic rapist, an oxymoron if there ever was one. He ties her wrists with ribbons; he takes her from behind; he holds her long hair in his fist and forcibly buries her face in a pillow:

> He separated and entered her. Both of them could hear the rip of her, the wet broken plunder, a spray of blood across the tiny room. She screamed. . . . It thrilled him, the possession of her. He only wished she were so black as not to have a face at all.

In making Sally's rape pornographic for a contemporary audience—she is headless, ripped, bleeding—and in making it a modern sadomasochistic scene as well, Erickson, a white writer, erases the institutional reality of being human chattel. Sally's complicity, always necessary as an implicit justification of the rape, takes the form of her experiencing orgasm after several more hand-tied, violent attacks:

> [W]hen she came she knew, with fury, that this was the ultimate rape, the way he'd make her give herself not just to his pleasure but to her own. Then he turned her over and plunged himself into her. But it was too late. If he'd intended to make his own possession of her complete, she had also, if only for a moment, felt what it was like not to be a slave.

In other words, for a woman orgasm is freedom. Or, as Marie Antoinette said, "If they don't have bread, let them eat cake."

Max Byrd's 1993 novel, *Jefferson*, takes the position of most pre-Brodie scholars: Jefferson could not have had sexual intercourse with Sally because Jefferson was a hero. The logic is elliptical and cloyingly male.

The story of Jefferson's sexual possession of his slave was first published in 1802, while Jefferson was president, by a political enemy. Published more than once, it got more checking and fact-checking than the *Washington Post* and *The New York Times* demand now; but it was suppressed by historians who wanted Jefferson unstained, uncompromised by miscegenation or venal exploitation. In 1873, an Ohio newspaper printed the narrative of Madison Hemings, Sally's third son with Jefferson born at Monticello in 1805. According to Madison, Sally—who had been sent to Paris to accompany one of Jefferson's daughters—refused to return to Virginia with Jefferson because she wanted her legal freedom. Still a young girl, she was nearly fluent in French. Jefferson promised her a high place in his household and to free her children at the age of twenty-one. Sometime before leaving France, she became pregnant by Jefferson. Had she stayed in France she would have faced penury, social dislocation, and the omnivorous violence of the French Revolution. On returning to Monticello with Jefferson, she gave birth to their first son, Tom, who physically resembled his father. One Hemings son, according to Jefferson's legitimate white grandson, Thomas Jefferson Randolph, "might have been mistaken for Mr. Jefferson." Jefferson did not free Sally's children; he let them run away, which put them in more jeopardy than if he had freed them.

And here is a fact with which to reckon—in the words of Brodie, who broke the boy-historians' covenant of silence with her careful and thorough investigation of Jefferson's life: Sally Hemings "was not mentioned in Jefferson's will, and after his death [in 1826] she appeared on the official slave inventory of 1827 as worth $50. She was fifty-four."

THE RAPIST CREATES SOCIAL REALITY:
DOMINANCE AND OPPRESSION, SPEECH AND SILENCE

Asked why Thomas Jefferson did not send the slaves who looked just like him to another Jefferson-owned plantation "to keep them out of public sight," Jefferson's legitimate grandson answered:

> Mr. Jefferson never betrayed the least consciousness of the resemblance and although [the grandson and his mother] would have been very glad to have them thus removed, that both and all venerated Mr. Jefferson too deeply to broach such a topic to him. What suited him satisfied them.

Jefferson, like a deity, created reality and imposed it on others through what he acknowledged and what he ignored. He was known never to discuss what he preferred to avoid—which goes to the heart of speech and democracy, especially with respect to men and women. The power to determine the silence of others is the power of a tyrant: a power Jefferson and his peers had, one the Bill of Rights reified. Empirically real rights were not enunciated in the Bill of Rights; they were articulated in the social and sexual relations at Monticello. Jefferson's free speech depended on the coerced silence of his white and black subordinates: women white and black, slaves male and female. His speech required their silence. The law itself seemed to follow nature, not to be imposed on it: the enslaved were willing or weak or inferior or wanton; submission must have meant love; silence was consent. What could Sally Hemings, or Jefferson's wife or daughters or sisters or mother, have had to say?

The new democracy did not just exclude black slaves and white women formally so that when they finally were recognized to be persons they could be added in; the exclusion of blacks and women was the organizing principle on which the legal system itself was built. Blacks and women were the hidden foundation, made invisible so that white men could continue to steal their labor and love. This was a material exile from rights, the cruelty of which was camouflaged by a rhetoric of liberty: freedom from, not freedom to. Having speech meant having the power to define as well as promulgate it. And what was it that the government must not intrude on? Was it writing letters? reading books?— or might it include the photograph of an Asian girl, naked, her breasts bound in thick ropes, hanging from a tree?

Amerikan law was set up to confirm already existing power, pander to white men's wealth, and let white men rape fourteen-year-old black girls. Democratic rights have expanded: men of all colors are now entitled, though a double standard still prevails; it takes less wealth to be a protected rapist; fourteen is old now; and the girls, too, can be any color. The right-wing militias lately being scrutinized because of the bombing of the federal building in Oklahoma City understand the framers' Constitution exactly. They know that rights were intended for white men with land and guns, and that the goal was freedom from the federal government. They hate the blacks and the women using federal power since the sixties and spreading it everywhere, like hosts of a contagion; and it was stinkingly ugly that a woman attorney general ordered the attack on the Branch Davidian compound in Waco, Texas, using armed federal force to wipe out a classic patriarch (guns, land, women, children—childbearing servants). They want the framers' country back. They want Jefferson's power (though not his erudition): the power to define what reality is. But they put their money on the wrong amendment (the Second) and their faith in the wrong political lobby (NRA). Liberals, representing themselves as advocates for women and blacks, found the speech clause of the First Amendment more amiable: they could talk the talk of equality but they did not have to walk the walk. Naive babes in the woods, not hardened by playing soldier on weekends, the liberals blabbed while the pornographers, snakes in the garden of happy talk, bought the speech clause right out from under them. With hard cash, pornographers deployed an army of lawyers into state and federal courts to litigate as if their sexual exploitation of women for profit were a federally protected speech right. The ACLU, which claims to defend civil liberties, colluded with these pimps to shield their for-profit exploitation as "speech."

It worked because speech is a right we all think we have. It is counterintuitive to think of speech as a negative right, *freedom from*: how can a speech right be anything other than *freedom to*? Most of us think that the founders' speech implied or included or anticipated our own. Freedom of speech became a progressive political beachhead, the preeminent right that implied all others. At the same time, liberals and lawyers for the pimps could decry government interference in a culture of hostility to government—a distinctly Amerikan political hostility easy to manipulate to virtually any purpose.

As substantive equality became harder and harder to make real for women and African Americans, speech became a substitute for equality and a diversion from the tough political work of redistributing power and wealth. Speech covered up the structural wrongs in our constitutional system: its valuing of property over people; its intractable antagonism to the personhood of women and blacks; and the absence of a legal mandate to racial and sexual equality, affirmative and unequivocal.

Liberals became gutless wonders who, instead of having a material standard for equality based on human dignity, accepted the dehumanization, humiliation, and injury of women in the sex industry as entertainment; liberals let women's bodies become the speech of pimps, a new chattel status—women's bodies became pimps' words and sentences and paragraphs, under law. The use of pornography in crimes of violence against women was ignored; but when terrorists attacked abortion clinic doctors, New York City Planned Parenthood advertised its discovery that "words kill" and "words are like bullets." Patricia Ireland, the current president of NOW, refused to denounce pornography's role in rape to *The New York Times* in a news feature on pornography and racist hate speech; yet she was photographed carrying a sign saying

"Gangsta Rap Is Rape" in a demonstration. Molly Ivins, in a law school forum, conceded that pornography "probably does harm people . . . probably, all those ugly pictures do encourage violence against women"; but she went on to say, "What should we do about it? Well, my answer is, not a goddam thing. The cure for every excess of freedom of speech is more freedom of speech." While Ivins's bold indifference to violence against women is heartbreaking enough, her "excess of freedom of speech" is a euphemism for exploited and hurt women, actual women. If the pimps gag one, should we gag two? There's more freedom of speech for you.

Meanwhile, the political Right, willing to attack pornography as obscene or indecent, will not support any policy that repudiates pornography as male dominance. In response to feminist activism defining pornography as an issue of equality, the political Right has increasingly committed itself to a free speech absolutism that is libertarian and militant.

With both liberals and the political Right converging to defend pornography, law protects money and power, consistent with the framers' vision: speech *is* defined as the photograph of an Asian girl, naked, breasts bound in thick ropes, hanging from a tree. And when such a child is found, hung and tied just like that, dead, no one says "words are like bullets" or even "right-to-life."

Liberals, hearing inflammatory talk linked to abortion clinic terrorism, began to reject what they called hate speech: to question just how expressive some people had the right to be. But they had already collaborated in protecting the for-profit hate of women, the brutality and terrorism of pornography, its role in rape, battery, incest, prostitution; they had not minded the hate involved in spreading the legs of a contemporary Sally Hemings—or lynching her or beating her or raping her or cutting her or mutilating her—for a consumer, or a million consumers, who want photographs of the violation, now called "speech." Ain't nobody heard her voice yet.

WOMEN IN THE PUBLIC DOMAIN

Sexual Harassment and Date Rape

THE PROSTITUTION PARADIGM

In the European tradition, men have tried to keep women from working for money except as prostitutes. As with so many enduring Western ideals, the roots of this social model can be found in the Athenian city-state. The most protected woman was the married woman, a prisoner in her own home, except, of course, that it was not hers, any more than the cage belongs to the bird. She had no rights and no money. She did, however, have responsibilities. It was her duty to submit to intercourse, have sons, and run the house. Her virtue was maintained by keeping her an isolated captive. She was physically confined to the house to guarantee the husband that his legal children were his biological issue.

Any woman less isolated was more collectively owned. Foreign women taken as plunder were slaves. Adult Athenian women who were not married were, in the main, either high-class prostitutes, social and sexual companions to a male elite, or prisoners in brothels. The high-class prostitutes were the only women with any real education or any freedom of movement. The courtesan class in many societies was the social location of women of accomplishment and foreshadowed the professional woman of advanced capitalism: highly educated compared

196

with other women, highly skilled, she worked for money and appeared to exercise choice.

The wife was the private woman in the private (domestic) sphere, protected inside, legally bound there. *Inside* meant confinement, captivity, isolation; high value; a reproductive as well as a sexual function; a privatized ownership. The prostitute was the public woman—publicly owned. She lived outside the home. *Outside* meant the breaching of one's body by more than one, how many and under which circumstances depending on one's closeness to or distance from the male elite—the small, wealthy ruling class. The low-class prostitute, kept in a brothel, was outside the bounds of human recognition: an orifice, a nonentity, used for a mass function. *Outside*, money paid for acts and access. *Outside*, women were for sale. *Inside* meant that a woman was protected from the commerce in her kind; the value of a woman was high only when she was immune from the contamination of a money exchange. A woman who could be bought was cheap. This cheapness signified her low value and defined her moral capacity. A woman was her sexual function; she was what she did; she became what was done to her; she was what she was for. Any woman born outside or left outside or kicked outside deserved what she got because she was what had happened to her. For instance, the rape of a lady stole her value from her but she was not the aggrieved party. Her husband or her father had been injured, because the value of his property had been destroyed. Once used, she might become the wife of the rapist, or she was cast out, exiled to the margins, newly created common property. Rape could create a marriage but more often it created a prostitute. The deeper her exile, the more accessible to men she was—the more accessible, the cheaper. This was an economic fact and an ontological axiom, status and character determined by the degree of her sexual vulnerability. In the public domain by virtue of the male use of her, she became venal by male definition and design, according to male power and perception.

These zones—private and public, inside and outside—continue to suggest a real geography of female experience under the rule of men. The insularity of the domestic sphere for women has been treasured or honored or valued even in poor or working-class families; a man's honor is compromised or contaminated when his wife works outside the home for money. The gender-specific exclusiveness of housework creates a literal and symbolic synthesis between woman and house. She is wedded to it as much as to him. The repetitive, menial work by which she is judged—her competence, her devotion, her womanhood—establishes the house as her indigenous habitat. Her tribe, woman, carries the housekeeping gene. By nature, she rubs and she scrubs. The male lives out his wider life in the wider world, a hunter (he brings home the bacon) with a biological imperative to spread his sperm. He works for money by right, and with it goes freedom of action. After work he can range over miles, bar to bar, or library to library; he roams the big world. When finally he enters the domicile where she belongs as a natural, unpaid worker, he is both master and guest. He eats, he sleeps, he dirties the floor. Inside the domestic sphere, she lives the best life for her. Too much association with the obligations of the domestic sphere make his life too small for him. He resents the taming of his wild nature; he will not accept the limits appropriate to a female life. He will not do housework. He will not jack her loose from it. Her association with the home is nativist and in the wider world, which is his real domain, she is an unwanted alien, at best a guest worker with a short-term visa, a stigmatized immigrant.

In the workplace, her money is seen to supplement his. He is first, she is second. She is paid less than men are paid for the same work, if men do the same work; she may be segregated into female-only work, menial and low-paid. Usually, whatever her work she makes less than her husband whatever his work. Two features of female labor are so familiar that they seem to have all the permanence of gravity, or is it gravy stains?—(1) she does unpaid work in the home, a lot of it, and (2) in the marketplace she lines the bottom. This makes her poor relative to him; this makes women poor relative to men. Women, then, can buy less shelter, less food, less freedom than men. Women, then, need men for money, and men require sexual access to make the exchange. Women's poverty means that women stay sexually accessible to men, a submission seen as natural instead of economically coerced.

The Athenian ethic prevails, however camouflaged. Working women are attached in marriage to the *inside*, mostly by cleaning it. The ideal is still the isolated captive but she is increasingly honored in the breach, since both the isolation and the captivity have been massively rejected by Western women. Ideologically, the Right continues to promote the house as the natural, even exclusive, locus of virtue for a woman. The media, construed to be liberal in their social advocacy, continue to insist that working for money outside the home makes women depressed, infertile, stressed, more prone to heart disease and earlier death, while all extant studies continue to show the opposite (see Faludi, *Backlash*, Crown, 1991; Barnett and Rivers, "The Myth of the Miserable Working Woman," *Working Woman*, February 1992). The Left—ever visionary—continues to caretake the pornography industry, making the whole wide world—street, workplace, supermarket—repellent to women. And while men use pornography to drive women out of the workplace, civil libertarians defend it as speech (it is, indeed, like "Get out, nigger"); and some ask, "Why can't a woman be more like a man?" i.e., why can't a woman flourish in a workplace saturated with pornography? Thus, each tried-and-true political tendency combines the best of its theory with the best of its practice to force women out of the workplace, back into the house, door locked from the outside. Pretending to argue, they collude. And if one don't get you, the other will.

And we, the women, of course, remain touchingly naive and ahistorical. We believe that women are in the workplace to stay, even though men have engineered massive and brutal social dislocations to keep women poor and powerless or to return us there. In Europe, the mass slaughter of the witches over a 300-year period was partly motivated by a desire to confiscate their property, their money—to take what wealth women had. During the Crusades, women took over land, money, aspects of male political sovereignty—and were pushed out and down when the men returned. In the United States, of course, Rosie the Riveter was pushed out of the factory and into the suburbs, unemployed. We have been playing Giant Steps throughout history, trying to advance on the man while his back was turned. Each time we get an economic leg up, the man finds a way to break our knees. Of course it will be different this time; of course. We want equal pay for equal work and we wait, patiently, quietly; let them have one more war. Especially, we believe that the workplace is a gender-neutral zone, a fair place; we believe that we leave gender behind, at home, with the polish on the linoleum; we believe that a woman is a person, at work to work, for money. We may wear our little skirts but we do not expect them to mean anything, certainly not that the men will try to look up them. Even though we know that we have had to fight bias to get the job and to get the money, we present ourselves at work as workers, a final prayer for fairness. We have given up on the streets; we have given up at home. But, this time, we entered the workplace *after* some legislative promises of fairness, and we believe in law, we believe the promise. Our immutable assumption, synonymous with our deepest hope, is that we do not go into the workplace sexed: which means, always in our experience, as a target.

But the men, classics scholars each and every one, honor the old road map: a woman outside, a woman in public, is more collectively owned than a woman inside. Each woman may be bound to her husband by the rites and rituals of domesticity, but when she crosses the periphery, exits the door, she belongs to them that see her: a little or a lot, depending on how the men are inclined. The eyes own her first; the gaze that looks her up and down is the first incursion, the first public claim. The single woman inhabits this old territory even more fully. She is presumed to be out there looking for him, whomever—his money, his power, his sex, his protection (from men just like him). There is virtually no respect for a woman without a man and there is virtually no recognition that a woman's life is fully human on its own. Human freedom has him as its subject, not her. Always, she is an adjunct. Her integrity is not central to the imperative for human rights or political rights or economic rights. And, indeed, this is what matters. It may be all that matters. The solitary woman must incarnate for us what it means to be human; *she* must signify all the dimensions of human value; she must set the standard. The inability to conceptualize her individuality amounts to a morbid paralysis of conscience. Without her as a whole human being in her own right, a sovereign human being, the predations of men against women will appear natural or justified. The tolerance of these predations depends on the woman's life being, in its essence, smaller, less significant, predetermined by the necessities of a sexual function, that function itself formed by the requirements of male sexual tyranny, a reductive and totalitarian set of sexual demands.

So, outside, the woman is public in male territory, a hands-on zone; her presence there is taken to be a declaration of availability—for sex and sexual insult. On the street, she may be verbally assaulted or physically assaulted. The verbal assaults and some physical assault are endemic in the environment, a given, an apparently inevitable emanation of the male spirit—from the breast-oriented "Hey, momma" to, as I saw once, a man in a suit walking rapidly down the street punching in the stomach each young, well-dressed woman he passed—wham, bam, punch, hard, they keeled over one after another as he barreled by them—each was incredulous even as she folded over, and he was gone before I could take in what I had clearly seen on rush-hour crowded streets. It is a fiction that male assaults against women are punished by law. In any woman's life, most are not. The casual, random violence of the stranger has nearly as much protection as the systematic, intimate violence of the lover, husband, or father. None of us can stand up to all of it; we are incredulous as each new aggression occurs. We hurry to forget. It can't have happened, we say; or it happens all the time, we say—it is too rare to be credible or too common to matter. We won't be believed or no one will care; or both.

In the workplace, the woman hears the beat of her unsexed heart: I am *good* at this, she says. She is working for money, maybe for dignity, maybe in pursuit of independence, maybe out of a sense of vocation or ambition. The man perceives that she is close to him, a physical and mental proximity; under him, a political and economic arrangement that is incontrovertible; poorer than he is, a fact with consequences for her—he perceives that she is in the marketplace to barter, skills for money, sexuality for advancement or advantages. Her genitals are near him, just under that dress, in the public domain, his domain. Her lesser paycheck gives him a concrete measure of how much more she needs, how much more he has. In the academy, a grade is wealth. In each arena, she is a strange woman, not his wife or daughter; and her presence is a provocation. His presumption is a premise of patriarchy: she can be bought; her real skills are sexual skills; the sexuality that inheres in her is for sale or for barter and he has a right to it anyway, a right to a rub or a lick or a fuck. Once outside, she is in the realm of the prostituted woman. It is an economically real realm. The poor trade sex for money, food, shelter, work, a chance. It is a realm created by the power of men over women, a zone of women compromised by the need for money. If she is there, he has a right to a piece of her. It is a longstanding right. Using his power to force her seems virile, masculine, to him, an act of civilized conquest, a natural expression of a natural potency. His feelings are natural, indeed, inevitable. His acts are natural, too. The laws of man and woman supersede, surely, the regulations or conventions of the workplace.

Every regular guy, it turns out, is a sociobiologist who can explain the need to spread the sperm—for the sake of the species. He is a philosopher of civilization, a deep thinker on the question of what women really want—and he thinks old thoughts, rapist thoughts, slave-owning thoughts. He thinks them deeply, without self-consciousness. He is a keeper of tradition, a guardian of values: he punishes transgression, and the woman outside has transgressed the one boundary established to keep her safe from men in general, to keep her private from him. If she was at home, as she should be, she would not be near him. If she is near him, his question is why; and his answer is that she is making herself available—for a price. She is there for money. The workplace is where a woman goes to sell what she has for money. Her wages suggest that her job skills do not amount to much. Indisputably, she is cheap.

It stuns us, this underlying assumption that we are whoring. Here we are, on our own, at last, so proud, so stupidly proud. Here he is, a conqueror he thinks, a coward and a bully we think, using power to coerce sex. We feel humiliated, embarrassed, ashamed. He feels fine. He feels right. Manly: he feels manly. And, of course, he is.

MALE SEXUALITY

Now, I have had this experience. In my work I have described the sexual philosophies of Kinsey, Havelock Ellis, de Sade, Tolstoy, Isaac Bashevis

Singer, Freud, Robert Stoller, Norman Mailer, Henry Miller. Each has an ethic of male entitlement to women's bodies. Each celebrates male sexual aggression against women as an intrinsic component of a natural, valuable, venerable masculinity. Each suggests that women must be conquered, taken by force; that women say no but mean yes; that forced sex is ecstatic sex and that women crave pain.

I have written about the gynocide of the witches, one thousand years of Chinese footbinding, serial rape and serial killing.

I have written about the misogyny in the Bible and in pornography, about the advocacy of rape in male supremacist psychology, theology, philosophy, about the cruelty of dominance and submission, including in intercourse.

In every case, I have used the discourse of men as a source, without distorting it. I have said what men say about women, about the nature of sex, about the nature of nature. The men remain cultural heroes, Promethean truth-tellers; surely they mean no harm. I am excoriated (surely I mean some harm) for saying what they say but framing it in a new frame, one that shows the consequences to women. The ones they do it to have been left out. I put the ones they do it to back in. In exposing the hate men have for women, it is as if it becomes mine. To say what they do is to be what they are, except that they are entitled, they are right in what they do and what they say and how they feel. Maybe they are tragic but they are never responsible: for being mean or cruel or stupid. When they advocate rape, that is normal and neutral. When I say they advocate rape, I am engaging in the equivalent of a blood libel (this is the meaning of the "man hating" charge); I slander them as if I invented the sadism, the brutality, the exploitation that they engage in and defend.

Now: men describe their masculinity as aggressive, essentially rapist. Feminists have challenged the rape itself. We have agitated for changes in law so that we can prosecute all acts of forced sex. Men continue to speak as if we are ultimately irrelevant; they say that force is a natural part of sex and a normal expression of masculinity. We say that force is rape. Men continue to rationalize the use of force in intercourse as if force indicates the degree of desire, the intensity of the urge. Feminists are charged with hating sex (rape) because we hate forced sex. We are charged with confusing the horrible crime of rape (rape with the most brutality imaginable) with intercourse (which involves less force, though how much less the men will not say), thereby making it impossible to prosecute real rape, horrible rape (rape done by someone else) because the force a good guy (me) might use can be confused by some nasty or dumb woman with the worse force used by a real rapist (not me).

Until about twenty years ago, men did what they wanted and called it what they liked. They decided all meaning and value. (Not all men decided all meaning and value; but men, not women, decided.) They could describe sex as conquest, violence, violation, and themselves as rapists (without using the word), because they were never accountable to us for what they said or did. Men were the law; men were morality; men decided; men judged. Now we have pushed our way out from under them, at least a little. We see them owning and naming. We have a critical new distance. Still screwed in place as it were, we have swiveled loose a little, and we see the face where before we only felt the heavy breathing. We see the brow knotted in exertion, the muscles of the brain flexing in what passes for thought: discounting us, ignoring us, ignorant of us, celebrating rape and leaving out the cost to us. In the last two decades, feminists have built a real political resistance to male sexual dominance, i.e., to male ownership of the whole wide world; and it is clear that we are not saying no because we mean yes. We mean no and we prosecute the pigs to prove it. More and more of us do, more and more. We prosecute and sue our fathers, lovers, bosses, doctors, friends, as well as the ubiquitous stranger. For all our cultural brazenness, men have learned that no might mean no because we take them to court. It started as a rumor. The rumor spread. The bitches are really pissed.

Uses of force that men consider natural, necessary, and fair are being confronted by women who take those same uses of force to be intolerable violations without any possible extenuation. In 1991, two events clarified the state of conflict between male sexual hegemony and female political resistance: Anita Hill charged Clarence Thomas with sexual harassment; and William Kennedy Smith was prosecuted for rape.

   Clarence Thomas was George Bush's nominee for the Supreme Court, an African-American conservative whose origins were rural and poor, in the segregated South. Anita Hill was a law professor who came from the same background. She had been Thomas's subordinate at the EEOC, the administrative agency responsible for pursuing complaints of sexual harassment and other civil rights violations. In other words, Clarence Thomas was in charge of vindicating the rights of victims. His record at the EEOC was one of extreme lethargy. Feminists saw a relationship between his record, a poor one, and his own behavior as alleged by Hill—he was a perpetrator. Hill described a continuing pattern of verbal assault, especially the recounting of pornographic movies that featured rape, women being penetrated by animals, and large-breasted women. In one incidence of harassment, Thomas asked who had left a pubic hair on a Coke can. Ms. Hill could not make sense of the remark but those of us who study pornography identified it immediately: there are films in which women are penetrated by beverage cans. Mr. Thomas talked about the size of his penis and his ability to give women pleasure through oral sex. These confidences were forced on Ms. Hill in the workplace, in private, without witnesses. Ms. Hill was Mr. Thomas's chosen target, a smart, ambitious African-American woman whose future was linked with his. In the narrow sense, their political destinies were linked. He was a favorite of the Republicans and she could travel with him: up. In the wider sense, as an African-American conservative, he was pioneering the way for other black conservatives, especially women who would follow because they could not lead—Mr. Bush has shown no interest in even the token empowerment of African-American women. The verbal assaults humiliated Ms. Hill and pushed her face in her sexual status. They emphasized the servility that went with being female. They put her in her place, which was under him; in the office; in the movie; in life—her life.

   Anita Hill testified before the Senate Judiciary Committee and fourteen white men evaded the issues her testimony raised. Right-wing senators, with deft diagnostic skills, said she was psychotic. He was a lunatic if he did it but he could not be a lunatic and therefore he could not have done it. He would have to be morally degenerate to watch such films and he could not be morally degenerate. They sputtered trying to say what she must be—to bring the charges. *Psychotic* was their kindest conclusion. Left-wing senators, presumably out to destroy Clarence Thomas the black conservative by any means necessary, did not ask him questions on his use of pornography, though the answers might have vindicated Anita Hill. The topic was barely mentioned and not pursued. The claims of sexual harassment were essentially ignored; they were buried, not exposed. Panels of women were brought forward to say that Clarence Thomas did not sexually harass them. When I rob my neighbor, I want all the neighbors I did not rob to be asked to testify; I am very kind to my neighbors, except for the one I robbed. The chairman of the committee, Democrat Joseph R. Biden Jr. from Delaware, who is sponsoring the first federal bill to treat rape and battery as the sex-based crimes they are (the Violence Against Women Act), said that terrible things always come to his attention during confirmation hearings. He specifically mentioned charges of wife-beating (the aforementioned "battery" of the Violence Against Women Act). The press ignored this information; no one demanded to know which men confirmed by the Senate Judiciary Committee and then the whole Senate beat their wives. Clarence Thomas himself was reported to have beaten his first wife, an African-American woman, though she did not come forward to make the charge in public.

Clarence Thomas was confirmed and is now a sitting Supreme Court Justice.

Mr. Bush gave several interviews in which he deplored the sexually explicit testimony. His granddaughters, he said, could turn on the television and hear this dirty talk. He did not seem to mind the dirty behavior or having institutionalized it by putting an accused pornophile on the court that would make the law that would govern his granddaughters. If Clarence Thomas enjoys films in which women are fucked by animals, George Bush's granddaughters, like the rest of us, are in trouble.

Since the fourteen white men on the Senate Judiciary Committee did not ask, we do not know if Clarence Thomas still uses pornography. (This presumes that he would tell the truth, which presumes a lot. He stated under oath that he had never discussed *Roe* v. *Wade*, the decision legalizing abortion in the United States. My cat hasn't discussed it.) Thomas's friends from college confirm that he used pornography when he was in law school at Yale (1971–1974). Then, and even in the early 1980s when Anita Hill alleges he detailed the pornographic scenarios to her, pornography showing women being penetrated by animals was still underground. It was available in film loops in stalls in adult bookstores and live-sex theaters. A man goes to the prostitution-pornography part of town; he finds the right venue; he occupies a private stall with the film loops—women being fucked by animals or pissed on or whipped; he keeps depositing tokens or quarters to see the loop of film, which keeps repeating; when he leaves, someone mops up the stall—usually he leaves semen. Clarence Thomas asserted the absolute privacy of what he called his bedroom when one senator broached the topic of pornography. If he used the pornography when his friends say he did, his bedroom includes a lot of geography. That is one big bedroom. The patriarchal standard the Bush administration wants to defend is a familiar one: a man's privacy includes any sexual act he wants to do *to women* wherever he wants to do it; a woman's privacy does not even extend to her own internal organs. The pornography Clarence Thomas was accused of using is viciously woman hating; it is the KKK equivalent of destroying women for the fun of it, annihilating women for sport. The President used every resource at his command to defend Thomas's nomination. So did the right-wing senators. The liberals sacrificed the women of this country to the usual imperatives of male bonding. How many—left, right, or center—harass the very low-paid, low-status women who work for them (they exempted themselves from the reach of sexual harassment laws)? How many use pornography? How many, in fact, beat their wives?

William Kennedy Smith, thirty, a rich white man, recently graduated from medical school, nephew of Senator Edward M. (Ted) Kennedy, was prosecuted for rape in December 1991. The woman who accused him was white, his approximate age and social status, an unmarried mother of one. They met in a chic bar in Palm Beach, Florida, Smith accompanied by his uncle and his cousin Patrick, a Rhode Island state legislator. The woman went with Smith to the Kennedy home in Palm Beach. (Who would not think it safe? Which citizen would not go?) According to her, Smith tackled her and forced himself on her. His defense was that she had had intercourse. The jury believed him and acquitted him with less than an hour of deliberation. He had a story that was consistent; she had memory lapses. The judge refused to allow testimony from an expert on rape trauma that would have explained how commonplace such memory losses are in victims of rape. The trial was televised. The woman's face was obscured from view. The shock to the nation, the shock to ruling-class men, the shock to male dominance was that Mr. Smith was prosecuted at all. Feminists call the crime date rape or acquaintance rape. In the good old days, in the 1950s and 1960s as well as in the Athenian city-state, rape was a crime of theft; the woman belonged to a man, her husband or father; and raping her was like breaking her, smashing a vessel, a valuable vase; the man's property was destroyed. Until two decades ago, men raped women and men made and administered the laws against rape. Rape law protected the interests of men from the aggressions of other men; it punished men for getting out of line by taking a woman who belonged to someone else. With the advent of the women's movement, rape was redefined as a crime against the woman who was raped. This seems simple but in fact it overturned over two thousand years of male supremacist rape law.

In order for the crime to have happened to her, she had to be someone (when it happened to him, she was something). In order for her to be someone, the law had to revise its estimation of her place: from chattel to person in her own right. As a person, then, she began to say what had happened to her, in the courtroom but also in books, in public meetings, among women, in the presence of men. She began to say what had happened, where, how, who had done it, when, even why. The old law of rape, it seemed, barely touched on the reality of rape. The crime had been defined by male self-interest. Men had demanded as a legal standard that women be prepared to die rather than to submit; this degree of resistance was required to show, to prove, that she did not consent; her visible injuries had to prove that she might have died, because he would have killed her. Resisting less, she would be held responsible for whatever he had done to her. Her testimony had to be corroborated—by witnesses or by physical evidence so overwhelming as to be incontrovertible. The legal presumption was that women lied, used false rape charges to punish men. One of the law's purposes was to protect men from vindictive women, which all women who charged rape were presumed to be. In practice, every effort was made to destroy any woman who prosecuted a rapist. A woman's sexual history was used to indict her. The premise always has been that loose women—prostitutes, sluts, sexually active women—could not be raped; that the public woman was for sexual consumption however achieved, by money or by force; that any woman who "did it" was dirt, took on the status of the act itself (dirty)—that she had no value the law was required to honor or protect. If a woman could not prove her virtue, she could be found culpable for the lack of it, which meant acquittal for the rapist. Empirically speaking, it did not matter if she had been forced to do what it was presumed she would be happy to do anyway—even if under different circumstances or with someone else. If the rapist's lawyer could show that the woman had had sex—was not a virgin or a faithful wife—she was proved worthless. No one would punish the accused, hurt his life, for what he had done to a piece of trash—unless he needed to be punished for some other reason, for instance, his race, or social hubris, or some other scapegoating reason, in which case she would be used to put him away.

The reforms seemed so minor; frankly, so inadequate. We need more and better but the changes have had an impact. Trial rules were changed so that the woman's past sexual history was generally inadmissible. Corroboration was no longer required—the woman's testimony could stand on its own. The procedures involved in collecting and keeping physical evidence were scrutinized and standardized so that such evidence could not be lost, contaminated, or tampered with. Before, evidence had been collected in a haphazard way, giving the rapist a big headstart on an acquittal. Doctors in emergency rooms and police were trained in how to treat rape victims, how to investigate for sexual abuse. Rape crisis centers were created, some in hospital emergency rooms; these gave victims expert counseling and a sympathetic peer on the victims' side in dealing with the police, doctors, prosecutors, in going through the ordeal of a trial, in surviving the trauma of the event itself. In some states, the definition of consent was changed so that, for instance, if a woman was drunk she could *not* give legal consent (rather than the old way: if she was drunk, she had consented—to whatever would be done to her; she deserved whatever she got). Laws that protected rape in marriage—the right of a husband to penetrate his wife against her will, by force—were changed so that forced intercourse in marriage could be prosecuted as what it was: the act of rape. "But if you can't rape your wife," protested California state senator Bob Wilson in 1979, "who can you rape?" The answer is: no one. And women began to sue rapists, including husbands, under civil law: to expose the crime; to get money damages. The law remains tilted in favor of the rapist. For instance, prior convictions for rape are not admissible as evidence. The woman still almost always looks wrong, stupid, venal, and the prejudices against women—how women should dress, act, talk, think—are virulent, nearly deranged by any fair standard. Most rapists are acquitted. Usually this means that the woman is told by a jury, as Smith's accuser was, that she had intercourse. (In some cases, the jury acquits because it believes that the wrong man has been apprehended; it accepts that the woman has been raped.) The acquittal that declares she was not raped, she had intercourse, upholds and reifies the patriarchal view of rape: a monstrous act committed by a monster (invariably a stranger), it is an excess of violence outside the force sanctioned in intercourse; the woman is, in fact, subjected to so much violence that no one could interpret her submission as voluntary or think it was at her invitation, for her pleasure. Just some violence does not take the act out of the realm of normal intercourse for male supremacists because, for them, sex is a sometimes mean dance, and aggression against the woman is just a fast and manly way of dancing.

The progress is in this: that, increasingly, incursions against women are prosecuted as rape; that rape is now a crime against the woman herself; that the use of force is enough to warrant a prosecution (if not yet a conviction); that a date, a friend, an acquaintance, will be prosecuted for the use of force—even if he is rich, even if he is white, even if he is a doctor, even if his family is powerful and lionized. And the progress is also in this: that a woman could go out, outside, past the periphery, at night, to a bar, chat with men, drink—a woman who had been sexually abused as a child, who had worked for an escort service, who had had three abortions—and still, force used against her was taken to be rape—by prosecutors, hard-asses who do not like to lose.

Feminists have achieved what amounts to a vast redefinition of rape based on women's experience of how, when, and where we are raped—also, by whom; and we have achieved a revised valuation of the rape victim—someone, not something. Male society, once imperial in its authority over women and rape, having operated on the absolutist principle of the divine right of kings, has not taken the change with good grace.

"Feminists," says the right-wing *National Review* (January 20, 1992), "have attempted to strengthen the likelihood of conviction by inventing the concept of 'date rape,' which means not simply rape committed by an escort, but any sexual contact that a woman subsequently regrets." Regret, then, not force, is the substance of this charge we thought up; Pied Piper–like, we lead and the little children—the police, district attorneys—charmed by our music, follow.

Neo-con writer Norman Podhoretz claims that date rape does not exist; that feminists, in order to make men sexually dysfunctional, are putting unfair, unnatural, unreasonable constraints on masculinity. There is "a masculine need to conquer," an "ever restless masculine sex drive," in conflict with the "much more quiescent erotic impulses" of women (*Commentary*, October 1991)—we don't push and shove? In other words, so-called date rape is, in fact, normal intercourse using normal force, misunderstood by women who are misled by feminists into thinking they have been forced (raped) when they have just been fucked (forced). Mr. Podhoretz singles me out as a particularly noxious example of a feminist who repudiates women's being force-fucked, call it what you will; I am indecent, castrating, and man hating in my refusal to accept male force and male conquest as a good time. The liberal *Tikkun* praises Mr. Podhoretz for trying to off me; then, with dim logic but shining arrogance, claims that "the psychic undergirding of so much neo-conservatism" has been "the fear of women's power, the fear that women's wishes and desires may have to be given equal weight with those of men" (November/December 1991). Ain't I a woman? What undergirds *Tikkun*?

In *The Wall Street Journal* (June 27, 1991), Berkeley professor Neil Gilbert, a very angry man, seriously undergirded, claims that we lie about rape as a way of lying about men. In particular, we lie about the frequency of rape. We make up statistics in order to "broadcast a picture of college life that resembles the world of 'Thelma and Louise,' in which four out of six men are foul brutes and the other two are slightly simpleminded." We do this because we have a secret agenda: "to change social perceptions of what constitutes acceptable intimate relations between men and women . . . It is an effort to reduce the awesome complexity of intimate discourse between the sexes to the banality of 'no' means 'no.'" Actually, being force-fucked is pretty banal. Didn't Hannah Arendt write a book about that?

"The awesome complexity" of getting a woman drunk to fuck her has lost some ground, since if a woman is drugged she is held incapable of consent in some states.

"The awesome complexity" of owning her body outright in marriage has lost ground because marital rape is now criminalized in some states.

"The awesome complexity" of driving a woman into prostitution through forced sex, however, holds its ground, it seems, since incest or other child sexual abuse appears to be a precondition for prostitution and prostitution thrives. Claiming that date rape—rape defined from women's experience of sexual coercion at the hands of an acquaintance—has created a "phantom epidemic of sexual assault" (*The Public Interest*, spring 1991), Mr. Gilbert opposes funding rape crisis centers on college campuses. A press release for Mr. Gilbert proudly states: "In a similar vein four years ago, Gilbert criticized sexual abuse prevention training for small children. Partly as a result of Gilbert's research, Governor Deukmejian last year canceled all state funding for the school-based prevention programs." The awesome simplicity of Mr. Gilbert's public discourse is more venal than banal: neither women nor children should have any recourse; keep the rapist's discourse awesome by keeping the victim helpless and silent.

Male hysteria over date rape (its recognition, stigmatization, punishment) was especially provoked in the media by date-rape charges on college campuses: where boys become men. Outstanding numbers of young women said that boys could not become men on them; by coercing them. Take Back the Night marches and speak-outs proliferated. Women named rapists and reported rapes, though college administrators mostly backed up male privilege. Even gang rapes rarely got a penalty more punishing than the penalty for plagiarism. At Brown University, women wrote the names of male students who had coerced them on the walls of women's bathrooms. To men, First Amendent absolutists in defense of pornography, this suggested a logical limit on free speech. It seemed clear to them. In a slyly misogynist profile of an actual date rape at Dartmouth College, *Harper's* (April 1991) characterized student activism against rape this way: "Sexual-abuse activists are holding workshops to help students recast the male psyche."

Indeed, male rage against date-rape charges originated in the conviction that men had a right to the behaviors constituting the assaults; but also, that manly behavior, manhood itself, required the use of force, with aggression as the activating dynamic. The redefinition of rape based on women's experience of being forced is taken by men to be a subversion of their right to live peaceably and well-fucked, on their own terms. "The trend in this complicated arena of sexual politics is definitely against us, gentlemen," warns *Playboy's* Asa Baber (September 1991). "A lynch mob could be just outside your door. In William Kennedy Smith's case, a lynch mob has already placed the rope around his neck." Well, hardly. The boy had the best due process money could buy.

Men cannot live without rape, say these organs, so to speak, of male power. Men cannot be men without using some force, some aggression, or without having the right to use some force, some aggression. Men need rape, or the right to rape, to be men. Taking away the right to rape emasculates men. The charge of date rape is an effort to unsex men.

This male rage also derives from the perception that college-age women experience what used to be normal, sanctioned coercion as rape—real rape. These charges are not ideological. They do not come from the first generation of this wave's feminists, the sadder-but-wiser flower children who wondered why all the peace-now men pushed and shoved and what it meant. Male aggression is being experienced by young women now as violation. The pushing and shoving is taken to be hostile and unfair, wrong and rotten. This is proof of feminism's success in articulating the real experiences of women, so long buried in an imposed silence. We older ones looked at our lives—the forced sex that was simply part of what it meant to be a woman, the circumstances under which the force occurred, who he was (rarely the famous stranger). Male lies all around us celebrated force as romantic rape; male laws protected force used against women in rape and battery; in this very unfriendly world we enunciated, at risk and in pain, the meaning of our own experience. We called it rape. The younger women vindicate us. They are not bewildered as we were—stunned by how ordinary and commonplace it is. They are not intimidated by the rapist, who can be any man, any time, any place. They are traumatized by the force, as we were. The unwanted invasion repels them, as it did us. But we were quiet, during and after. The rapes were covered over by so much time, so many desperate smiles. The younger women know what date rape is. They publicly charge it, publish it, prosecute it, because it is the truth. And, as the angry men know, these young women are the future.

The male strategy in undermining the claim is simple, rapelike verbal attacks on women as such: on the inherent capacity of women to say what we mean, to know what has happened, to say anything true. The old rape jurisprudence protected men from rape charges by so-called vindictive women (any woman they might know). To undermine the validity of date rape, male supremacists claim that all women are vindictive women; that date rape is a vindictive social fantasy, a collective hysteria, invented by that mass of vindictive women, feminists. The whole political spectrum, gendered male, claims that women are emotional illiterates (heretofore the province of men; see, they can learn to give up territory). *National Review* defined date rape as any sex that a woman later regretted. Over a year earlier, *Playboy* (October 1990) made the same charge (in an article penned by a woman, *Playboy*-style, to break our hearts): ". . . the new definition of rape gives women a simple way of thinking about sex that externalizes guilt, remorse or conflict. Bad feelings after sex become someone else's fault. A sexual encounter is transformed into a one-way event in which the woman has no stake, no interest and no active role." Actually, the rapist defines the woman's role (the very essence of rape) and it is about time that the guilt was externalized. He can have the remorse, too. We can share the conflict. *Playboy*'s prolonged propaganda campaign against date rape predates the mainstream backlash—usually the verbiage is in unsigned editorial copy, not written by the token girl. *Playboy* has the political role of developing the misogynist program that is then assimilated, one hand typing, into news journals left and right. The point of view is the same, *National Review* or *Playboy*, with the left political magazines paying better lip service (for women who like that sort of thing) to feminist sensibilities while ripping us apart by critiquing our so-called excesses. Underlying virtually all of the date-rape critiques is the conviction that women simply cannot face having had consensual sex. A genetic puritanism (it travels with the housekeeping gene) makes us sorry all the time; and when we are sorry we retaliate—we call it date rape, sexual harassment, we tear the pornography off the walls. Any way one looks at it, these boys ain't great lovers. Women are not left quivering, begging for more (waiting by the phone for his call). The old-type vindictive woman used to want the man to stay but he left; she retaliated for being betrayed or abandoned. The new vindictive woman—on college campuses, for instance—can't get far enough away from him; she appears to retaliate because he has shown up. Surely, this is different. Male privilege seems to be at stake here, not any woman's sense of regret. (That is a different girls' club. Men one wants to sleep with can be bastards, too.) Regret tends to be an identifiable emotion, one even dumb women (a redundancy in the male-supremacist lexicon) can recognize. It has taken us longer to identify garden-variety rape because use of us against our will was so protected for so long. Now we know what it is; and so will he. Count on it.

Date rape and sexual harassment have emerged together—in 1991 because of the coincidence of Anita Hill's charges against Clarence Thomas and the prosecution for rape of William Kennedy Smith; politically because each challenges men's right to have sexual access to women who are not hidden away, to women who are out and about. Both date rape and sexual harassment were, as Gloria Steinem says, just life—until women turned them into crimes. Each is defended as essential masculine practice, necessary to the expression of male sexuality—

he chases, he conquers. The proscribing of each is repudiated by those who defend rapist sexuality as synonymous with male sexuality. "Enough is enough," writes *Playboy*'s hired girl, this time on sexual harassment (February 1991). "An aggressively vehement sexual-harassment policy, whether in the workplace, on campus or in high school, spreads a message that there is something intrinsically evil about male sexuality. It preaches that men must keep their reactions (and their erections) bottled up tightly, that any remnant of that sexuality (in the form of a look, a comment, a gesture, even a declaration of interest) is potentially dangerous, hurtful, and now, criminal." (A bottle is fine; in high schools they can be found in the chemistry lab.) Sexual harassment laws and policies are gender-neutral, in keeping with a basic ethic of contemporary United States law. The existence of the laws and policies does not indict men; but the frenzied repudiation does indict men—it is a male supremacist repudiation of conscience, fairness, and, of course, equality. Some feminists say "please." Some feminists say "put up or shut up." But it is the defenders of male privilege who say that it is the nature of men to aggress against women; that male sexuality requires such aggression. It is the defenders of male privilege who say that male sexuality is essentially rapist. Feminists say that laws against date rape and sexual harassment are fair laws. No man of conscience will use force against a woman nor will he use his power to harass, pursue, humiliate, or "have" her. Men raised in a rapist culture, in conflict with it but also having internal conflict, wanting to be fair, wanting to honor equality, will not want to rape or to sexually harass; these laws will set standards and show the way. It was good of us, and generous, to pursue remedies in a principled way, without shedding blood. These things have been done to us. They will stop.

But Thomas was confirmed and Smith was acquitted. Now the question is: how do we nail them? Think.

ISRAEL

Whose Country Is It Anyway?

It's mine. We can put the question to rest. Israel belongs to me. Or so I was raised to believe.

I've been planting trees there since I can remember. I have memories of my mother's breast—of hunger (she was sick and weak); of having my tonsils out when I was two and a half—of the fear and the wallpaper in the hospital; of infantile bad dreams; of early childhood abandonment; of planting trees in Israel. Understand: I've been planting trees in Israel since before I actually could recognize a real tree from life. In Camden where I grew up we had cement. I thought the huge and splendid telephone pole across the street from our brick row house was one— a tree; it just didn't have leaves. I wasn't deprived: the wires were awesome. If I think of "tree" now, I see that splintery dead piece of lumber stained an uneven brown with its wild black wires stretched out across the sky. I have to force myself to remember that a tree is frailer and greener, at least prototypically, at least in temperate zones. It takes an act of adult will to remember that a tree grows up into the sky, down into the ground, and a telephone pole, even a magnificent one, does not.

Israel, like Camden, didn't have any trees. We were cement; Israel was desert. They needed trees, we didn't. The logic was that we lived in the United States where there was an abundance of everything, even trees;

in Israel there was nothing. So we had to get them trees. In synagogue we would be given folders: white paper, heavy, thick; blue ink, light, reminiscent of green but not green. White and blue were the colors of Israel. You opened the folder and inside there was a tree printed in light blue. The tree was full, round, almost swollen, a great arc, lush, branches coming from branches, each branch growing clusters of leaves. In each cluster of leaves, we had to put a dime. We could use our own dimes from lunch money or allowances, but they only went so far; so we had to ask relatives, strangers, the policeman at the school crossing, the janitor at school—anyone who might spare a dime, because you had to fill your folder and then you had to start another one and fill that too. Each dime was inserted into a little slit in the folder right in the cluster of leaves so each branch ended up being weighed down with shining dimes. When you had enough dimes, the tree on the folder looked as if it was growing dimes. This meant you had collected enough money to plant a tree in Israel, your own tree. You put your name on the folder and in Israel they would plant your tree and put your name on it. You also put another name on the folder. You dedicated the tree to someone who had died. This tree is dedicated to the memory of. Jewish families were never short on dead people but in the years after my birth, after 1946, the dead overwhelmed the living. You touched the dead wherever you turned. You rubbed up against them; it didn't matter how young you were. Mass graves; bones; ash; ovens; numbers on forearms. If you were Jewish and alive, you were—well, almost—rare. You had a solitary feeling even as a child. Being alive felt wrong. Are you tired of hearing about it? Don't be tired of it in front of me. It was new then and I was a child. The adults wanted to keep us from becoming morbid, or anxious, or afraid, or different from other children. They told us and they didn't tell us. They told us and then they took it back. They whispered and let you overhear, then they denied it. Nothing's wrong. You're safe here, in the United States. Being a Jew is, well, like being an Amerikan: the best. It was a great secret they tried to keep and tried to tell at the same time. They were adults—they still didn't believe it really. You were a child; you did.

My Hebrew school teachers were of two kinds: bright-eyed Jewish men from New Jersey, the suburbs mostly, and Philadelphia, a center of culture—mediocre men, poor teachers, their aspirations more bourgeois than Talmudic; and survivors from ancient European ghettos by way of Auschwitz and Bergen-Belsen—multilingual, learned, spectral, walleyed. None, of course, could speak Hebrew. It was a dead language, like Latin. The new Israeli project of speaking Hebrew was regarded as an experiment that could only fail. English would be the language of Israel. It was only a matter of time. Israel was the size of New Jersey. Israel was a miracle, a great adventure, but it was also absolutely familiar.

The trick in dedicating your tree was to have an actual name to write on your folder and know who the person was to you. It was important to Amerikan Jews to seem normal and other people knew the names of their dead. We had too many dead to know their names; mass murder was erasure. Immigrants to the United States had left sisters, brothers, mothers, aunts, uncles, cousins behind, and they had been slaughtered. Where? When? It was all blank. My father's parents were Russian immigrants. My mother's were Hungarian. My grandparents always refused to talk about Europe. "Garbage," my father's father said to me, "they're all garbage." He meant all Europeans. He had run away from Russia at fifteen—from the Czar. He had brothers and sisters, seven; I never could find out anything else. They were dead, from pogroms, the Russian Revolution, Nazis; they were gone. My grandparents on each side ran away for their own reasons and came here. They didn't look back. Then there was this new genocide, new even to Jews, and they couldn't look back. There was no recovering what had been lost, or who. There couldn't be reconciliation with what couldn't be faced. They were alive because they were here; the rest were dead because they were there: who could face that? As a child I observed that Christian children had lots of relatives unfamiliar to me, very old, with honorifics unknown to me— great-aunt, great-great-grandmother. Our family began with my grandparents. No one came before them; no one stood next to them. It's an incomprehensible and disquieting amnesia. There was Eve; then there is a harrowing blank space, a tunnel of time and nothing with enormous murder; then there's us. We had whoever was in the room. Everyone who wasn't in the room was dead. All my mourning was for them—all my trees in the desert—but who were they? My ancestors aren't individual to me: I'm pulled into the mass grave for any sense of identity or sense of self. In the small world I lived in as a child, the consciousness was in three parts: (1) in Europe with those left behind, the dead, and how could one live with how they had died, even if why was old and familiar; (2) in the United States, the best of all possible worlds—being more-Amerikan-than-thou, more middle-class however poor and struggling, more suburban however urban in origins, more normal, more conventional, more conformist; and (3) in Israel, in the desert, with the Jews who had been ash and now were planting trees. I never planted a tree in Camden or anywhere else for that matter. All my trees are in Israel. I was taught that they had my name on them and that they were dedicated to the memory of my dead.

One day in Hebrew school I argued in front of the whole class with the principal; a teacher, a scholar, a survivor, he spoke seven languages and I don't know which camps he was in. In private, he would talk to me, answer my questions, unlike the others. I would see him shaking, alone; I'd ask why; he would say sometimes he couldn't speak, there were no words, he couldn't say words, even though he spoke seven languages; he would say he had seen things; he would say he couldn't sleep, he hadn't slept for nights or weeks. I knew he knew important things. I respected him. Usually I didn't respect my teachers. In front of the whole class, he told us that in life we had the obligation to be first a Jew, second an Amerikan, third a human being, a citizen of the world. I was outraged. I said it was the opposite. I said everyone was first a human being, a citizen of the world—otherwise there would never be peace, never an end to nationalist conflicts and racial persecutions. Maybe I was eleven. He said that Jews had been killed throughout history precisely because they thought the way I did, because they put being Jews last; because they didn't understand that one was always first a Jew—in history, in the eyes of the world, in the eyes of God. I said it was the opposite: only when everyone was human first would Jews be safe. He said

Jews like me had had the blood of other Jews on their hands throughout history; that had there been an Israel, Jews would not have been slaughtered throughout Europe; that the Jewish homeland was the only hope for Jewish freedom. I said that was why one had an obligation to be an Amerikan second, after being a human being, a citizen of the world: because only in a democracy without a state religion could religious minorities have rights or be safe or not be persecuted or discriminated against. I said that if there was a Jewish state, anyone who wasn't Jewish would be second-class by definition. I said we didn't have a right to do to other people what had been done to us. More than anyone, we knew the bitterness of religious persecution, the stigma that went with being a minority. We should be able to see in advance the inevitable consequences of having a state that put us first; because then others were second and third and fourth. A theocratic state, I said, could never be a fair state—and didn't Jews need a fair state? If Jews had had a fair state wouldn't Jews have been safe from slaughter? Israel could be a beginning: a fair state. But then it couldn't be a Jewish state. The blood of Jews, he said, would be on my hands. He walked out. I don't think he ever spoke to me again.

You might wonder if this story is apocryphal or how I remember it or how someone so young made such arguments. The last is simple: the beauty of a Jewish education is that you learn how to argue if you pay attention. I remember because I was so distressed by what he said to me: the blood of Jews will be on your hands. I remember because he meant what he said. Part of my education was in having teachers who had seen too much death to argue for the fun of it. I could see the blood on my hands if I was wrong; Jews would have nowhere; Jews would die. I could see that if I or anyone made it harder for Israel to exist, Jews might die. I knew that Israel had to succeed, had to work out. Every single adult Jew I knew wanted it, needed it: the distraught ones with the numbers on their arms; the immigrant ones who had been here, not there; the cheerful more-Amerikan-than-thou ones who wanted ranch houses for themselves, an army for Israel. Israel was the answer to near extinction in a real world that had been demonstrably indifferent to the mass murder of the

Jews. It was also the only way living Jews could survive having survived. Those who had been here, not there, by immigration or birth, would create another here, a different here, a purposeful sanctuary, not one stumbled on by random good luck. Those who were alive had to find a way to deal with the monumental guilt of not being dead: being the chosen this time for real. The building of Israel was a bridge over bones; a commitment to life against the suicidal pull of the past. How can I live with having lived? I will make a place for Jews to live.

I knew from my own urgent effort to try to understand racism—from the Nazis to the situation I lived in, hatred of black people in the United States, the existence of legal segregation in the South—that Israel was impossible: fundamentally wrong, organized to betray egalitarian aspirations—because it was built from the ground up on a racial definition of its desired citizen; because it was built from the ground up on exclusion, necessarily stigmatizing those who were not Jews. Social equality was impossible unless only Jews lived there. With hostile neighbors and a racial paradigm for the state's identity, Israel had to become either a fortress or a tomb. I didn't think it made Jews safer. I did understand that it made Jews different: different from the pathetic creatures on the trains, the skeletons in the camps; different; indelibly different. It was a great relief—to me too—to be different from the Jews in the cattle cars. Different mattered. As long as it lasted, I would take it. And if Israel ended up being a tomb, a tomb was better than unmarked mass graves for millions all over Europe—different and better. I made my peace with different; which meant I made my peace with the State of Israel. I would not have the blood of Jews on my hands. I wouldn't help those who wanted Israel to be a place where more Jews died by saying what I thought about the implicit racism. It was shameful, really: distance me, Lord, from those pitiful Jews; make me new. But it was real and even I at ten, eleven, twelve needed it.

You might notice that all of this had nothing to do with Palestinians. I didn't know there were any. Also, I haven't mentioned women. I knew they existed, formally speaking; Mrs. So-and-So was everywhere, of course—peculiar, all held in, reticent and dutiful in public. I never saw one I wanted to become. Nevertheless, adults kept threatening that one day I had to be one. Apparently it was destiny and also hard work; you were born one but you also had to become one. Either you mastered exceptionally difficult and obscure rules too numerous and onerous to reveal to a child, even a child studying Leviticus; or you made one mistake, the nature of which was never specified. But politically speaking, women didn't exist, and frankly, as human beings women didn't exist either. You could live your whole life among them and never know who they were.

I was taught about *fedayeen*: Arabs who crossed the border into Israel to kill Jews. In the years after Hitler, this was monstrous. Only someone devoid of any humanity, any conscience, any sense of decency or justice could kill Jews. They didn't live there; they came from somewhere else. They killed civilians by sneak attack; they didn't care whom they killed just so they killed Jews.

I realized only as a middle-aged adult that I was raised to have prejudice against Arabs and that the prejudice wasn't trivial. My parents were exceptionally conscious and conscientious about racism and religious bigotry—all the homegrown kinds—hatred of blacks or Catholics, for instance. Their pedagogy was very brave. They took a social stance against racism, for civil rights, that put them in opposition to many neighbors and members of our family. My mother put me in a car and showed me black poverty. However poor I thought we were, I was to remember that being black in the United States made you poorer. I still remember a conversation with my father in which he told me he had racist feelings against blacks. I said that was impossible because he was for civil rights. He explained the kinds of feelings he had and why they were wrong. He also explained that as a teacher and then later a guidance counselor he worked with black children and he had to make sure his racist feelings didn't harm them. From my father I learned that having these feelings didn't justify them; that "good" people had bad feelings and that didn't make the feelings any less bad; that dealing with racism was a process, something a person tangled with actively. The feelings were wrong and a "good" person took responsibility for facing them down. I was also taught that just because you feel something doesn't make it true. My parents went out of their way to say "some Arabs," to emphasize that there were good and bad people in every group; but in fact my education in the Jewish community made that caveat fairly meaningless. Arabs were primitive, uncivilized, violent. (My parents would never have accepted such characterizations of blacks.) Arabs hated and killed Jews. Really, I learned that Arabs were irredeemably evil. In all my travels through life, which were extensive, I never knew any Arabs: and ignorance is the best friend of prejudice.

In my mid-thirties I started reading books by Palestinians. These books made me understand that I was misinformed. I had had a fine enough position on the Palestinians—or perhaps I should say "the Palestinian question" to convey the right ring of condescension—once I knew they existed; long after I was eleven. Maybe twenty years ago, I knew they existed. I knew they were being wronged. I was for a two-state solution. Over the years, I learned about Israeli torture of Palestinian prisoners; I knew Jewish journalists who purposefully suppressed the information so as not to "hurt" the Jewish state. I knew the human rights of Palestinians in ordinary life were being violated. Like my daddy, on social issues, the policy questions, I was fine for my kind. These opinions put me into constant friction with the Jewish community, including my family, many friends, and many Jewish feminists. As far as I know, from my own experience, the Jewish community has just recently—like last Tuesday—really faced the facts—the current facts. I will not argue about the twisted history, who did what to whom when. I will not argue about Zionism except to say that it is apparent that I am not a Zionist and never was. The argument is the same one I had with my Hebrew school principal; my position is the same—either we get a fair world or we keep getting killed. (I have also noticed, in the interim, that the Cambodians had Cambodia and it didn't help them much. Social sadism takes many forms. What can't be imagined happens.) But there are social policy questions and then there is the racism that lives in individual hearts and minds as a prejudgment on a whole people. You believe the stereotypes;

you believe the worst; you accept a caricature such that members of the group are comic or menacing, always contemptible. I don't believe that Amerikan Jews raised as I was are free of this prejudice. We were taught it as children and it has helped the Israeli government justify in our eyes what they have done to the Palestinians. We've been blinded, not just by our need for Israel or our loyalty to Jews but by a deep and real prejudice against Palestinians that amounts to race-hate.

The land wasn't empty, as I was taught: oh yes, there are a few nomadic tribes but they don't have homes in the normal sense—not like we do in New Jersey; there are just a few uneducated, primitive, dirty people there now who don't even want a state. There were people and there were even trees—trees destroyed by Israeli soldiers. The Palestinians are right when they say the Jews regarded them as nothing. I was taught they were nothing in the most literal sense. Taking the country and turning it into Israel, the Jewish state, was an imperialist act. Jews find any such statement incomprehensible. How could the near-dead, the nearly extinguished, a people who were ash have imperialized anyone, anything? Well, Israel is rare: Jews, nearly annihilated, took the land and forced a very hostile world to legitimize the theft. I think Amerikan Jews cannot face the fact that this is one act—the one act—of imperialism, of conquest that we support. We helped; we're proud of it; here we stand. This is a contradiction of every idea we have about who we are and what being a Jew means. It is also true. We took a country from the people who lived there; we the dispossessed finally did it to someone else; we said, they're Arabs, let them go somewhere Arab. When Israelis say they want to be judged by the same standards applied to the rest of the world, not by a special standard for Jews, in part they mean that this is the way of the world. It may be a first for Jews, but everyone else has been doing it throughout recorded history. It *is* recorded history. I grew up in New Jersey, the size of Israel; not so long ago, it belonged to Indians. Because Amerikan Jews refuse to face precisely this one fact—we took the land—Amerikan Jews cannot afford to know or face Palestinians: initially, even that they existed.

As for the Palestinians, I can only imagine the humiliation of losing to, being conquered by, the weakest, most despised, most castrated people on the face of the earth. This is a feminist point about manhood.

When I was growing up, the only time I heard about equality of the sexes was when I was taught to love and have fidelity to the new State of Israel. This new state was being built on the premise that men and women were equal in all ways. According to my teachers, servility was inappropriate for the new Jew, male or female. In the new state, there was no strong or weak or more or less valuable according to sex. Everyone did the work: physical labor, menial labor, cooking—there was no, as we say now, sex-role stereotyping. Because everyone worked, everyone had an equal responsibility and an equal say. Especially, women were citizens, not mothers.

Strangely, this was the most foreign aspect of Israel. In New Jersey, we didn't have equality of the sexes. In New Jersey, no one thought about it or needed it or wanted it. We didn't have equality of the sexes in Hebrew school. It didn't matter how smart or devout you were: if you were a girl, you weren't allowed to do anything important. You weren't allowed to want anything except marriage, even if you were a talented scholar. Equality of the sexes was something they were going to have in the desert with the trees; we couldn't send them any because we didn't have any. It was a new principle for a new land and it helped to make a new people; in New Jersey, we didn't have to be quite that new.

When I was growing up, Israel was also basically socialist. The kibbutzim, voluntary collectives, were egalitarian communities by design. The kibbutzim were going to replace the traditional nuclear family as the basic social unit in the new society. Children would be raised by the whole community—they wouldn't "belong" to their parents. The communal vision was the cornerstone of the new country.

Here, women were pretty invisible, and material greed, a desire for middle-class goods and status, animated the Jewish community. Israel really repudiated the values of Amerikan Jews—somehow the adults managed to venerate Israel while in their own lives transgressing every radical value the new state was espousing. But the influence on the children was probably very great. I don't think it is an accident that Jewish children my age grew up wanting to make communal living a reality or believing that it could be done; or that the girls did eventually determine, in such great numbers, to make equality of the sexes the dynamic basis of our political lives.

While women in the United States were living in a twilight world, appendages to men, housewives, still the strongest women I knew when I was a child worked for the establishment, well-being, and preservation of the State of Israel. It was perhaps the only socially sanctioned field of engagement. My Aunt Helen, for instance, the only unmarried, working woman I knew as a child, made Israel her life's cause. Not only did the strong women work for Israel, but women who weren't visibly strong—who were conformist—showed some real backbone when they were active on behalf of Israel. The equality of the sexes may have had a resonance for them as adults that it couldn't have had for me as a child. Later, Golda Meir's long tenure as prime minister made it seem as if the promise of equality was being delivered on. She was new, all right; forged from the old, visibly so, but herself made new by an act of will; *public*; a leader of a country in crisis. My Aunt Helen and Golda Meir were a lot alike: not defined in terms of men; straightforward when other women were coy; tough; resourceful; formidable. The only formidable women I saw were associated with and committed to Israel, except for Anna Magnani. But that's another story.

Finally in 1988, at forty-two, on Thanksgiving, the day we celebrate having successfully taken this land from the Indians, I went to Israel for the first time. I went to a conference billed as the First International Jewish Feminist Conference. Its theme was the empowerment of Jewish women. Its sponsors were the American Jewish Congress, the World Jewish Congress, and the Israel Women's Network, and it was being organized with a middle-class agenda by middle-class women, primarily Amerikan, who were themselves beholden to the male leadership of the sponsoring groups. So the conference looked to secular Israeli feminists organizing at the grassroots level—and so it was. Initially, the secular Israeli feminists intended to organize an alternate feminist conference to repudiate the establishment feminist conference, but they decided instead to have their own conference, one that included Palestinian women, the day after the establishment conference ended.

The establishment conference was designed not to alienate Orthodox Jewish women. As far as I could see, secular Jewish women, especially Israelis, were expendable. What the hell? They could be counted on to keep working—keep those battered women's shelters going, keep those rape crisis centers open—without being invited *into* the hotel. They couldn't afford to come anyway. The wealthier excluded the poor and struggling; the timid (mainstream) excluded the grassroots (really mainstream but as socially invisible and despised as the women they represent and serve); the religious excluded the secular; Jewish excluded Palestinian; and, to a considerable degree, Amerikans, by virtue of their money and control of the agenda, excluded Israelis—feminists, you know, the ones who do the work in the country, on the ground. Lesbians were excluded until the last minute by not being specifically included; negotiations with those organizing what came to be called the post-conference put a lesbian on the program speaking as such, though under a pseudonym because she was Israeli and it was too dangerous for her to be known by her real name. War-and-peace issues were underplayed, even as the establishment conference was held in the occupied West Bank; even though many feminists—organizers and theorists—consider both militarism and masculinity feminist issues—intrinsically feminist, not attached to the agenda because of a particular political emergency.

I went because of grassroots Israeli feminists: the opportunity to meet with them in Haifa, Tel Aviv, and Jerusalem; to talk with those organizing against violence against women on all fronts; to learn more about the situation of women in Israel. I planned to stay on—if I had, I also would have spoken at and for the rape crisis center in Jerusalem. In Haifa, where both Phyllis Chesler and I spoke to a packed room (which included Palestinian women and some young Arab men) on child custody and pornography in the United States, women were angry about the establishment conference—its tepid feminist agenda, its exclusion of the poor and of Palestinian feminists. One woman, maybe in her sixties, with an accent from Eastern Europe, maybe Poland, finally stood up and said approximately the following: "Look, it's just another conference put on by the Amerikans like all the others. They have them like clockwork. They use innocents like these"—pointing to Phyllis and me—"who don't know any better." Everyone laughed, especially us. I hadn't been called an innocent in a long time, or been perceived as one either. But she was right. Israel brought me to my knees. Innocent was right. Here's what compromised my innocence, such as it was.

1 THE LAW OF RETURN

Jewish women attended the establishment conference from many countries, including Argentina, New Zealand, India, Brazil, Belgium, South Africa, and the United States. Each woman had more right to be there than any Palestinian woman born there, or whose mother was born there, or whose mother's mother was born there. I found this morally unbearable. My own visceral recognition was simple: I don't have a right to this right.

The Law of Return says that any Jew entering the country can immediately become a citizen; no Jew can be turned away. This law is the basis for the Jewish state, its basic principle of identity and purpose. Orthodox religious parties, with a hefty share of the vote in recent elections, wanted the definition of "Jewish" narrowed to exclude converts to Judaism not converted by Orthodox rabbis, according to Orthodox precepts. Women at the establishment conference were mobilized to demonstrate against this change in the Law of Return. The logic used to mobilize the women went as follows: "The Right is doing this. The Right is bad. Anything the Right wants is bad for women. Therefore, we, feminists, must oppose this change in the Law of Return." Fight the Right. In your heart you know the fight is for the sake of women, but don't tell anyone else: not Shamir, not the Orthodox rabbis, not the press; but especially not the Amerikan Jewish boys who are sponsoring your conference, who are in Israel right then and there to lobby Shamir and to keep an eye on the girls. Fight the Right. Find an issue important to Jewish men and show up as the women's auxiliary. Make them proud. And don't offend them or upset them by making them stand with you—if they want you there—for the rights of women.

Protesting the change in the Law of Return was presented at the establishment conference as "taking a first step" against the power of the Orthodox rabbis. Because the power of these men over the lives of Jewish women in Israel is already vast and malignant, "taking a first step" against them—without mentioning any of the ways in which they are already tyrants over women—wasn't just inadequate; it was shameful. We needed to take a real step. In Israel, Jewish women are basically—in reality, in everyday life—governed by Old Testament law. So much for equality of the sexes. The Orthodox rabbis make most of the legal decisions that have a direct impact on the status of women and the quality of women's lives. They have the final say on all issues of "personal status," which feminists will recognize as the famous private sphere in which civilly subordinate women are traditionally imprisoned. The Orthodox rabbis decide questions of marriage, adultery, divorce, birth, death, legitimacy; what rape is; and whether abortion, battery, and rape in marriage are legal or illegal. At the protest, feminists did not mention women.

How did Israel get this way—how did these Orthodox rabbis get the power over women that they have? How do we dislodge them, get them *off* women? Why isn't there a body of civil law superseding the power of religious law that gives women real, indisputable rights of equality and self-determination in this country that we all helped build? I'm forty-four; Israel is forty-two; how the hell did this happen? What are we going to do about it now? How did Jewish feminists manage not to "take a first step" until the end of 1988—and then not mention women? The first step didn't amount to a feminist crawl.

2   THE CONDITION OF JEWISH WOMEN IN ISRAEL IS ABJECT

Where I live things aren't too good for women. It's not unlike Crystal Night all year long given the rape and battery statistics—which are a pale shadow of the truth—the incest, the pornography, the serial murders, the sheer savagery of the violence against women. But Israel is shattering. Sisters: we have been building a country in which women are dog shit, something you scrape off the bottom of your shoe. We, the "Jewish feminists." We who only push as far as the Jewish men here will allow. If feminism is serious, it fights sex hierarchy and male power and men don't get to stand on top of you, singly or in clusters, for forever and a day. And you don't help them build a country in which women's status gets lower and lower as the men get bigger and bigger—the men there and the men here. From what I saw and heard and learned, we have helped to build a living hell for women, a nice Jewish hell. Isn't it the same everywhere? Well, "everywhere" isn't younger than I am; "everywhere" didn't start out with the equality of the sexes as a premise. The low status of women in Israel is not unique but we are uniquely responsible for it. I felt disgraced by the way women are treated in Israel, disgraced and dishonored. I remembered my Hebrew school principal, the Holocaust survivor, who said I had to be a Jew first, an Amerikan second, and a citizen of the world, a human being last, or I would have the blood of Jews on my hands. I've kept quiet a long time about Israel so as not to have the blood of Jews on my hands. It turns out that I am a woman first, second, and last—they are the same; and I find I do have the blood of Jews on my hands—the blood of Jewish women in Israel.

Divorce and Battery

In Israel, there are separate religious courts that are Christian, Muslim, Druze, and Jewish. Essentially, women from each group are subject to the authority of the most ancient systems of religious misogyny.

In 1953 a law was passed bringing all Jews under the jurisdiction of the religious courts for everything having to do with "personal status." In the religious courts, women, along with children, the mentally deficient, the insane, and convicted criminals, cannot testify. A woman cannot be a witness or, needless to say, a judge. A woman cannot sign a document. This could be an obstacle to equality.

Under Jewish law, the husband is the master; the woman belongs to him, what with being one of his ribs to begin with; her duty is to have children—preferably with plenty of physical pain; well, you remember the Old Testament. You've read the Book. You've seen the movie. What you haven't done is live it. In Israel, Jewish women do.

The husband has the sole right to grant a divorce; it is an unimpeachable right. A woman has no such right and no recourse. She has to live with an adulterous husband until he throws her out (after which her prospects aren't too good); if she commits adultery, he can just get rid of her (after which her prospects are worse). She has to live with a batterer until he's done with her. If she leaves, she will be homeless, poor, stigmatized, displaced, an outcast, in internal exile in the Promised Land. If she leaves without formal permission from the religious courts, she can be judged a "rebellious wife," an actual legal category of women in Israel without, of course, any male analogue. A rebellious wife will lose custody of her children and any rights to financial support. There are an estimated 10,000 *agunot*—"chained women"—whose husbands will not grant them divorces. Some are prisoners; some are fugitives; none have basic rights of citizenship or personhood.

No one knows the extent of the battery. *Sisterhood Is Global* says that in 1978 there were approximately 60,000 reported cases of wife-beating; only two men went to prison. In 1981 I talked with Marcia Freedman, a former member of the Israeli parliament and a founder of the first battered-women's shelter in Israel, which I visited in Haifa. At that time, she thought wife-beating in Israel occurred with ten times the statistical frequency we had here. Recent hearings in parliament concluded that 100,000 women were being beaten each year in their own homes.

Marcia Freedman was in Haifa when I was. I saw only some of what she and other feminists had accomplished in Israel and against what odds. There are now five shelters in Israel. The shelter in Haifa is a big building on a city street. It looks like the other buildings. The streets are full of men. The door is locked. Once inside, you climb up several flights of steps to come upon a great iron gate inside the building, a gate you might find in a maximum-security prison for men. It is locked all the time. It is the only real defense against battering men. Once the iron gate is unlocked, you see women and children; big, clean, bare common rooms; small, immaculate rooms in which women and their children live; an office; a lounge; drawings by the children who live there—colorful, often violent; and on the top floor a school, the children Palestinian and Israeli, tiny, young, perfect, beautiful. This shelter is one of the few places in Israel where Arab and Jewish children are educated together. Their mothers live together. Behind the great iron bars, where women are voluntarily locked in to stay alive, there is a living model of Palestinian-Israeli cooperation: behind the iron bars that keep out the violent men—Jewish and Arab. Feminists have managed to get housing subsidies for women who have permission to live outside the marital home, but the process of qualifying can take as long as a year. The women who run the shelter try to relocate women fast—the space is needed for other women—but some women stay as long as a year. At night the women who run the shelter, by now professionals, go home; the battered women stay, the great iron gate their lone protection. I kept asking what if— what if he comes? The women can call the police; the police will come. The cop on the beat is nice. He stops by sometimes. Sometimes they give him a cup of coffee. But outside, not too long ago, a woman was beaten to death by the husband she was escaping. The women inside aren't armed; the shelter isn't armed; this in a country where the men are armed. There isn't any network of safe houses. The locations of the shelters are known. The women have to go out to find jobs and places to live. Well, women get beaten—and beaten to death—here too, don't they? But the husband doesn't get so much active help from the state—not to mention the God of the Jews. And when a Jewish woman is given a divorce, she has to physically back out of her husband's presence in the court. It is an argument for being beaten to death.

A draft of Israel's newly proposed Fundamental Human Rights Law—a contemporary equivalent of our Bill of Rights—exempts marriage and divorce from all human rights guarantees.

Pornography

You have to see it to believe it and even seeing it might not help. I've been sent it over the years by feminists in Israel—I had seen it—I didn't really believe it. Unlike in the United States, pornography is not an industry. You find it in mainstream magazines and advertising. It is mostly about the Holocaust. In it, Jewish women are sexualized as Holocaust victims for Jewish men to masturbate over. Well, would you believe it, even if you saw it?

Israeli women call it "Holocaust pornography." The themes are fire, gas, trains, emaciation, death.

In the fashion layout, three women in swimsuits are posed as if they are looking at and moving away from two men on motorcycles. The motorcycles, black metal, are menacingly in the foreground moving toward the women. The women, fragile and defenseless in their near nudity, are in the background. Then the women, now dressed in scanty underwear, are shown running from the men, with emphasis on thighs, breasts thrust out, hips highlighted. Their faces look frightened and frenzied. The men are physically grabbing them. Then the women, now in new bathing suits, are sprawled on the ground, apparently dead, with parts of their bodies severed from them and scattered around as trains bear down on them. Even as you see a severed arm, a severed leg, the trains coming toward them, the women are posed to accentuate the hips and place of entry into the vaginal area.

Or a man is pouring gasoline into a woman's face. Or she's posed next to a light fixture that looks like a shower head.

Or two women, ribs showing, in scanty underwear, are posed in front of a stone wall, prisonlike, with a fire extinguisher on one side of them and a blazing open oven on the other. Their body postures replicate the body postures of naked concentration camp inmates in documentary photographs.

Of course, there is also sadism without ethnicity, outside the trauma of history—you think Jewish men can't be regular good ol' boys? The cover of the magazine shows a naked woman spread out, legs open, with visual emphasis on her big breasts. Nails are driven through her breasts. Huge pliers are attached to one nipple. She is surrounded by hammers, pliers, saws. She has what passes for an orgasmic expression on her face.

The woman is real. The tools are drawn. The caption reads: Sex in the Workshop.

The same magazine published all the visual violence described above. *Monitin* is a left-liberal slick monthly for the intelligentsia and upper class. It has high production and aesthetic values. Israel's most distinguished writers and intellectuals publish in it. Judith Antonelli in *The Jewish Advocate* reported that *Monitin* "contains the most sexually violent images. Photos abound of women sprawled out upside-down as if they have just been attacked."

Or, in a magazine for women that is not unlike *Ladies' Home Journal,* there is a photograph of a woman tied to a chair with heavy rope. Her shirt is torn off her shoulders and upper chest but her arms are tied up against her so that only the fleshy part of the upper breasts is exposed. She is wearing pants—they are wet. A man, fully dressed, standing next to her, is throwing beer in her face. In the United States, such photographs of women are found in bondage magazines.

For purists, there is an Israeli pornography magazine. The issue I saw had a front-page headline that read: ORGY AT YAD VASHEM. Yad Vashem is the memorial in Jerusalem to the victims of the Holocaust. Under the headline, there was a photograph of a man sexually entangled with several women.

What does this mean—other than that if you are a Jewish woman you don't run to Israel, you run from it?

I went to the Institute for the Study of Media and Family on Herzelia Street in Haifa: an organization built to fight violence against women. Working with the rape crisis center (and desperately fund-raising to stay alive), the institute analyzes the content of media violence against women; it exposes and fights the legitimacy pornography gets by being incorporated into the mainstream.

There is outrage on the part of women at the Holocaust pornography—a deep, ongoing shock; but little understanding. For me, too. Having seen it here, having tried to absorb it, then seeing stacks of it at the institute, I felt numb and upset. Here I had slides; in Israel I saw the whole magazines—the context in which the photographs were published. These really were mainstream venues for violent pornography, with a preponderance of Holocaust pornography. That made it worse: more real, more incomprehensible. A week later, I spoke in Tel Aviv about pornography to an audience that was primarily feminist. One feminist suggested I had a double standard: didn't all men do this, not just Israeli men? I said no: in the United States, Jewish men are not the consumers of Holocaust pornography; black men aren't the consumers of plantation pornography. But now I'm not sure. Do I know that or have I just assumed it? Why do Israeli men like this? Why do they do it? They are the ones who do it; women aren't even tokens in the upper echelons of media, advertising, or publishing—nor are fugitive Nazis with new identities. I think feminists in Israel must make this "why" an essential question. Either the answer will tell us something new about the sexuality of men everywhere or it will tell us something special about the sexuality of men who go from victim to victimizer. How has the Holocaust been sexualized for Israeli men and what does this have to do with sexualized violence against women in Israel; what does it have to do with this great, dynamic pushing of women lower and lower? Are Jewish women going to be destroyed again by Nazis, this time with Israeli men as their surrogates? Is the sexuality of Israeli men shaped by the Holocaust? Does it make them come?

I don't know if Israeli men are different from other men by virtue of using the Holocaust against Jewish women, for sexual excitement. I do know that the use of Holocaust sex is unbearably traumatic for Jewish women, its place in the Israeli mainstream itself a form of sadism. I also know that as long as the Holocaust pornography exists, only male Jews are different from those pitiful creatures on the trains, in the camps. Jewish women are the same. How, then, does Israel save us?

All the Other Good Things

Of course, Israel has all the other good things boys do to girls: rape, incest, prostitution. Sexual harassment in public places, on the streets, is pervasive, aggressive, and sexually explicit. Every woman I talked with who had come to Israel from some other place brought up her rage at being propositioned on the street, at bus stops, in taxis, by men who wanted to fuck and said so. The men were Jewish and Arab. At the same time, in Jerusalem, Orthodox men throw stones at women who don't have their arms covered. Palestinian boys who throw stones at Israeli soldiers are shot with bullets, rubber-coated or not. Stone throwing at women by Orthodox men is considered trivial, not real assault. Somehow, it's their right. Well, what isn't?

In Tel Aviv before my lecture, I talked with an Israeli soldier, maybe nineteen, part of the occupying army in the West Bank. He was home for Sabbath. His mother, a feminist, generously opened her home to me. The mother and son were observant; the father was a secular liberal. I was with the best friend of the mother, who had organized the lecture. Both women were exceptionally gentle people, soft-spoken and giving. Earlier, I had participated with about 400 women in a vigil in Jerusalem against the occupation. For a year, feminists in Haifa, Jerusalem, and Tel Aviv had held a vigil each week called Women in Black, women in mourning for the duration of the occupation. The father and son were outraged by the demonstrations. The father argued that the demonstrations had nothing to do with feminism. The son argued that the occupation had nothing to do with feminism.

I asked the son about something that had been described to me: Israeli soldiers go into Palestinian villages and spread garbage, broken glass, rocks in the streets and make the women clean up the dangerous rubble bare-handed, without tools. I thought the son would deny it or say such a thing was an aberration. Instead, he argued that it had nothing to do with feminism. In arguing, he revealed that this kind of aggression is common; he had clearly seen it or done it many times. His mother's head sank; she didn't look up again until the end. What it had to do with feminism, I said, was that it happened to women. He said that was only because Arab men were cowards, they ran and hid. The women, he said, were strong; they weren't afraid, they stayed. What it had to do with feminism, I said, was that every woman's life, for a feminist, had the same high value. Feminism meant that the Arab woman's life was worth as much as his mother's. Suppose the soldiers came here now, I said, and made your mother go out on the street, get down on her knees, and clean up broken glass with her bare hands?

I said feminism also had to do with him; what kind of man he was or was becoming, what hurting other people would do to him; how callous or sadistic it would make him. He said, with perfect understanding: you mean, it will be easier to rape?

He said the Arabs deserved being shot; they were throwing stones at Israeli soldiers; I wasn't there, I didn't know, and what did it have to do with feminism anyway? I said that Orthodox men were throwing stones at women in Jerusalem because the women's arms weren't covered down to the wrist. He said it was ridiculous to compare the two. I said the only difference I could see was that the women didn't carry rifles or have any right to shoot the men. He said it wasn't the same. I asked him to tell me what the difference was. Wasn't a stone a stone—for a woman too? Weren't we flesh; didn't we bleed; couldn't we be killed by a stone? Were Israeli soldiers really more fragile than women with bare arms? Okay, he said, you do have a right to shoot them; but then you have to stand trial the same way we do if we kill Arabs. I said they didn't have to stand trial. His mother raised her head to say there were rules, strict rules, for the soldiers, really there were, and she wasn't ashamed of her son. "We are not ashamed," she said, imploring her husband, who said nothing. "We are not ashamed of him."

I remember the heat of the Jerusalem sun. Hundreds of women dressed in black were massed on the sidewalks of a big public square in Jerusalem. Women in Black began in Jerusalem at the same time as the intifada, with seven women who held a silent vigil to show their resistance to the occupation. Now the hundreds of women who participate each week in three cities are met with sexual derision and sometimes stones. Because the demonstrations are women-only, they are confrontational in two ways: these are Israelis who want peace with Palestinians; these are women who are standing on public ground. Women held signs in Hebrew, Arabic, and English saying: END THE OCCUPATION. An Arab vendor gave some of us, as many as he could reach, gifts of grapes and figs to help us fight the heat. Israeli men went by shouting insults—men called out insults from passing cars—the traffic was bumper to bumper, with the men trying to get home before Sabbath eve, when Jerusalem shuts down. There were also men with signs who screamed that the women were traitors and whores.

Along with most of the demonstrators, I had come from the post-conference organized by the grassroots, secular feminists. The post-conference was chaired by Nabila Espanioli, a Palestinian woman who spoke Hebrew, English, and Arabic. Palestinian women came out of the audience to give first-person testimony about what the occupation was doing to them. They especially spoke about the brutality of the Israeli soldiers. They talked about being humiliated, being forcibly detained, being trespassed on, being threatened. They spoke about themselves and about women. For Palestinian women, the occupation is a police state and the Israeli secret police are a constant danger; there is no "safe space." I already knew that I had Palestinian blood on my hands. What I found out in Israel is that it isn't any easier to wash off than Jewish blood—and that it is also female.

I had met Nabila my first night in Israel, in Haifa, at the home of an Israeli woman who gave a wonderful welcoming party. It was a warm, fragrant night. The small, beautiful apartment open to the night air was filled with women from Jerusalem, Tel Aviv, Haifa—feminists who fight for women, against violence. It was Sabbath eve and there was a simple feminist ceremony—a breaking of bread, one loaf, everyone together; secular words of peace and hope. And then I found myself talking with this Palestinian woman. She talked a mile a minute about pornography. It was her field of study and she knew it inside out, recognized herself in it, under it, violated by it. She told me it was the focus of her resistance to both rape and sexualized racism. She, too, wanted freedom and it was in her way. I thought: with this between us, who can pull us apart? We see women with the same eyes.

In Israel, there are the occupied and the occupied: Palestinians and women. In the Israel I saw, Palestinians will be freer sooner. I didn't find any of my trees.

THE U.S. HOLOCAUST
MEMORIAL MUSEUM

Is Memory Male?

In early September 1993 I went to the United States Holocaust Memorial Museum in Washington, D.C., to do research for a book on scapegoating, especially of Jews and women in anti-Semitism and woman hating. In November I went back to the museum because *Ms.* asked me to write about it. I consider myself not-a-civilian in the world of Holocaust memory, no stranger. A survivor's knowledge of the women's camp and killing center at Auschwitz-Birkenau was passed on to me by an aunt having flashbacks—graphic, detailed, of rapes, murders, tortures—when I was ten, a child without intellectual defenses. In a tiny room in Camden, New Jersey, I saw what she said was happening—what she was seeing—as she reexperienced her captivity. I still see it. Many of my teachers in Hebrew school were survivors, and they were different from everyone else. In the 1950s, closer to the real events, they lived more there than here: they shook, they cowered, they suffered—beyond understanding, in silence, without explanation. They lived in terror.

For me, the *Shoah*, the Hebrew word for "annihilation," is the root of my resistance to the sadism of rape, the dehumanization of pornography. In my private heart, forever, rape began at Auschwitz; and a species of pornography—sexualized anti-Semitic propaganda—was instrumental in creating the hate. My adult heart knows that Julius Streicher, who joined with Hitler in 1921, was executed at Nuremberg for his part in the genocide of the Jews because he published the rabid, pornographic, Jew-hating tabloid *Der Stürmer*, which was used by the Nazi party, then Hitler's regime, to fuel aggression against the Jews. Streicher was convicted of committing a crime against humanity.

I nside, the museum building is purposefully uncomfortable to the eye, to consciousness. Prisonlike elements are part of the design: cold, institutional brick walls made colder by exposed steel girders; windows obscured by metal bars or grates or louvered slats. There is a visual eloquence that does not let the mind drift, because the eye cannot find anywhere not prison-inspired to land. The interior, developed by the architect to suggest physical elements of Auschwitz, is ruthless: it demands alertness and suggests both danger and oppression.

The permanent exhibition is on three floors of a five-story building. One takes an elevator to the fourth floor: Nazi Assault, 1933–1939 (Hitler's ascendance and the German conquest of Europe). The third floor is dedicated to illustrating and explicating the facts of the Final Solution, 1940–1944; and the second floor is the Aftermath, 1945 to the present.

Standing in line for an elevator, I am encouraged to take a card on which is a photograph of a Holocaust victim, his name, his biography. Other women fingering through the cards ask each other, where are the women? Why aren't there biographies of women? They express a muted outrage—not wanting to call attention to themselves yet unable to accept that among the hundreds of cards there are no women. A museum employee (a woman) explains that the cards of women have all been used. We are supposed to be able to pick a biography of someone like ourselves and, with interactive computer technology, find out what happened to our person at various stages of the exhibit. The card machines were not in use (and have since been discontinued); but the absence of women's lives from the biographies was part of an old program, a familiar invisibility and absence, a simple carelessness to get more cards printed or a more malignant indifference.

I went to the United States Holocaust Memorial Museum with questions about women. Where, how, in what numbers were women raped? Where, how, in what numbers were women prostituted—the brothels in forced labor and concentration camps, where were they, who were the women, who used them? Where, how, in what numbers were women used in medical experiments, and with what results? Who were the inmates in Ravensbrück, a camp for women from many occupied countries but that earlier in Hitler's reign held German political prisoners, prostitutes, and lesbians—how did they get there, what happened to them? What exactly was done to Jewish women at Auschwitz-Birkenau or to the Jewish women held at Bergen-Belsen in 1944? How did the hatred of Jews and women intersect, not abstractly but on their bodies? How was the sadism against Jewish women organized, expressed?

There were no answers to my questions in the permanent exhibition's story of the rise of Hitler or the genocide of the Jews or the mass murders of the Poles, Gypsies (Roma), and other stigmatized groups; nor in the "aftermath," what happened in Europe when the Nazis were defeated. Although there were films and photographs of women, often naked, terribly brutalized, and there was first-person testimony by women survivors, there was no explanation or narrative of their persecution as women; nor was there any coherent information in the computers in the Wexner Learning Center, intended to be an electronic encyclopedia of the Holocaust; nor in any side exhibits. (One temporary exhibit, for children, is on the fate of a young Jewish boy. Another documents the efforts of a brave male intellectual to rescue mostly male intellectuals from Nazi-dominated France. In both, the romance of male significance mobilizes feelings and attention.)

I was given research materials that demonstrated the museum's commitment to documenting the egregious persecution of homosexuals; included were biographies of eight gay men and one lesbian. The museum's first conference—held in December 1993 on "The Known, the Unknown, the Disputed, and the Reexamined"—eliminated women altogether by disappearing the one lesbian. There were talks at the conference on "Nazi Anti-Homosexual Policies and Their Consequences for

Homosexual Men" and "The Pink Triangle: Homosexuals as 'Enemies of the State.'" There was scholarship on "The Black Experience in the Holocaust Period"; but nothing on women—not on Jewish women or Gypsy women or women political prisoners; not on female perpetrators, SS volunteers, for instance, some of whom were convicted of war crimes; not on Hitler's social policies on women's reproductive rights; not on the relentless early suppression of the feminist movement in Germany. Women were apparently neither known nor unknown, a common enough condition but no less heartbreaking for that.

In the museum, the story of women is missing. Women are conceptually invisible: in the design of the permanent exhibition, by which I mean its purpose, its fundamental meaning; in its conception of the Jewish people. Anti-Semites do not ignore the specific meaning or presence of women, nor how to stigmatize or physically hurt women as such, nor do those who commit genocide forget that to destroy a people, one must destroy the women. So how can this museum, dedicated to memory, forget to say what happened to Jewish women? If this genocide is unique, then what happened to Jewish women was unique; attention must be paid. If not here, where?

Genocide is different from war. In a genocide, women and children are primary targets, not accidental victims or occasional combatants. This museum, governed in its narrative choices by a courteous, inclusive politics of sensitivity to ethnic and political persecution, leaves out the story of the Nazis' hatred of women. The role of misogyny in the organized sadism of these men must be articulated: because women's lives were destroyed by careful plan; and because that sadism continues to contaminate and compromise what it means to be human. The Nazi invasion of the human body—the literal and metaphoric castration of subjugated men, the specter of the sexualized, tortured, emaciated "Jewess," mass plundered, mass murdered—is still the touchstone for an apparently depoliticized social sadism, a fetishized rapism that normalizes sexual humiliation and mass dehumanization. Sex tourism is one contemporary example—Thai women and children kept in brothels for the use of male consumers from developed countries.

This is what it means to pay attention to the sadism of the Nazis in the context of the Holocaust museum. Germans with disabilities were the first victims of secret, systematic murder—from October 1939 to August 1941 at psychiatric clinics. Groups of fifteen to twenty would be gassed in carbon monoxide chambers. In the permanent exhibition, there is a photograph of children being killed by lethal injection, their awful steel beds, the restraints. Behind this photo is another—smoke comes out of the chimney of Hartheim, a storybooklike castle near Linz, one of the clinics.

There is a photo of a naked girl, probably adolescent, "mentally handicapped," taken before she was killed. She is standing up, facing the camera, full-frontal, but she does not have the strength to stand on her own—her rib cage is all bones—so a nurse in a conventional white uniform holds her up by force; the pain on the girl's face is horrible. The photograph itself is Nazi child pornography—no breasts, no hips, not enough food for that, no paint or makeup, just a naked body and pure suffering; child pornography for real sadists, those who do not want their victims to smile. And there is a photo of an eight-year-old boy, also "mentally retarded," also naked, also full-frontal, this too child pornography Nazi-style, the camera complicit in the torturer's pride, his monument to memory.

Concerning disability, so-called Aryans turned in their own, not a dreaded racial "other." This was the first place where murder could hide behind doctors who would legitimize it. I heard a woman say, "It makes you wonder about Dr. Kevorkian." Yes, it does; and also about oneself—how complicit am I in devaluing those with disabilities, how much fear and prejudice are part of that complicity? I asked myself a lot of hard questions. I was able to ask them because the museum told the story. Those who don't see that pornography is, at its core, the appropriation of another person's body, identity, life might also begin to have questions.

The museum uses words, photographs, documents, films, and artifacts to create a discourse vivid with detail. Archival film and photographs from the period have been transferred to videotape for display. Some exhibits feature photographs mounted on walls. There are more than 10,000 artifacts, ranging from concentration camp uniforms to leaflets confiscated by the Nazis to children's drawings and paintings made during the years 1932–1944. The artifacts are startling, often beautiful. In telling the story of how the Nazis persecuted and murdered the Gypsies, there is a wagon, with a violin. "Yeah, this is the kind of wagon I saw going along the Danube in 1935," said a man behind me. The violin belonged to Miodrag Djordjević-Tukalia, a Roma musician executed by the Germans in October 1941. Each time a name is attached to an artifact, one is made to remember that everything happened to someone. It is as hard to remember the individuality of the victims as it is to take in the mass nature of the slaughter.

There are clothes and ornaments that belonged to Roma women; photographs of Roma prisoners being deported to Poland; and a film of Roma children used in so-called racial research. They are clothed and still vibrant, many smiling. Almost all of the Gypsy children at Auschwitz were killed.

Approaching the concentration camp area, I stop thinking. None of it is unfamiliar to me; but here is a real boxcar used to transport Jews, a real barrack from Auschwitz-Birkenau. Film is not easier. There are films of the mass killings by mobile killing squads: a line of naked women standing in front of an already-dug mass grave, naked women shot, falling, piled on top of each other, ravines filled with misshapen bodies. Months later, this will be what I wish I had not seen.

Before one enters the boxcar, there are artifacts from the Warsaw Ghetto uprising, Passover 1943: a 1929 Mauser rifle, fuses for the two unused Molotov cocktails, two 75mm artillery shells, a pistol. Near the boxcar, to its side, is a workbench that concealed a hiding place for Polish Jews in the house of Stefan Petri near Warsaw; a handcart used to transport heavy loads and dead bodies in the ghetto; a manhole cover, from Warsaw, because Jews hid in the sewers.

There is a wall of photographs of Jews and Gypsies being deported, from internment camps and ghettos to concentration camps and killing centers; still photos of the trains that transported them, all preface to the actual boxcar. Now one must choose to walk through it or around it. The boxcar is set up this way so that Holocaust survivors do not have to walk through it.

The freight car is clean now. I wonder if they had to scrub it out. It is smaller than I could have imagined. It is dark inside. There is nowhere to sit. Aunts and uncles and cousins of mine were here.

There is a wrought-iron gate to a camp, with its wrought-iron arch, *Arbeit Macht Frei* ("Freedom Through Labor"). In front of it are piles of things taken from the victims: scissors, can openers, strainers, graters, mirrors, toothbrushes, razors, clothes, hangers, hairbrushes, shoe brushes, knives, forks, spoons; and a photo of confiscated suitcases, duffel bags, prayer shawls, canes, leg braces, and artificial limbs. One walks under the arch—through the gate—to a real barrack from Auschwitz-Birkenau, one of the more than 200. This barrack held Jews from Theresienstadt Ghetto in Czechoslovakia.

There are benches to sit on, before going in. I sit. The bench is peaceful, the floor a hard, smooth, shiny stone surface with lovely pastels in it. Then I see the identification of the very floor under my feet: "A path connecting Treblinka killing center with a nearby forced labor camp was paved with the crushed remains of tombstones from Jewish cemeteries. Below is a casting from a section of the path; Hebrew letters are visible in several pieces." Behind me there is sound: a glass-enclosed room, also with benches, with photos of the physical plant at Auschwitz-Birkenau, and from speakers in the floor come the voices of survivors of Auschwitz saying what happened to them there, the small details of degradation, narratives of humiliation, torture, and overwhelming loss. I walk on the casting of the crushed tombstones from Treblinka into the Auschwitz-Birkenau barrack where, had I been born earlier, I might have been with the majority of my family on both sides. The bunks are wood, almost slats—but then, they didn't have to bear much weight, did they? I have seen photos with the inmates stacked-in lying flat, but the eye plays a trick: one thinks the bunks must have been bigger to hold so many. There is no smell. This too must have been scrubbed down.

In the center of the barrack are cement walls about four feet high behind which are video displays of some of the medical experiments: photos of dismembered bodies and of bodies and body parts preserved in vats; films of skeletal boys used in medical experiments by Dr. Josef Mengele, known in Auschwitz as "the Angel of Death"; photos of skeletal girls with bruises and open sores all over them. There is a Ravensbrück woman; a single man at Dachau being used for experiments at extremes of air pressure; a Gypsy man being injected with seawater right into his heart; a Jewish dwarf who was subsequently stabbed to death to study his bone structure; a Jewish woman used in sterilization experiments. The low walls are supposed to conceal these videos from children.

There are bowls the prisoners ate from; Zyklon B canisters that were used in Auschwitz-Birkenau and Majdanek; a scale model of Crematorium II at Auschwitz-Birkenau that shows how vast it was, and also where the victims undressed, were gassed, were cremated.

You pass an exhibit on why the U.S. War Department, when bombing military targets only five miles away, refused to bomb the train tracks to Auschwitz to stop delivery of Jews. Though Jewish groups in the U.S. repeatedly begged for this bombing, Assistant Secretary of War John J. McCloy said it "would be of such doubtful efficacy that it would not warrant the use of our resources." You pass through a steel passageway with a glass floor and the names of victims etched in glass panels on the walls. You move into an area with brick walls and a steel floor. You round a corner and there is a smell, strange and bad, thick and heavy, almost suffocating. But you walk onward and then on each side of you there are shoes, thousands of shoes: to your left and your right, the shoes of the dead brought from Auschwitz to be on exhibit here. "We are the shoes, we are the last witnesses," says a poem by Yiddish poet Moses Schulstein inscribed on a wall. It is almost unbearable. Then there is a wall of photographs—just arms with tattooed numbers. The arms face a wall with smaller photographs of emaciated prisoners.

Covering another wall there is a huge color photograph of the hair they cut off the women at Auschwitz, a mountain of human hair; adjacent to it, a black-and-white photo of this hair as it was baled for sale. Facing the mountain of hair are photographs of Hungarian Jewish women with their heads shorn. There is a casting of a table on which gold fillings were removed from corpses; castings of crematorium ovens from Mauthausen; a stretcher used to move bodies, a crematorium poker.

When the war ended in 1945, two-thirds of Europe's Jews had been murdered. According to Deborah Dwork in *Children With a Star*, "a mere 11 percent of European Jewish children alive in 1939 survived the war; one and a half million were killed."

The museum honors the "Rescuers," those who tried to save Jewish lives: a whole village, Le Chambon-sur-Lignon, in France, that saved 5,000 refugees, including several thousand Jews (the Bible of its pastor, André Trocmé, is on display); Raoul Wallenberg, a Swedish diplomat who worked relentlessly to rescue the Jews of Budapest; an underground Polish group code-named Zegota that provided money, false identity papers, and hiding places for 4,000 Jews; and the Danes, who refused en masse to collaborate with the Nazis. On display is a boat used by the Danes to smuggle Jews to safety in Sweden. According to the museum, "Among the Nazi-occupied countries, only Denmark rescued its Jews." The Danes raised over $600,000 to help the hunted escape; 7,220 Jews were saved; nearly 500 were deported to Theresienstadt Ghetto—and all but fifty-one survived.

And there are sadder stories of resistance. In Lidice, Czechoslovakia, on May 27, 1942, Reinhard Heydrich, former chief of Reich security police, an architect of the genocide, was shot (he died later). In retaliation, all the male villagers were murdered, the women sent to concentration camps, the children jailed in Lodz Ghetto or, if blond enough, put in German homes. The two Czech resistance fighters who killed Heydrich committed suicide rather than surrender. The Nazis, never camera-shy, photographed the executions of the villagers.

There were thirty-two parachutists trained by the British in Palestine and sent to Hungary and the Balkans as saboteurs. These fighters also wanted to rescue Jews under German occupation. None was more committed to this cause than the poet Hannah Senesh, a Zionist who emigrated from Hungary to Palestine as a teen-ager. Commissioned as an officer in the British army, she fought in Yugoslavia with the resistance. On crossing the border into Hungary, Senesh was arrested by the Nazis as an enemy soldier and jailed by the Gestapo in a military prison in Budapest. The Nazis also jailed her mother, Catherine Senesh, who was still living in Hungary, in the same prison, and threatened Hannah with the torture and killing of her mother. But it was Hannah, who never broke, whom they tortured and, after five months, executed on November 7, 1944. Her last poem read in part: "I could have been twenty-three next July;/I gambled on what mattered most,/The dice were cast. I lost." The museum displays her words but does not tell her story.

There was the White Rose, students identified by the museum as the only German group to demonstrate and leaflet against the genocide of the Jews. The leaders, Sophie and Hans Scholl, sister and brother, were beheaded in 1943. (I keep a remembrance of them—an enamel white rose raised on a background of black and gray beads—in front of the German editions of my books.)

The permanent exhibition ends in an open amphitheater, on the screen survivors, in good health, strong, fleshy, spirited, with stories of agony and unexpected uplift. They speak with calm and authority, only one with the constant nervous tremble I remember in survivors when I was a child. This is a triumph: to have forged a way of telling. It is impossible to overestimate how hard this must have been. The Nuremberg trials, the historians, gave the survivors some ground on which to stand; but they had to find both words and the will to speak. Many overcame their shame—the internalized humiliation of anyone so debased, in captivity. But many have not spoken, maybe because here too men have established the standard for what can be said.

In the last two decades, feminists have learned how to talk with raped, prostituted, and tortured women—what they need to be able to speak, how to listen to them. This museum was in formation for the second of those two decades, a ten-year period of research, investigation, discovery—finding artifacts, deciding which to use and how, which stories to tell and how. No use was made of feminist work on sexual abuse or bodily invasion and violation—neither the substance of this knowledge nor the strategies used to create the safety in which women can bear remembering. I know Holocaust survivors who have not spoken out: women who were raped or sexually hurt. This museum did not become a safe place for women's testimony about the sadism of sexualized assault. One rationale for building it was that soon the survivors would pass on, and the burden of memory would be passed from them to all the rest of us. But because the museum did not pay attention to women as a distinct constituency with distinct experience, what women cannot bear to remember will die with them; what happened will die with them. This is a tragedy for Jews and for women, with miserable consequences for Jewish women. The conceptual invisibility of Jewish women is the kind of erasure that is used—indefensibly, with a prejudiced illogic of its own—to justify yet another generation of second-class status for women in Jewish communities and in Israel. The torment of women in the Holocaust was not second-class, and it cannot translate into second-class rights. Acknowledgment and respect are necessary; the conceptually invisible have neither.

Perhaps the threat of seeking this knowledge is that some of the sadism is familiar, even familial; not confined to camps or genocide. Better to avoid any crime against women that men who are not Nazis still commit. Or perhaps women are conceptually invisible because of the continuing and belligerent sexism of the men who run Jewish institutions now—but the blinding arrogance of sexism has no place in this museum. I want the suffering and endurance of women—Jewish or not Jewish, in Auschwitz or Ravensbrück, Bergen-Belsen or Dachau, Majdanek or Sobibor—reckoned with and honored: remembered. I want the rapes documented, the brothels delineated, the summary murders of pregnant women discussed. I want the medical experiments—excision of genitals, injections into the uterus—explained, exposed. I want the humiliation rituals—forced nakedness, cutting and shaving of hair, punishments of hundreds or thousands of women standing naked in the cold for twelve hours at a time—articulated. I want the beatings, the whippings, the forced hard labor and slave labor narrated. I need to know about those who resisted and those who escaped; there were some. I need a heritage on the female side. I want this museum changed so that remembrance is not male. I want to know the story of women in the Holocaust.

ACKNOWLEDGMENTS

I thank the editors who gave me an opportunity to write and publish the essays and articles in this book, especially Allison Silver of the *Los Angeles Times* and Robin Morgan during her tenure at *Ms.* as editor-in-chief.

I thank Phyllis Chesler for getting me invited to the feminist conference in Israel in 1988 that gave rise to "Israel: Whose Country Is It Anyway?" And I'm particularly indebted to Howard Zinn's *A People's History of the United States* for the quantitative information about the founding fathers that I use in "Race, Sex, and Speech in Amerika"; so this is also my chance to thank Gerry Spence for telling me to read it.

I am profoundly grateful to Nikki Craft, activist and provocateur extraordinaire, for setting up The Andrea Dworkin On-Line Library on the Internet (http://www.igc.apc.org/womensnet/dworkin) and for her support and friendship. She has a special place in my heart.

I thank Melissa Farley, who has consulted me on a host of research issues concerning prostitution and post-traumatic stress syndrome. I am grateful to Evelina Giobbe, Susan Hunter, Ann Simonton, and Cookie Teer for their political knowledge, hard work, and courage.

I thank Pat Butler, Twiss Butler, Merle Hoffman, Kathrin Scheerer,

251

and Jan Philipp Reemtsma for political and economic support and for friendship and kindness.

I thank my buddies, especially Anne Simon, Gloria Steinem, Gretchen Langheld, Elsa Dorfman, Sally Owen, Michael Moorcock, Henk Jan Gortzak, and Catharine A. MacKinnon, for their help, conversation, and political clarity. I thank Robin Morgan for the raucous times we spend discussing literature.

I thank the organizers of conferences and lectures who invited me to speak in these last years, and I thank the women I've met in cities and towns throughout North America for teaching me so much.

I thank Elaine Markson, my friend and literary agent, for her endurance, patience, commitment, and generosity. I thank my father, Harry Dworkin, for his love and support. I thank John Stoltenberg for his love and for our life together.

I thank my editor at The Free Press, Susan Arellano, for her commitment, which has stood the test of time, to publishing my work. I thank her associate Norah Vincent for valuable suggestions with respect to this book. And I thank Adam Bellow and Michael Jacobs of The Free Press for the intellectual integrity that allowed them to recognize and publish this and two future books.

INDEX

253